Islam, Kurds and the Turkish
Nation State

Islam, Kurds and the Turkish Nation State

Christopher Houston

Oxford • New York

First published in 2001 by
Berg
Editorial offices:
150 Cowley Road, Oxford, OX4 1JJ, UK
838 Broadway, Third Floor, New York, NY 10003-4812, USA

Berg is an imprint of Oxford International Publishers Ltd.

Library of Congress Cataloging-in-Publication Data
A catalogue record for this book is available from the Library of Congress.

British Library Cataloguing-in-Publication Data
A catalogue record for this book is available from the British Library.

ISBN 1 85973 472 3 (Cloth)
       1 85973 477 4 (Paper)

Typeset by JS Typesetting, Wellingborough, Northants.
Printed in the United Kingdom by Antony Rowe.

Contents

Contents

Acknowledgements

It is a genuine pleasure to thank so many people for their collaboration in the long process of researching and writing a book. Writing of any kind is a collective activity, and the collective – disunited, rowdy and dispersed as it is – involved in the producing of this book is rather large. First I wish to express my gratitude to neighbours and friends in Kuzguncuk, who made living there for the most part a truly happy experience. Second I would like to thank my interviewees, many of whom became close friends, for their patience and forbearance at my leading questions, repetitive confusions and muddle-headed presumptions. They tried to set me aright, with varying success. Third I wish to offer special thanks to Şeyhmus and his family, whose door (and fridge) were permanently open to their Australian guest. And to Suheyla *abla* in particular for treating me as warmly as a son. Fourth I wish to thank the staff at Boğazici University for their kind advice and support, especially Ayşe Hanim, who let me share her study, at considerable inconvenience to her daily programme.

Without the insights, friendship and helpfulness of them all Istanbul would not be the second home it so happily became.

I acknowledge here too the support of the Commonwealth Government of Australia, whose research scholarship enabled me to pursue my academic interests in Turkey. The Turkish Consul in Melbourne agreed to my request for a research visa, for which I am grateful. I am deeply grateful too for the intellectual inspiration of my colleagues, Joel Kahn, Rowan Ireland and Chris Eipper, whose sage comments made the decisions of composition so much clearer. And let me not forget Charlie Ambrose, computer trouble-shooter *extraordinaire*, who pulled me out of more crashes than I care to remember.

Last I wish to name my family, to thank them for their support during the period of the research. Here of course I include my partner Esma. You are as much a part of the book as its punctuation.

Prologue

Republic Day, 29 October 1994, Istanbul

Red flags filing into Taksim Square: teeming on the flagpoles outside the five-star hotels, draped over the balconies of offices, promenading down the boulevards. Shaking the hands of children sitting on their fathers' shoulders, swishing like snappy red butterflies across the face of the Atatürk Cultural Centre, as fearless as acrobats high over the unfinished hole of the Istanbul Metro. Flags pinning up the sky.

Slogans pasted around the square:

'What happiness to be living in Atatürk's Turkey.'
'Today think of Mustafa Kemal and the Republic.'
'Without ceasing we will protect Turkish independence and the Turkish Republic.'
'The Republic is the future.'

Music, popstars, celebrities, personalities! Pledges prancing on the stage. 'We love Atatürk and the Republic.' Banks of howling speakers, spotlights, cameras, cheers. Brackets of songs stitched together with the compère's prattle. 'Republic Day, our greatest celebration!' The voice of the crowd, the voice of the singer, echoes bouncing off the buildings. Fireworks, oohs, aahs, whistles, roars. Silence. The national anthem. 'What Happiness to say, "I am a Turk"', in huge flaming letters on the roof of the Concert Hall. Green laser light shooting across the dark of the Metro hole to play on the glass backdrop of the Marmara Hotel, 'Independence or Death!' Atatürk's famous silhouette trudging up the building, forever establishing the Republic. Music spraying the crowd, Carl Orff's *Carmina Burana* with bass drums booming, 'Next stop the Aegean' flickering on the wall. Fireworks. More fireworks!

Acrid smoke drifting over the nation, to be taken home with the children and thrown over the chair with the clothes to be worn all of the 30th of October.

Introduction

During the two years of my research in Istanbul (October 1994–December 1996) I lived, more by chance than design, in the small suburb of Kuzguncuk, a district squashed up hard against the Bosphorus by the Muslim, Jewish and Christian cemeteries on its surrounding slopes. In Turkish Kuzguncuk means the 'grille in the prison door', and Kuzguncuk did seem to peer out on the broad expanse of the sea channel from its narrow neighbourhood beneath the hills.

I had wanted to live in Fatih, an ancient suburb within the historic peninsula on one of Istanbul's seven hills, noted for its religious affectations. But the price and poor quality of housing was a deterrent and Kuzguncuk, which falls within the electoral boundaries of the Üsküdar Council, seemed on first reconnaissance as good a base as any from which to pursue research. For Üsküdar (on the other side of the Bosphorus from Fatih) had been won by the 'Islamist' Refah (Welfare) Party in the 1994 Istanbul local government elections, and thus appeared a propitious place from which to examine the workings of the Islamist movement. Ironically, Fatih was won by Refah, only to be lost in a re-election, and so was controlled by the Motherland Party.

As it turned out, Kuzguncuk itself probably did not deliver many votes to the Refah Party in either the local elections of 1994 or the general election of 1996: party meetings at a local coffee-house during the campaign for the 1996 election were not well attended, and on one particularly disappointing occasion had to be cancelled when only the convener and I turned up. Refah's women's section in Kuzguncuk was more successful, organizing meetings over a meal at various women's houses to publicize the programme and recruit members. In Istanbul alone, the Refah Party claims to have over 300,000 women members. 'We are organized in every county of Istanbul province, down to individual neighbourhoods. Each member's name is on our computers,' says the head of Refah's Istanbul Women's Commission (*Turkish Daily News*, 15 Dec., 1995).

The Islamist movement does not exist in a vacuum though, and its dimensions, ambiguities and self-constitution are explicable only in relation to state or other oppositionary discourses. Kuzguncuk proved an extremely fertile neighbourhood in which to encounter people's embellishment of these discourses. Further, there was a small, unpopular but active group of 'Islamists' living in Kuzguncuk. They refused to perform the daily prayer ritual (*namaz*) in the mosque, and were also extremely cynical about the Islamic pedigree of the Refah Party, which was supposed to be pursuing their political vision. Like most suburbs of Istanbul, Kuzguncuk was far from being impervious to the siren appeal of Islamist politics.

For most of the two years of my fieldwork in Istanbul I attended the Koran study organized by this group, whose members took turns to host our twice-weekly readings. Not all were convinced of my sincerity when I told Ahmet *ağabey*, their enthusiastic leader, that I wanted to learn about Islam. But my ignorance and status was on the whole forgiven as we worked our way through the text with the aid of various *tefsir* (commentaries). Still, I probably disappointed those who had hoped that our labour might result in my Islamic enlightenment. I confess that I remained a Christian, if not a particularly pious one, throughout my fieldwork.

Other participants were nonplussed when I said I wished to understand what an Islamist movement does. Perhaps because not all of them interpreted their earnest study of the Koran as contributing to the wider enlivening of Islam in Istanbul. Yet by contrast with Paul Stirling's experience as an object of suspicion in rural Turkey – as recounted by his research assistant Emine Inciroglu (1994) – in nearly all my many interviews with Islamist journalists, activists and scholars, my being a non-Muslim did not present itself as a problem. True, the word 'Christian', like the word 'Muslim', can signify a multiplicity of creeds, practices and political commitments. Yet my willingness to discuss the finer points of doctrinal difference between Christianity and Islam – the idea of the Trinity, for example – with those who insisted meant that my conscientiousness as a believer, if nothing else, was respected. Comprehension was another matter: as most theologians would admit, even God struggles to explain the Trinity.

I sometimes wondered too if being from Australia was fortuitous, particularly when questioning Turkish and Kurdish Muslims about how the Kurdish situation was conceptualized within political Islam. No one could seriously accuse the Australian government of sponsoring Kurdish, Islamist or Secularist tyrants against the good people of Turkey. As will be seen, Part III examines Islamist responses to the Kurdish problem, as well as the possibility of Islamist multiculturalism. This is sensitive territory indeed, and I fear I may well offend everybody. Part I investigates Islamist practices in the context of state republicanism, a topic that many card-carrying secularists, and also other more liberal Istanbulites, might not find particularly edifying. More than once I detected the laicist suspicion that foreigners like myself were pandering to the Islamist social movement, even propagating its message. Antipodean or not, no researcher can avoid participation in the political worlds he or she describes.

In part, then, this book presents a study of the views and historical interpretations of those who conceive themselves to be most mis-recognized by the Turkish Republic. In so doing it runs the risk of presenting Turkish-republican discourse as the possession of an activist elite, whose manufacture of the nation minimizes the creativity of other agents as they too constitute themselves modern. In various places I have tried to draw attention to a response from below that picks up and runs with the project of the state, a response that Nükhet Sirman has described as individuals' 'aspirations to westernism and modernity' (1995: 170), and Chris Hann as their 'domestication of the state' (1990: 66). I have tried to show, too, how shared sentiments often make secularist and Islamist concerns less oppositional than they appear. Nevertheless, I have not dwelt on the self-creation of subjects who have complemented in their own lives the state-sponsored civilizational shift. That might well be a task for an ethnography of Kemalism, or even for a study of Republican autobiography.

Chapter 1 begins with an emblematic account of two suburbs in Istanbul and their varying responses to the shaming of the Turkish flag. This leads us into a more general discussion of the difficulty of locality-making in the context of national and global projects seeking to create certain kinds of Turkish subjectivity. It concludes with a thumbnail sketch of recent developments in the built environments of Istanbul and Ankara. Chapter 2 examines the production of alternative localities in the suburb of Kuzguncuk, Istanbul's oft-proclaimed 'last heaven'. Chapters 3 and 4 analyse varying attempts to construct new spaces and forms of Islamist conviviality. At the same time, class distinctions may also become highlighted, making the Islamist movement's attempt to forge a cross-class coalition more difficult. Chapter 5 explores the boisterous orders of Islamist and Republican carnival, before returning to Kuzguncuk and the question of its relative autonomy.

Part II of the study signals a shift in concern, from a concentration on the republicanism of the state and its Islamist critics to a focus on its nationalism and its Kurdish ones. Chapter 6 sketches out three competing interpretations of the nation's founding mythology. Chapter 7 looks more closely at the Kurdish problem, including the various ways it might be conceptualized. Chapter 8 returns us to Istanbul, the most populous Kurdish city in the world, where it charts the world of one particular family. In the rich confusion of its members' lives an intimation of the range of dilemmas constituting Kurdish urbanity in Turkey is revealed.

Part III attempts to bring these two dimensions together, to ascertain the relationships, both practical and theoretical, between Islamist and Kurdish movements. Chapter 9 describes the damning self-analysis, by those Islamists concerned enough to ponder it, of the reasons for Turkish Muslims being so lax in showing their solidarity with Kurdish Muslims in Turkey. Chapters 10, 11 and 12 present three contrasting Islamist approaches to the Kurdish problem, which I have labelled statist, Islamist and Kurdish Islamist respectively. Chapter 13 closes the study by reflecting on the prospects for a truly multicultural Islamist movement, a movement forced to democratize through a pluralization of the aims of its struggle.

Part I

–1–

Global Cities, National Projects, Local Identities

A Tale of Two Suburbs

Kuzguncuk gives the impression of being physically straitjacketed by its human geography. The grounds and mansion of the Koç business empire dominate it from the hill at the rear, cemeteries surround it on three sides and the high wall of Fetih Paşa Korusu (Forest) constrict it on the fourth. A little way up the Bosphorus the soaring steel technology of the Suspension Bridge overwhelms the skyline, leaving Kuzguncuk crouched in its shadow. Around the bridge and extending back to the far edge of Kuzguncuk is an exclusive military zone: walking along the road separating the military and civil spaces one recoils from the blank gaze of the sentries, machine-guns in their arms.

If Kuzguncuk appears somewhat self-contained compared to most other suburbs, it seems appropriate to ask whether such urban segregation allows the neighbourhood much autonomy to 'produce its own locality' (to invoke a phrase of Appadurai). This is no idle reverie pandering to a misbegotten anthropological desire to minimize the effect of 'outside' forces on a discrete, self-reproducing community. On the contrary the question is to ascertain the extent to which Kuzguncuk functions as a conduit for the nation-state's project of producing 'citizen-subjects' (or subject citizens). For it can be argued that neighbourhoods are where the 'heavy' work of nationalism is done. From the state's perspective, their role is 'to incubate and reproduce compliant national citizens' (Appadurai 1995: 214). How variable the state's success is in any given area depends of course on numerous factors.

This was visually demonstrated when the Turkish flag was thrown to the floor at the legal Kurdish party's general conference in Ankara in 1996.[1] In immediate indignant response Kuzguncuk was festooned with

---

1. The perpetrator of the crime was sentenced to 22 years in gaol: the head of the party and the chairperson of that particular session were given 6 years apiece.

the national flag for days afterwards, criss-crossing streets, obscuring the merchandise in shop windows, hanging off balconies, even fluttering on the rusty pole sticking out at right angles over the gateway to the mosque. No doubt this was a spontaneous outburst of patriotism – except that the state printing office was simultaneously pumping out posters adorned with the national flag, vowing 'While you are, we will be.' And then there was the even more chilling banner strung across the prime shopping streets: '*Memleket bölünmez. Esan susmaz. Bayrak indirmez*' ('The nation won't be split. The call to prayer silenced. The flag thrown down'). This from the supposedly secular party of the ruling coalition. By contrast, in the Istanbul suburb of Gazi Osman Paşa, where earlier riots in 1995 ended in a massacre by security forces, the refusal to fly the flag in reaction to its desecration was vilified by the republican press as an act of betrayal. The production of locality by recent Kurdish and Alevi migrants clashed here with the state's ambition to subordinate local neighbourhoods to its own national logic, to nationalize all space within its sovereign territory. Kuzguncuk's identification with the state's project, then, becomes as significant (and peculiar) as Gazi Osman Paşa's apparent resistance to it.

In fact during most of my fieldwork access to certain areas of Gazi Osman Paşa was strictly limited. Checkpoints manned by special police controlled the comings and goings of inhabitants and their visitors. The riot, which resulted in 23 protesters being shot dead by state security forces, ended only when the army occupied the suburb and clamped down on all unauthorized civil associations. Clearly, then, acquiescence in the civilizing project of the state was greater in Kuzguncuk than in Gazi Osman Paşa. And equally clearly, without the horrifying contrast of Gazi before us, we would be hard-pressed to discern the naturalizing effects of nation-state discourse, in which the achievement of state legitimacy resides in the very concealment of the artifice underlying its production.[2]

Globalizing Istanbul

We may still find it strange that two districts within the one city (Kuzguncuk and Gazi Osman Paşa) can be so different in terms of their susceptibility to the seductive charms of national identity. For after all, both neighbourhoods

---

2. June Starr, in a follow-up to her research in the Bodrum area in the late 1960s, writes self-accusingly: 'to my astonishment, a decade later, some of what I had taken as fixed had been challenged and undergone radical change at the top (the parliament, public stability, the Constitution' (Starr 1992: 174). She then affixes a quote from Marx's *Grundrisse*: 'everything social that has a fixed form merely is a vanishing moment in the movement of society' (ibid., p. 175).

have been exposed to the full repertoire of the Turkish nation-state's techniques for producing an homogeneous citizenry: a standardized and nationalist school curriculum; a calendar year punctuated by national holidays like October 29th; the colonization of public space by monuments and memorials honouring the nation's founding heroes; the encouragement of a collective remembering and forgetting; the endless repetition of the narrative of the nation's birth, including the important genre of battle-accounts; the censorship – often by the proprietors – of the mass media in the name of national self-interest; the registration of residential permits by state-appointed functionaries; the omnipresence of police stations, gendarmeries, and military zones; the formalization of the 'cultural' sphere (particularly in the areas of folk-dance and music); the naming and re-naming of streets, suburbs, public buildings, parks; even the permissibility of children's names, etc.

But different suburbs of the same city – and certainly different regions within the state's borders – get caught up in the national imaginary in contrary ways over a period of time. The character of the various Istanbul neighbourhoods is affected by a multiplicity of factors. These include the degree of development of the local productive forces and the accompanying class struggles, as well as the incorporation or expulsion of trade unions from state mechanisms for negotiating labour issues. The radicalization of segments of the labour force resulting from the liberalization of the economy too is important, as is the ability of the state to lock in the loyalty of workers whose 'hold on citizenship has been dependent on jobs in manufacturing and other sectors protected and subsidized by national economic managers' (Beilharz 1996: 94). Significant too is the extent of ethnic segmentation in the division of labour, and competition between workers from different regions of the country for control of local jobs. We might think here, to bring us down to earth, of Eminönü porters or Kasımpaşa stevedores. Lastly, changes in the state's cultural policies and consequent effects on the politicization/reconstruction of ethnic and religious identities, including war, forced migration and mass urbanization, affect the kinds of locality constructed by inhabitants of a neighbourhood. Such factors test local sentiment towards solutions propounded by the state to the problems facing residents (or constituting them as problems!).

In this sense any particular neighbourhood's task of producing locality ('as a structure of feeling, a property of social life, and an ideology of situated community' Appadurai 1995: 213) is under duress as much from the identity-forming discourse of the Turkish nation-state as from that ensemble of economic and cultural transformations most conveniently labelled globalization. Since the watershed of the 1980 military coup and the liberalization of the Turkish economy, the elites of Istanbul have re-positioned it as the only Turkish metropolis capable of becoming a 'global city'. In this process a newly imagined Istanbul has been re-defined *vis-à-vis* Ankara, while the national-developmentalist project coordinated from the Turkish capital falters, in both the economic and cultural spheres.

Yet if the present conjuncture of the world economy confers on [port] cities that manage to insinuate themselves into the transnational economy the possibility of greater autonomy from national capitals, not every neighbourhood within the city will be equally affected – or enthusiastic. Talk of a 'global city' may be misleading, unless the uneven processes of actual factory development, service operations, and sites of investment are seen as one of its hallmarks. As most studies show, global cities are intrinsically unequal cities, in terms of their citizens' variable exposure to, and the redistribution of, income, property, access to services – and life chances and risk. Global cities are likewise producers of inequality by their incorporation into a hierarchical global urban system, whereby cities 'function as production sites and market-places for global capital' (Sassen 1994: 45).

Incorporation of influential cities within circuits of global capital accumulation is often taken to mean a corresponding crisis in the nation-state itself, which is unable to control the movements of capital within its borders. This in turn is assumed to herald the 'erosion of the capability of the nation-state to monopolize loyalty', opening up such things as a renewal of civic pride over against national affiliation (Appadurai 1993: 421). Yet obviously such renewals, if indeed they do exist, will be as unevenly distributed, even within particular neighbourhoods, as the selective transformation of the city and its economy by global forces. As Sassen points out, 'processes of economic globalization [are thereby] reconstituted as concrete production complexes situated in specific places containing a multiplicity of activities and interests, *many unconnected to global processes*' (1994: 44 – my emphasis).

In this process the scope for local autonomy, if any, in the art of producing locality needs to be re-visited. The question is not so much how global forces impinge on local communities, as if such communities were always there. Ethnography should not concern itself with attending to the integration/transformation of forms of cultural life it first has imaginatively to re-create. Rather we might wish to study the very construction of locality by such forces, to trace how 'much of the promotion of locality is in fact done from above or outside' (Robertson 1995: 26). In like manner, the constitution of those same 'global forces' may be best analysed by studying their embodiment in local sites, as in adding themselves they become indigenized. Here the disparate projects of national elites in the politics of state formation and their relative success in implementing them at the local level is a vital (mediating) third moment of analysis.

Global cities can be imagined, then, as urban mosaics, but mosaics in which both the colour and contours of the tiles keep changing, so that such cities become nodal points for global capital and cultural flows that re-shape them into contested spatial terrains.

National Construction and Islamist Whitewash

It is a considerable irony, then, that in order to become a global city – i.e. a city to which 'overly irritable capital which is technologically disposed to hyper-mobility' is persuaded to relocate – cities are exhorted to appro-priate or re-package or even invent a specialty by which to sell themselves (Keyder and Öncü 1994: 391). Thus 'those who are in a position to engage in this entrepreneurship will have to carefully think about the niche where the city will present itself, and will have to come up with an image of the city to advertise, and indeed to sell'. Or again 'successful cities have all engaged in such a sales effort; those cities which lack the power structure, or the vision, or are too encumbered by conflict that makes the evolution of such a vision difficult, fall behind in the competition . . .' (1994: 391) What can a city sell that makes it unique? Certainly not cowed labour, or tax-free havens, or well-organized infrastructure, or consumer services for a new global political class, though of course it needs to sell all these as well. What it can sell is its particular 'localness'.

In Istanbul's case this has entailed a re-structuring inspired by the global discourse of heritage conservation, in which the historic peninsula has been reconceived as an open-air museum, a 'consumption-artifact' (1994: 412). Touristification has involved the clearing of slum dwellings, the creation of parks, the restoration of old churches, bazaars, mosques and significant Ottoman wooden houses, as well as the construction of highways, overpasses and broad thoroughfares to enable quick access to the 13 new five-star hotels put up since 1983 on prime sites overlooking the Bosphorus.

Here the diffusion of a global discourse concerning the 'expectation of uniqueness of identity' (Robertson 1990: 50), and a commodification of a particular interpretation of history combine to legitimize the trans-formation of urban space in Istanbul. In this process the selective retention and appropriation of 'localness' no longer conform mainly to nation-state requirements for constituting a national culture, but also to the market's sponsorship of commodity localism. Localisms 'remembered' by the nation, and localisms 'remembered' by the market do not always coincide in terms of their logic – this despite the close links between political and business elites. The marketing for consumption of symbols that signify the national-culture – that is, their circulation as commodities in a process of de-etatism – means that the actual definition of the national culture is inherently plural. Further, it is obvious that the Republican state itself is not totally unified, but open to influence ('infiltration' if one does not like the directions of the change) by interests not necessarily linked to the reformist bureaucracy and its cultural project. Here class, cultural and political agendas interact in complex ways that make historiography in particular, and related attempts to symbolize those histories in monumental architecture and spatial practice, a vital part of current political struggle.

Yet historiography is not merely instrumental for present-day struggles. The acceptance or otherwise of a historical interpretation by groups or individuals who are also invited to become the subject of the narrative is a complex affair. People give their assent to a historical narrative because their experiences, lives and hopes confirm the possibility of the truth of the interpretation. In the same way, the constitution and consolidation of historical narratives in architectural design and built interventions in the public domain enter into the contest over the organization of the individual's 'interior space' (identity). Certain kinds of political hegemonies are effective to the extent that they bring into conformity exterior politicization of space with agents' subjectivity, and inefficient to the extent that people resist such efforts.

Stokes sums up the changes initiated in the late 1980s by Istanbul's controversial mayor Bedrettin Dalan as 'an explicit attempt to reconstruct Istanbul as the Islamic and Ottoman capital of the age of conquest . . .', so that 'monuments in public space, once exclusively and conspicuously reserved for Atatürk, now focused upon the conqueror [of Constantinople], Mehmet II, as an image of an outwardly oriented and very different kind of Turkey' (Stokes 1994a: 25). We might note in passing that such urban renewal practices trace a long pedigree in 'Islamic' cities. Both Henri Prost in Morocco and later in Istanbul, and Le Corbusier in Algiers and Izmir, displayed in their work what Rabinow calls a discourse of 'techno-cosmopolitanism', which entails a philosophical commitment to archi-tectural (and cultural) conservatism. Neither architect was a technocratic modernist, suppressing (or simply bypassing) in the name of efficiency the earlier built traces of life, history or material culture. As Çelik puts it, Le Corbusier's Algiers projects were 'an attempt to establish an ambitious dialogue with Islamic culture, albeit within a confrontational colonial framework' (Çelik 1991: 60). Meanwhile, Abu-Lughod argues, the redeeming grace of Prost was his 'sensitivity to the aesthetic values intrinsic to the older Moroccan towns' (Abu-Lughod 1980: xvii).

But more significantly, the history preserved or commemorated by 'techno-cosmopolitanism', as a theoretical urbanization practice, is always a politicized conservation: history (monuments, styles, culture) becomes in this context the ground upon which 'society's future form could be legitimated' (Rabinow 1989: 12). Imagined spaces conjure up imagined communities to inhabit them, and vice versa. 'Cities, like dreams, are made of desires and fears, even if the thread of their discourse is secret', writes Calvino (1974: 44).

The Republicans under Atatürk had indeed imagined a new citizen, and legislated for the metamorphosis. One of the National Assembly's first decrees was to disestablish Islam and abolish the institution of the Caliphate. In the same bill members of the last Ottoman Sultan's family were 'forever forbidden within the frontiers of the Turkish Republic, the Ministry of Religious Affairs was disbanded, the historic office of the Sheikh of Islam ceased to exist, the revenues of the Pious Foundations were confiscated; all the religious schools were transferred to the secular arm' (Kinross 1964: 385–86). A month later the religious courts of the *Şeriat* were closed, Swiss civil law replacing its jurisdiction in family, marriage, divorce and inheritance matters.

As part of the secularization programme, the Republicans made museums out of many of the monasteries of the Dervish sects, including the most famous at Konya, home of the Whirling Dervishes, whose performances had already been drastically touristified in the nineteenth century. The most symbolic of these transformations, declaring the Sancta Sophia mosque – once the greatest church of Byzantium – a national museum, occurred in 1930. This touristifying of Islam was, ironically, remarked upon critically by Le Corbusier in 1925: 'and already today we have Ankara, and the monument to Mustapha Kemal! Events move fast. The die is cast: one more centuries-old civilization goes to ruin. No more whitewash in Turkey for a long time to come!' (Çelik 1991: 65). Le Corbusier saw, it seems, in the first flush of the Republic's earliest anti-Islamism an inferior form of techno-cosmopolitanism, one not preservative enough.

The symbolic gesturing towards a revived Ottomanism by Dalan's Istanbul was implicated in both the re-arrangement of relations between Islam and the State that occurred after the 1980 coup, and those between Ankara and Istanbul. The new capital, Ankara, had already made its rendez-vous with 'techno-cosmopolitanism', even if the 'history' celebrated in its design was rather more transparently a political invention. One thinks immediately of the huge Hittite-inspired sculpture placed on the apex of Atatürk Boulevard, an artwork proclaiming the pre-Islamic origins of Turkish civilization. Or more importantly, Atatürk's mausoleum, spotlit on its hill the whole year round, which must be approached along an avenue lined with large 'pseudo-Hittite' stone lions (see Vale 1992; Meeker 1997). If Dalan in Istanbul was inspired to 'colonize' a history in order to re-invent it, the Turkish republicans in Ankara invented a history to colonize. For a time the new capital's public buildings – for example the original National Assembly complex – were informed by what Bozdoğan calls the 'first-national' or 'neo-Ottoman renaissance' style (till the onset of the worldwide depression of 1929). The demise of 'neo-Ottomanism' prefigured Ankara's decoration with Hittite and Turkish-nationalist motifs, neo-Ottomanism's Islamic connotations being 'simply not palatable for the populist and westernizing undercurrent in the Kemalist politics of identity' (Bozdoğan 1994: 41).[3]

Yet if Ankara's [mis]appropriation of a past is best understood as complicit in the architectural and metaphorical nation-building project, Dalan's claiming of *Fatih* Sultan Mehmet ('the Conqueror' of Constantinople) as symbol of a newly-envisioned and newly-commodified Istanbul has been built on and transformed by the Refah Party. Since winning control of the Greater Istanbul City Council in 1994 Refah has celebrated an annual May 5th *Fetih Gecesi* (Conquest Night) at İnönü Stadium, Istanbul's largest enclosed venue. Whilst Refah's presentation of the conquest of Constantinople as the 'coming of civilization' is particularly offensive to the few remaining Rum (Eastern Orthodox) families in Kuzguncuk, the spectacle's polemical 'Christians' are not the Orthodox but the secular elite. Though carefully vague to escape the possibility of prosecution the message is crystal-clear: 'We need a new *Fetih*,' (which casts the Republic in the role of the Byzantines) said Necmettin Erbakan, leader of the Refah Party at the 1996 rally. 'With the arrival of Islam we are celebrating the onset of tolerance,' and 'We are feeling the same excitement tonight as *Fatih* Sultan Mehmet's soldiers did 543 years ago.' The events of the rally were carefully orchestrated: Erbakan's triumphant entry into the stadium like a

3. Interestingly it was replaced briefly by more modish 'cubist' architecture, with its accompanying universal claims to functional and technological rationality. Nationalist architects like Sedad Hakkı Eldem criticized this in turn for its 'cosmopolitanism', as the state-sponsored and newly formalized national culture rediscovered in the 'Turkish House' an abiding ethnic essence. Other vernacular styles, as Bozdoğan notes, were conveniently forgotten in the process.

conquering sultan, after the crowd had been worked over by a fireworks extravaganza, march music, and the pulling around the stadium's athletic track of a twenty-metre model warship by young men in Ottoman costume re-enacting the audacious carrying of ships over the Karaköy peninsula and into the Golden Horn by *Fatih*'s soldiers. Finally, after speeches and greetings from invited Islamist guests from the whole Muslim world, a mock castle manned by soldiers with large crosses on their 'period' dress was stormed by sea and land in an epic battle. God's will and human determination had once again triumphed.

Ankara, too, has not been immune from these more recent re-workings of historical claims. The Refah Party, on winning local government there too in 1994, managed to exchange the Hittite Sun symbol of the greater city council for one featuring a mosque and citadel. This despite the protests of a 'Let's take responsibility for our city and Hittite Sun' campaign organized by the 'Platform for a Contemporary Turkey' group. In their petition, signed by 175,000 people and handed to the city's Governor, the writers make the comment that

> Today, these beautiful symbols are being pushed aside, and are replaced by others as if they were the new industrial product of a famous brand. From a competition which the country's entire artistic community boycotted came an arabesque design which is touted as a new emblem. Here in the cause of Turkist and Islamist propaganda a racist and theocratic approach is being expressed (*Cumhuriyet*, 7 July 1995).

The petition critiques the proposed change in the City's symbol (which of course appears prominently displayed on all documents of a promotional nature, as well as on the Net) for treating the emblem as though it were as disposable as last year's fashions. If this was not enough, the new choice itself is derided as being 'arabesque', a term with a long and unsavoury history in cultural debates (see Stokes 1989, 1994b). Finally the referent of the new emblem, the 'history' conjured up by it, is explicitly rejected – but partly, as the petition letter goes on to make clear, in the name of a rival and more inclusive imagined community: 'the Hittite Sun, *being Anatolia's cultural symbol*, is natural for Ankara' (my emphasis).

Since winning Greater Istanbul Refah has not attempted, however, a major transformation of urban space. In this sense they have continued the more populist policies of Dalan's successor (Nurettin Sözen of the People's Social Party), concentrating on providing services, however inadequate, to the slums making up vast areas of the city. But they have not only relied on the bread of basic amenities or the circus of polemical and self-congratulatory rallies to create a political constituency. Refah has also, among other activities, sponsored the restoration of four or five very fine old Ottoman mansions, re-opening them to the public as *çay bahçesi* (tea gardens) and restaurants, one of them in Fetih Paşa Korusu, the 'forest' bordering Kuzguncuk.

Here the Refah Party's self-identity, and its vision of the type of citizen it imagines will occupy the public space created by such facilities, is on display. What Refah cannot totally control, of course, is the actual consumption of such spaces. Their colonization by the public affects in turn the way the Party, or its most influential groups, are forced to think about themselves and the Islamist movement. For the tea garden in the forest has become a public space where young women wearing *türban* (headscarf) and *pardösü* (light overcoat) feel free to meet without male accompaniment, or chat with their like-minded religious boyfriends without 'social' supervision. Here the boundaries both of Islamist discourse on gender and secular discourse on the public sphere are being widened.

Let us now return to Kuzguncuk, where the machinery of nation, if not without hiccup, hums on determinedly: in the school, the bureau-cratized mosque, the local post office, even in the hard-working flags fluttering on the morning commuter ferries. Kuzguncuk, as we have seen in our brief tale of two suburbs, has not remained indifferent to the state's attempt to manufacture the nation. Neither, however, has it been unaffected by the struggle between the competing visions that seek to globalize Istanbul in their own image. Patently 'politicized conservation' is no longer the preserve of the reforming republican elite. Global tourism, as we have also seen, encourages the city to mime itself, to caricature its own past.

In the remainder of Part I we will tease out some of the tensions between the state's production of its desired civilians, the challenge of political Islam to such republican civility, and the locality-making activism of local Kuzguncuk players. We will do so in part by examining the Refah Party's initiative in Fetih Paşa Korusu (forest), as well as Kuzguncuk's rather surprising response to it.

–2–

Suburban Sequestration and the Making of Alternative Localities in Kuzguncuk

Historical Background

Kuzguncuk is in one way an arbitrary unit for analysis, once we admit that its inhabitants and boundaries are neither fixed nor impermeable. For in the production of locality we could have easily taken as problematic the ability of Üsküdar (the local council area) to force its claims upon its inhabitants as a place worth identifying with. Ethnography necessarily constructs boundaries in time and space, often imitating for various reasons the administrative divisions of the modern state, within which the actions of actors are assumed to have coherent meaning (or disappoint for failing to have). On the other hand, the zone of sociality called Kuzguncuk is not merely carved out of the body of the city by the ethnographer but is a reflection of its social construction by residents. That is, Kuzguncuk is a material entity, symbolized as such by its asymmetrical black outline in the architectural map on the *muhtar*'s[1] office wall, as well as by its incorporation as a unit within the administrative structures of the state. But it is also an imagined place, celebrated as different from other suburbs by those who live in it, as well as by others who do not, but know its reputation. This construction too is not arbitrary but stems from wider discourses of 'place' circulating within the society, as well as being determined by the historical development of Greater Istanbul, whose newer suburbs provide an ideological foil for the imagined significations placed upon Kuzguncuk.

As is attested by its cemeteries, Kuzguncuk is a multireligious and multicultural suburb. But mainly in the solidarity of death. For Kuzguncuk has also been a microcosm of the massive urbanization of Turkish society, of what we might as easily term its brave new making of locality. The first

---

1. The *muhtar*'s position is the lowest level in the State's administrative structure, responsible for registering voters, recording residential permits etc. Every suburb or village has a *muhtar*, who is popularly elected and paid a wage. Kuzguncuk's *muhtar* was beginning his 37th year in the job in 1997.

mosque in Kuzguncuk was begun only in 1952,[2] a year or two before the infamous riots against Christians in the Beyoğlu area on the other side of the Bosphorus led to an exodus of the Orthodox minority to Greece and the sudden availability of cheap housing in Kuzguncuk. The riots, ostensibly ignited spontaneously by the news (subsequently proved untrue) that Atatürk's birthplace in Salonika had been vandalized by Greek nationalists, led to numerous deaths and hundreds of pillaged and destroyed houses and businesses in the Christian quarters of the city. Kuzguncuk too was not immune from the riots. One of the effects of the rampage was the subsequent speeding up of the muslimification of the suburb.

Accounts of the damage in Kuzguncuk vary. Georgiou *amca* (uncle), when I asked him, said he stood outside his door all night to keep the rioters away.[3] He reported they came on boats from the other side of the Bosphorus but didn't touch his house. By contrast Zehra *teyze* (auntie) noted in a separate interview that

> Nobody was killed in Kuzguncuk on the 6–7 September. But there was a lot of destruction. In our district the Turks didn't let the looters in. They were like a lot of sheep. They looted my brother's café. My brother was injured and had to be taken to hospital. It lasted less than twenty-four hours . . . Everyone shut themselves up in their houses . . . Some were injured. They destroyed the priest's house. They tried to set fire to the church but it wouldn't burn . . . They did more damage in other places. We (the Greeks) were their main targets. But they also attacked Armenian and Jewish houses, probably without realizing. We were afraid they would attack again. That was when people gradually began to emigrate. Nobody from my family went then. But they went later. I have a brother in Greece. I went once, and stayed a couple of months (Bektaş 1996a: 148).

Where did this first large-scale Muslim movement to Kuzguncuk in the 1950s and thereafter come from, these migrants fortunate or canny enough to catch this wave of history? Generally from the western Black Sea environs, including the city of Kastamonu, one of the first regions in Turkey to experience land shortages when the availability of cultivable land along the coastal strip reached its natural limits. In this regard Kuzguncuk enabled a necessity (the need to leave the village) to be turned into a blessing, a boon not to be granted to later migrants to Istanbul. As a result

---

2. Even the Armenian Orthodox priest, whose church was next door, gave 500 Turkish lira towards its construction (Bektaş 1996a: 139).

3. All given names have been changed. I have changed the names, too, of the cities or regions from which my interviewees came, particularly in the Kurdish provinces.

Kuzguncuk was an early, though in some ways an atypical example of rural–urban migration, if we assume the 1960s, 1970s and 1980s explosion of *gecekondu* (literally 'put up in a night') housing erected on vacant state land on the outskirts of the major cities to be the norm. By contrast the people thinking of themselves today as Kuzguncuk locals, as distinct from more recently arrived middle-class or professional *yabancılar* (foreigners), are quite often living in buildings they did not put up themselves but bought cheaply from departing Christians and Jews. On the other hand, the residents' homogeneous origin reveals their chain migration from Kastamonu and the Black Sea region to Kuzguncuk, a pattern similar to that populating most of the large slums surrounding the major cities.[4]

Ruralization and Globalization of Istanbul

Despite this evidence for the similarity of the Muslim migration to Kuzguncuk and the heroic journey of later migrants to the newer suburbs of Istanbul, locals in Kuzguncuk tend to be rather dismissive of the city's 'Mehmet Come-latelies', especially those from the eastern provinces of Turkey. Fears about Istanbul's civility being undermined by country bumpkins and peasants are heard in such slurs. What is interesting about this selective amnesia is the way such claims are implicated in producing locality in Kuzguncuk, over against other imagined communities. For locals are fond of citing a newspaper article that calls Kuzguncuk Istanbul's *son cennet* ('last heaven'), in which the flavours of old Istanbul, the Istanbul alleged to be rapidly disappearing under the flood of peasants choking its insides and cluttering up its edges, can still faintly but sweetly be savoured. *Gayri müslim* (non-Muslims) figure prominently in these reminiscences of Kuzguncuk's former glory, even if it is said no longer to retain the charm of olden days. Although acknowledged by locals to be not as sociable as previously, when everyone knew each other and there was more community spirit, Kuzguncuk is still claimed as exceptional in Istanbul.

Yet it would be idle to suggest that Kuzguncuk's belief in the degeneration of Istanbul is unique. For it is striking how common the conviction is in all the more established quarters of the metropolis that recent migrants

4. The *muhtar* reports that of Kuzguncuk's 15 000 people, 20 per cent are from Inebolu, 15 per cent from Rize, 10 per cent from Trabzon, 10 per cent from Tokat, 10 per cent Kars, 10 per cent Sivas and the remainder from varied places, including Gümüşhane and Malatya. Kuzguncuk's more recent artists and architects generally originate from Istanbul or Ankara.

have ruralized the city, bringing their village mentality (*zihniyet*) and uncultured habits into even the prime sites of modernity. Such sentiments mirror a principal strand of the historic modernizing discourse that constituted the elite as republican, as well as justifying so much of that elite's programme for the civilizing of the people. Here the mode of modernization was also a forced Westernization, with taste, or cultural capital, operating as a social marker signifying both class position and one's degree of modernity. The state's obsession with crushing even symbolic resistance in local life (for example its legislation on dress code)[5] betrays its determination to produce homogenized and modern-looking national citizens. In this context the making of neighbourhood by Kuzguncuk locals, their self-image as *Kuzguncuklular*, shares something with the vision of the ideal community upheld by the Turkish state, as well as with other older and wealthier suburbs of Istanbul. On one level this reveals the success, in Kuzguncuk at least, of the Turkish-republican discourse's retaining the allegiance of those it hails as citizens.

It reveals too that Kuzguncuk, in its nostalgia for a civil past, is tempted to imbibe the same diagnosis of the present that is pulling Istanbul's middle class out of the city and into the housing estates. Paradoxically, the remaking of 'Ottoman' Istanbul in the heady years of the 1980s, when the middle classes 'rediscovered the aesthetics of their city's historical heritage', also revealed to them how 'disorderly, contaminated and polluted the familiar fabric of Istanbul's everyday life had become' (Öncü 1997: 57). The touristification of Istanbul as a global city facilitated at the same time the tourist gaze of the locals. A sanitized reconstruction of the past and its material culture (its romantic wooden houses, its quaint old neighbourhoods, its monumental works of architecture) rendered visible the unsanitary 'reality' of the present. Accordingly Istanbul's globalization has also entailed a major transformation in its urban structure, as the city's middle classes have deserted the older suburbs to move into new housing developments dotted along the highways exiting the city. As a result, there has been an increasing residential separatism and social uniformity, as class differentiation is re-constructed in the consumption of housing and the commodification of such housing's respective lifestyles. For example, an advertisement for a new luxury estate named *Akbulut* (White Cloud) asks 'Are you pleased with your present neighbours . . . are they culturally

---

5. That the politicization of clothing in particular is a live habit is illustrated nicely by a Refah Party parliamentarian's recent claim that 'to do *namaz* in a turban is eighty times more meritorious' (*Zaman*, 27 March 1997). Interestingly, Refah's general secretary immediately disassociated the party from his opinion.

up to your standards?' The pitch for Kemer Country Estate is only a little different: 'Who wouldn't want to work in Istanbul, but also go horse riding in the morning? Who wouldn't want to enjoy the relaxation of a swimming pool or a tennis court, to have breakfast by the lakeside and to have a cool drink in the evening in the garden? . . . All these things are possible within twenty minutes' reach of central Istanbul' (Aksoy and Robins 1994: 67–8).

One wonders in passing whether the trope of urban decay and the polluting, essential difference of 'newcomers' has not become a displaced but acceptable way of culturalizing poverty, of constructing as a cultural difference the skewed distribution of wealth and related opportunity that makes Turkey one of the most inequitable societies in the world.[6] In this case the virtue of tolerance is stressed, not as a ground for accepting difference, but for maintaining distinctions.

Istanbul's globalization, then, has rendered the historical heterogeneity of the city increasingly problematic in the eyes of its own inhabitants. Like all globalizing cities Istanbul is continuing to attract migration: 300,000 people a year, many with few skills to sell on the market other than their labour power. Like all globalizing cities Istanbul is exposed to an explosion of mass media technologies and flows of advertising: witness the tens of new radio stations and private TV channels, all based in Istanbul, all diffusing varied versions of global images of ideal homes and lifestyles. Like all globalizing cities Istanbul is being transformed by the 'segmentation and zoning of urban space on the basis of functionality' (Aksoy and Robins 1994: 58): giant malls to shop and play in (*Carousel, Capitol, Ak Merkez, Galeria* etc.), financial districts to work in, housing *siteler* (estates) to live in, and new highways and bypasses to join them all up.[7] And as in all globalizing cities, the search is on by strategic groups for ways to symbolize and sell the changes by new commodifications of its history: 'cosmopolitan Istanbul', at peace with its [Islamic?] past.

The exodus of the middle class suggests otherwise. For many such families, 'the emergent culture of the 1980s in Istanbul, with its "mixed" forms of music, grammar and dress, represents a half-bred world of pseudo-urbanism, one which contradicts and pollutes the cherished purity of their own "Westernized" way of life' (Öncü 1997: 69). Or, it might be added, the cherished purity of a truly Islamic way of life as well. For religious people too are sequestering themselves off from the 'arabesque' of the city, threatened in turn by its ambiguous accommodations with a secular lifestyle. Saktanber, for example, details the lives of middle-class

---

6. Cited from Ayata 1996.
7. Including plans for a third Bosphorus Bridge almost on top of Kuzguncuk.

Islamists who have built a private housing estate in Ankara, a complex in which members seek to pursue a mode of life in accordance with perceived Islamist precepts (Saktanber 1997). Istanbul too has its Islamist *siteler*. Such developments fracture the middle classes' uniformity of desire, as competing images of the 'good life' proliferate. (They also fracture the Islamist movement along class lines.) This can be explained in several ways – as an autonomization and diversification of civil society, as a partial dilution of the state's drive to recruit the private sphere into its cultural project of modernization, or even as the creation of a parallel economy with its marketing of a 'niche' Islam.

On the other hand, one would not wish to over-emphasize the differences in taste between the Islamist and secularist middle class. As Saktanber admits, in the messiness of everyday life 'the two competing world-views, Islam and modernity, cannot remain in their pure forms as they can at the ideological discursive level' (1997: 151). So one notes, for example, the central role ascribed to women in both secularist and Islamist discourse: in each women are bestowed with a mission that gives them a dignity beyond that which they are thought to possess in themselves. Charged with raising modern or Muslim children for the greater good of the nation or *ümmet*, women are honoured for (and reduced to?) their child-rearing function. Similarly in both discourses it is the next generation who will bring in the longed-for end of the teleological process: society will be modern, or Muslim, and only then will women be freed, presumably, from the urging of the state or *ümmet* to make their homes educational incubators. Society, women and children at last would just be. Such crossovers should, at the very least, make us wary of protagonists' claims to the mutual antipathy and exclusivity of Islamist and secularist visions and praxis. More importantly, they should leave us open as well to other responses to the changes restructuring the city.

Alternative Kuzguncuk: (1) Istanbul's Last Heaven?

Yet the diagnosis of the present made by many of Kuzguncuk's residents has resulted in a different cure to that of the spatial segregation pursued by those who can afford it, Islamist or laic. For there is in fact more than one imagined Kuzguncuk, and contending interpretations of its own history are important in creating multiple local views of itself, self-identities that sit uneasily with state-inspired elitist perceptions that situate it as a Shangri-La among the lost suburbs of peasantized Istanbul. In this rival version Kuzguncuk is Istanbul's *son cennet* (last heaven) precisely because it bears witness: not to a golden age that can never come again, but to a possibility that can be incarnated in present time, not resuscitated but created anew according to Kuzguncuk's changed conditions. Here the soul of the suburb is fought over, as nostalgia (and disdain for the present) grapples with grief (and hope for the present), though of course the two attitudes have much in common. Both contenders recall the fact that in Kuzguncuk the people of three faiths lived side by side with a sensitivity to, and mutual acceptance of, difference.[8]

Alternative imagined localities do not arise as a matter of course but require interest groups or organic intellectuals to articulate them. Kuzguncuk is no exception, the architect and community educator Cengiz Bektaş having lived there since 1978. Bektaş has been a major figure in the production of an oppositional locality in Kuzguncuk, both in his writings about Kuzguncuk and in the activities of groups with which he has been associated. As an architect he has been intimately associated with the project of conservation that has resulted in 300 of Kuzguncuk's 1,700 buildings being restored.[9]

Alternative Kuzguncuk's response to the perceived chaos and 'village-ization' of Istanbul has not been a flight to antiseptic, homogeneous housing complexes on the periphery of the city, but an attempted revitalization of the city's sociability in its 'heart'. As part of this process Cengiz Bektaş and others have organized numerous activities to persuade inhabitants of the suburb to participate in the restoration of community.[10] Similarly locals have been encouraged to beautify rather than sell their

---

8. Georgiou *amca* told me that when his generation were children they used to light the candles in the local synagogue (*havra*) on Friday evenings because of Jewish stipulations concerning work on the Sabbath.

9. According to the *muhtar*'s figures. A law protecting the historical integrity of the Bosphorus shoreline has been strictly enforced in Kuzguncuk (by contrast with other areas). Any demolished buildings have been replaced exactly as they were: no higher, no lower, no wider, of the same material, and with the same number and shape of windows and balconies etc.

10. These include shadow puppet (*karagöz*) shows, street theatre, a children's pots and pans band, wall-painting, the construction of a children's playground and basketball court on vacant land, a summer school (with painting, sculpture, poetry, literature, photography, and map-reading courses), a kite competition, fund-raising activities for the primary school (a fete, a football tournament, greeting cards, street markets, school dinners), a carnival, block printing in the square and an exhibition, pebble-paving of the mosque yard, the establishment of a public library and cultural centre (for concerts, theatre, conferences and exhibitions), communal dinners with *muhtar* candidates as guest speakers, picnics, and even a successful mobilization against a proposal to turn the suburb's market garden into a private hospital.

old houses – but not in order to re-inscribe Kuzguncuk as a tourist site.
As Bektaş himself comments, 'My plan included some things which seemed
very important at the time, but not so much now. For instance, I attached
excessive importance to physical change . . . But I had ignored the fact
that even the repair of communal facilities naturally followed on the repair
of human relations' (Bektaş 1996b: 29, 30)
But why do human relations need to be repaired at all?

> [Because] in 1985 the urban population [of Turkey] exceeded the rural
> population for the first time . . . Although city dwellers might be regarded as
> urbanized for statistical purposes, they are not so in social terms. Yet this city
> [Istanbul] has been a school of urbanization throughout its history. The people
> who have come here from rural areas have learnt to be urban dwellers . . .
> Today it is a matter of urgency that our cities assume the role of generating
> urban culture . . . in a more conscious way than ever before (1996b: 11).

Is there a difference, however, between the intellectuals who will develop
a progressive culture in the city, and the Republic's earlier generations of
schoolteachers charged with imparting modernity (in word and deed) to
the countryside? Has the mountain merely come to Muhammad?
Yes, there is a difference, if Kuzguncuk's urban educators heed Bektaş's
warning: 'the sole criterion of cultural validity for our intellectuals is the
avoidance of alienation from society as a whole. Participation by the people
in cultural production is a condition without which it cannot be said to
exist at all' (1996b: 11–12). Thus Cengiz Bektaş's invitation to Kuzguncuk
inhabitants to civilize themselves is important:

> only by participating in something, by achieving something together, by creating
> together, can human relations be repaired . . . Representational democracy does
> not permit participation in decisions . . . Perhaps 'neighbourhood groups' of
> around thirty houses could be formed . . . The method is not the essence of
> course. What matters is to bring about democratic participation by this or that
> method . . . So long as we do not take the decisions which affect ourselves,
> so long as we allow others to take decisions on our behalf, is there any hope
> of solving the problems we complain about today? (1996b: 158–9).

If participatory democracy is the prize, then tolerance is its patron.
Kuzguncuk naturally is the venue. 'The real Kuzguncuk [is] neither
the buildings, nor the walls, nor the windows nor the door . . . The real
Kuzguncuk is quite a different Kuzguncuk. Kuzguncuk is a model unit
in the heart of Istanbul that has something of vital importance to say to
the people of our time' (Bektaş 1996a: 143).

In sum, alternative Kuzguncuk proffers itself as worthy of preservation not just as a symbol of past tolerance but as a possible future one.[11] Here the perceived failure of the civilizing mission of the state results not in a quietist escape to the suburbs in the name of the unbridgeable [cultural] gap between the city's peasants and its urban[e] (Islamist and laic) middle classes, but in a proposal for mutual self-transformation. Similarly, difference is not essentialized but historicized, and change not foreclosed but facilitated. Equally importantly, though sharing some formal properties with historic Kemalist discourse, alternative Kuzguncuk as a project of civil society is imagined less as an object to be worked upon and more as a subject in process.

Alternative Kuzguncuk and the Selling of a Global City

One telltale sign of Istanbul's globalization resides, then, in its simultaneous production of new local identities. Kuzguncuk is a case in point: here its living heritage is discursively re-signified to produce a sense of locality related to, but different from, the city as a whole. Its residents once banded together to prevent Üsküdar Council unilaterally changing the name of one of the suburb's streets from Üryanizade Sokak to Perihan Abla Sokak. Perihan Abla was the name of a popular TV series shot in Kuzguncuk's Üryanizade Sokak after most of its houses (the ones used in the series) were restored. Perhaps not too much should be read into the protest – but Perihan Abla was filmed in Kuzguncuk precisely because it fulfilled the stereotype of what Istanbul used to be like (both architecturally and in its sociability) before its ruin. The refusal to change the name of their street suggests its inhabitants' dislike of the nostalgia of others, as well as their resistance to the bestowing of a new 'identity' by outsiders (in this case, Üsküdar Council, and the image industry).

Local identity is ensured through the discourse of conservation, as alternative Kuzguncuk's political and social vision is given built substance

11. In Cengiz Bektaş's first book about Kuzguncuk, there are many interviews with Kuzguncuk's older Greek Orthodox, Armenian, Jewish and Muslim residents, where they talk about the relations between the different religious and ethnic groups in Kuzguncuk before the 1955 riots. For example Mrs. N (Turkish, Muslim) said, 'Our neighbours were a Madam Donna and a Madam Ester. We got on very well. They would allow us to attend their circumcision feasts. They would also invite us to their Feast of the Passover. They would come to celebrate the Sacrificial and Ramazan feasts with us . . . They taught us how to make fig jam. We also learnt how to make apple and quince sweet. We would go to their baptism ceremonies' (Bektaş 1996a: 153). Bektaş's collecting and publicizing of memories is both a challenge and an encouragement to the suburb's residents.

by its architectural intervention in the physical space of the suburb. Local is as local does. Yet localization is meaningful only in a global context. Thus along with this initiative alternative Kuzguncuk, as much as global Istanbul, is driven to display its 'identity' to the gaze of a world audience. So Cengiz Bektaş's two books about the suburb (*Kuzguncuk, Another Name for Tolerance*, and *Don't Buy a House, Buy its Neighbours*) are printed in both Turkish and English. Kuzguncuk in this guise is presented as an inspiration not just to Turkey, but to a world gripped by the eminently modern idea of 'humanity as a racially and/or culturally fragmented category' (Kahn 1997: 1) and a corresponding terror of impending ethnic war.

Perhaps it is no coincidence, then, that Istanbul's presentation of itself as an 'open-air' museum for consumption by both foreigners and locals marshals some of the same slogans to market its uniqueness as are employed by alternative Kuzguncuk. So the city sold its bid for the 2000 Olympic Games with the blurb, 'Let's meet where the continents meet', playing on its image as a melting-pot of 'East' and 'West'. Within Istanbul's larger production of a civic identity, Kuzguncuk is appropriated, then, as an exemplary suburb, memorable for its historic tolerance. The Refah Party, on winning local government, has in its turn reworked the source of Istanbul's tolerance: assumed to be the fruit of an Islamic tree, Kuzguncuk (as a miniature Istanbul) can only be rejuvenated as a matter of course by the Islamization of society, however proposed. Refah's re-narrativization of local tolerance as a side-effect of Islamic tolerance is live ammunition in the struggle for 'history' without which people cannot constitute themselves as subjects. But has its pitch for ownership of Kuzguncuk's historic tolerance been successful? More particularly, how has Kuzguncuk's small group of Islamists responded to the production of locality by Cengiz Bektaş and friends? And has Refah's refurbishment of neighbouring Fetih Paşa Korusu's tea garden and restaurant seduced them into sampling its wares, into giving assent, however guarded, to Refah's particular vision of a civilized, liberal Islamism?

Alternative Kuzguncuk: (2) Islamist Localism

No one questions the desirability of being civilized. But it is clear that even in Kuzguncuk the secularist elite's hegemonic definition of what this means no longer stands unchallenged. The existence of a small but committed group of Kuzguncukites who meet to study the Koran and to encourage each other's experiment in living out a *şuurlu* (conscious) Islam testifies to the difficulty the Turkish state encounters in convincing citizens of the continued viability of its emancipatory project. The state's semi-withdrawal from the civilizing process has opened the way for the migration of the contest into the sphere of civil society itself: Atatürk clubs square off against Koran-study groups, secular women line up against Islamist women, non-religious symposiums, conferences, and media vie for audiences with religious ones. Its withdrawal paves the way, too, for the development of a contrasting locality to the alternative Kuzguncuk of Cengiz Bektaş and his colleagues, a rival community ill at ease with the prevailing sensibility in Kuzguncuk but without the resources or skills to remould the suburb physically.

At one stage the small Islamist community in Kuzguncuk were meeting twice a week in each other's homes to study the Koran, as well as several times a year with other like-minded groups from nearby suburbs. Their houses – liberated zones – were marked by a mixture of Islamist and non-Islamist practices. For example 'Ahmet' *ağabey* (elder brother), the leader of the study group, attempted to conform to the level of gender segregation enjoined by the Koran, with its advice about the degrees of male kinship amongst which women can appear uncovered. In Ahmet *ağabey*'s home the tea-tray would be left at the lounge room door, a discreet tap on its panels signalling to the host that he could bring it to the table and serve his guests. Other members were not as conscientious: one evening we met in the house of a man whose wife had been sent for the duration of the study to the home of another member (his son served the tea). The very next evening, when I met the son by chance and was invited home for dinner, we all ate together and then watched TV, his mother included. Apart from everything else, to live an Islamist life as a radical elaboration on social practices partly suffused by an Islamic 'idiom' is to invite inconsistency. As Saktanber says, 'The discourses of complementarity and modesty which inform Muslim women's gender identity can quite effectively find places of correspondence in both the official and civil discourses of patriarchal morality of modern Turkish society' (Saktanber 1994: 130). Of course the same applies to men. But sources of convergence do not mean that the living of an Islamist lifestyle is easy: at least in Kuzguncuk it requires repeated acts of will, which in the end can always become exhausted. Radicalness has the attraction of distinction; but its successful accomplishment often leads to routinization.

If their houses are designated by the local Islamists themselves (half jokingly) as 'liberated zones' (*kurtuluş bölgeleri*), Kuzguncuk too is coveted to become a 'liberated locality'. Until this happens, Ahmet *ağabey* and friends see themselves as living in internal exile, strangers in their home suburb of Kuzguncuk. In order to make Kuzguncuk resemble the place they desire it to be, the group at one stage were organizing weekly discussion meetings in a hall at the back of the mosque. However, problems with the *hoca* (hodja – the leader of prayers in the mosque and a religious bureaucrat on the state's payroll) forced their cancellation. Instead Ahmet *ağabey* was hoping to hire a local *kahvehane* (coffee-house) to continue the programme, but this too met with some resistance. Setbacks like these have led Ahmet *ağabey* to ponder the possibility that Muslims should have the right to set up an area of their own, an area in which Islamic law would be the basis of the legal system and anyone who wanted to join should be free to do so. This would be something akin to an Islamist housing estate, but on a bigger scale. Ahmet *ağabey* envisions a whole city, for example, being set aside for religious people who want the state to stop interfering in their way of life. Though the principles of Ahmet *ağabey*'s Islamist city are apparently democratic – self-recruitment and free association – its territorial nature implies boundaries and the production of a culturally exclusive politics. The hybridized nature of Istanbul's urban ecology once more incites separatist fantasies, even if they are grounded in perceived persecution. Consequently, the more this utopian Islamist city is imagined, the more life in Kuzguncuk is experienced by the religious community as a diaspora.

Living in diaspora implies the prior existence of a journey (if only in the soul), a separation from a homeland or community (that may not as yet exist). Christians in St Augustine's *City of God* are understood as a diasporic community, citizens of a yet to be realized polity. Politicized Muslims in a non-Islamist setting like Kuzguncuk both constitute themselves and are constituted as outsiders, their imagined homeland not a place but a time (*asrı saadet dönemi* – the period of the Prophet and the first four caliphs). Like Cengiz Bektaş's struggle to re-work the imagined historical tolerance of Kuzguncuk for the present day, the *asrı saadet* period too serves as an inspiration whose dimensions need to be re-imagined for modern times. Ahmet *ağabey*, despite the accusations of secularists, does not want to begin riding a camel.

But if Kuzguncuk's Islamists feel themselves to be in diaspora this is not to suggest they live an introspective life closeted off from the imperfections of their neighbours' behaviour. In fact during the day, especially in the warmer months, they congregate around the suburb's taxi-rank, where some shady trees and small stools from a tiny tea-shop provide a pleasant place to sit and chat. This is not exclusively Islamist or even male public space: many of the waiting taxi drivers, religious or otherwise, would join in the informal conversations, while in the early morning those same stools are occupied by the well-heeled and obviously secular women employees of the nearby bank sipping tea before opening hour.[12] Kuzguncuk's Islamists also played football every Saturday after-noon on the outdoor carpet with a number of us from the suburb who were not religious at all. The Koran-study members were keen to show off their piety, though, by wearing green and yellow shorts that hung well below their knees – modesty after all is an Islamist virtue.[13]

Despite this traffic between Islamists and others in Kuzguncuk, the group – or at least the idea of it – was not well liked by many locals, and my sitting with them at the taxi-rank on the main street frequently drew worried glances and concerned warnings. 'Don't believe what they tell you about Islam, they're ignorant,' I was often told. This not only by people who never read the Koran but also by conscientious Muslims, believers who prayed five times a day. And it was true that Ahmet *ağabey* and his friends boycotted the local mosque, refusing to pray with the state-employed religious functionary, even on the important ceremonial days when a large proportion of Kuzguncuk men attended morning prayer. This refusal was interpreted by others as an attempt to re-politicize Islam, the mosque according to secularist discourse having been evacuated of, even liberated from politics by its incorporation within the Religious Affairs department. The denial of the efficacy of prayer performed at the mosque was also seen as fractious, as a wilful splitting of local unity, religion serving not to bring the suburb's inhabitants together in a joint activity but to sunder them if taken too seriously. To the extent that Kuzguncuk's mosque was implicated in the state's work of ensuring that neighbourhoods continued to be useful 'producers of nationals', Ahmed *ağabey* and Co., in rejecting local activities in which they had once participated, were also splitters of national unity.

State Visions, Local Appropriations

This national unity as represented in Kuzguncuk is clearly not explicitly anti-religious: but neither are Kuzguncuk's Islamists unambiguously anti-nationalist. The struggle is over the definition and place of Islam within the state's production of (Turkish) nationality. Appadurai's point is fine as far as it goes: 'it is the nature of local life to develop partly by contrast

12. This reminds me of a story told by a friend. She explained that when attending an Islamist group in her teens, the teacher had banned them from sitting on any bus seat recently vacated by a man, in case of ritual pollution (and displaced sexual excitement).
13. If only that virtue had abounded on the battlefield of the soccer pitch!

to other neighbourhoods, by producing its own contexts of alterity (spatial, social and technical), contexts which may or may not meet the needs for spatial and social standardization prerequisite for the disciplined national citizen' (1995: 215).

But localities develop also by contrast to other localities within the same neighbourhood, where national movements and their oppositions attempt to put down roots, and local allegiances use their own resources (historical, ethnic, economic) to capitalize on, resist, or reinterpret state initiatives. Kuzguncuk's Islamists, then, are not pale imitators of the Refah Party's national strategy, and nor are they merely discursive 'affects' of a global Islamist discourse that is feared or celebrated as taking advantage of nation-state weakness to construct its own transnational 'citizens'. For the internationalization of national economies and the successful wooing of global capital flows (foreign investment) could just as easily bring a new ability to state elites to inscribe 'national' identities on the face of the city to an extent never managed before. Such a scenario should sober up those who fear that globalization is a threat to national or local identity (MacWorld), as if such identities express an abiding ethnic core somehow less historically constructed than that which would replace them.[14]

In the reconfiguration of power balances, alternative and Islamist Kuzguncuk may on some matters even share common interests, perhaps a mutual concern to prevent the expropriation of Kuzguncuk's localities as exemplary ciphers in the service of wider imagined communities such as the nation or the Muslim *ummah* (as constructed by Refah).

So there was, for example, an unanticipated but fascinating Christian–Muslim dialogue going on in the suburb, in which Ahmet *ağabey* and an equally enthusiastic Greek Orthodox friend would meet weekly to discuss their respective religious positions.[15] This was pursued very seriously: they would leave the taxi stand and march off to a secluded tea garden,

---

14. One may, on the other hand, decry for many other reasons the transformation of the democratic sociability of the city by state elites in their successful capturing of a portion of the capital washing around the globe in search of profit-making ventures.

15. Vassili refused to call himself Greek (*Yunan*), but described himself as Orthodox *Rum*. *Yunan* for him meant to be a citizen of Greece (*Yunanistan*), and though he was totally bilingual (Greek and Turkish) he did not have a Greek passport. On the contrary, he had done his 12-month military service in the Turkish Army. In fact Istanbul *Rum* have some problems with their status in Greece, where the Government does not look kindly on their 'abandoning' of Istanbul (Constantinople) to re-settle in Athens: the Greek state still maintains officially that Istanbul is theirs. Vassili reciprocated such hostility, claiming that Athens folk were inhospitable and rude. Even given his ascribed status as *gayri-Müslüman* (non-Muslim) and member of an official minority in Turkey, diaspora for him would mean living in Greece.

both of them with their notes, and pick up again from where they had left off the previous occasion, sometimes only the day before. The dialogue was possible because of the extraordinary character of each man – both were interested primarily in how the other was thinking, and perhaps in defeating his arguments, but there was little proselytizing intent in their discussions. I would meet with them sometimes as well, and for what it was worth put in my Protestant sixpence or two, so that the three of us would contradict each other or make temporary alliances in our arguments over the holy books or daily politics, over the nature of the regime, or the glory and disgrace of the histories of our own religions.

No doubt a cynic would see nothing illustrative in such an encounter, would disallow it any paradigmatic value in providing an explanation for the general phenomenon of Islamist revival, not just for Turkey but for the Muslim world as a whole. For though I would make the claim that such a dialogue was vital to the constitution of the Islamist movement in Kuzguncuk, the critic might reply that even so its dependency on the historical uniqueness of the suburb, its character as a unique happening, would disqualify it from carrying any wider significance. We shall see. But in what way could we say Vassili was an active player in the construction of an Islamist politics in Kuzguncuk, a politics that consequently made its constituents different from other Islamist groups in the vast suburbs of Istanbul?

Most importantly, Ahmet *ağabey*, the self-educated driving force behind the small Islamist group, could not accept the simplistic slogans circulating in the Islamist popular imagination regarding the Ottoman Empire. Vassili had made it clear for example that the mother of Sultan Fatih Mehmet (Ottoman conqueror of Constantinople) was *Rum*, and that Sultan Fatih could speak, read and write Greek. Ahmet *ağabey* had talked enough with Vassili then to acknowledge the 'intrusion' of non-Islamic elements into even the golden age of traditional Ottoman polity. Refah's ignoring of such complexities made him suspicious. Their slogan, *Biz Osmanlı Torunuyuz* ('we are the Ottoman grandchildren'), did not fill him with confidence – he interpreted it to mean they were more statist/ nationalist than Islamist. By contrast, a Refah Party member I met at the great rally in Inönü Stadium in celebration of *Fetih Günü* (Conquest Day) told me amidst all the excitement that Turkey would be rich and powerful in the future, would be the centre of the Islamic world once again, and that the Kurdish problem was a creation of Israel and the USA.

On the other hand, Ahmet *ağabey* and his friends' stress on the *asrı saadet* period seems to be in keeping with what Roy claims is the defining characteristic of Islamist movements all over the Muslim world: their inspiration by a 'political imagination dominated by a single paradigm: that of the first community of believers at the time of the Prophet and of the first four caliphs' (Roy 1994: 12). But the sharing of a common ideal (and its abbreviation to a slogan) is in fact no guarantee of a similar meaning's being encapsulated by its repetition in different contexts. (We will encounter this again in the chapters ahead, particularly in Part III: for example, in the contested meanings surrounding the universal Islamist phrase *Islam kardeşliği* (Islamic brotherliness)). Thus in the context of the production of a continuing nostalgia and mythology of the '*Pax Ottomana*' by more statist (Islamic or otherwise) organizations, Ahmet *ağabey*'s binding of the group to the imagined community of the *asrı saadet* is an implicitly anti-nationalist stance. But its deployment as an ideal by Islamist groups in Arab countries may well entail no such commitment. Conversely, in the parallel and common rejection by Arab Islamists of the Islamic credentials of the Ottoman Empire there may be scented more than a whiff of Arab nationalism. That is to say, Roy paints here with too wide a brush, assuming a global Islamist discourse that homogenizes not only Turkish but Arab local contexts. More self-conscious Shii communities, too, do not appreciate the perfection of the *asrı saadet*.

Pax Ottomana and State Nationalism

Nostalgia for the *Pax Ottomana* is, however, in the Turkish context neither artless nor naive. The rhetoric sometimes expresses an almost divine malignancy – the Balkan peoples, having allowed themselves to be provoked into rebellion by Western or Russian influence, have to face the continuing consequences of their unfaithfulness to the Ottoman Turks. Their ingratitude runs deep: 'there would be no Serbs, no Bulgarians, Romanians and Greeks, had not the Ottoman Turks conquered the Balkans. If the ever present and intimidating Catholic appetite had not been able to devour them, it has been so because of the Turkish invasion and conquest' (Ayverdi in Bora 1995: 106). Ahmet *ağabey*'s friendship with Vassili (among other things) does not allow him to accept such propositions. Islamist versions of the *Pax Ottomana* stress more the Islamic (rather than the Turkish) genius of the empire. But the same stories circulate. For example, the Refah-controlled Diyarbakır City Council sponsored the visit of a Polish historian and Muslim convert to a *Selahaddin-i Eyubbi* (Saladin) anniversary conference in Diyarbakır in 1996, who argued in his speech that the Muslim Turks didn't invade Europe but were invited there as a peace-keeping force by local peoples.

Hurt betrayal at the failure of others to express gratitude, however, presupposes *hizmet* (disinterested service) offered first to the peoples of the region, and secondly to Islam by the Ottoman Turks. Arab Muslims too can be ungrateful:

> So, Muslim civilization, assimilating the characteristics of the Seljukids, and thanks to the perfection of their government, to their social and cultural institutions, to the peace and safety they ensured, came to a new life and reached a new power, just as it was threatened with extinction. To conclude, the Turks have been the standard-bearers of Islam during ten centuries: they have conquered new countries for it; they have enabled Islam to take root in a huge domain from India to the Balkan peninsula (Köymen in Copeaux 1996: 109).

The quotation is taken from the 1990 Year 11 history textbook, although Copeaux makes it clear that notions of *hizmet* have permeated nationalist discourse throughout the Republic's history. These claims were secular-nationalist for most of the period, when for a long time the notorious 'history thesis' (*Tarih tezleri*) was taught in the schools.[16] But the slippage from benefactor of all of humanity to benefactor of Islam was present from the beginning as well, with the ascription of Turkish ancestry to many of the most notable Muslim leaders, scholars and philosophers, including even the Arab conqueror of Spain! This nervous tic is continuing – at that same *Selahaddin-i Eyubbi* conference the Governor of the province of Diyarbakır opened proceedings with the pronouncement that Saladin was a Turk. Neo-Ottomanism is a disreputable henchman of an old nationalistic theme, and Refah's flirtation with it (cf. Erbakan celebrating Conquest Day as the 'coming of tolerance and civilization') is revealing of the party's populist character. On these grounds, then, Refah can be accused of pandering to the Turk–Islam synthesis propagated by the state. On the other hand, its clever usage of Islamic expressions, for example *Hicret Gecesi* (the ceremony recalling Muhammad's flight from Mecca to Medina) as metaphors reveals its concern to appeal to less nationalistic sensibilities also. Ahmet *ağabey*'s refusal to get excited by the Refah Party's rhetoric is testimony to his friendship with Vassili, and to Kuzguncuk's continuing projection of itself as a parable of inter-faith tolerance.

16. 'The most conspicuous theme of the famous *Türk Tarihinin Ana Hatları* ("The Main Lines of Turkish History") is an alleged diffusion of the Turks towards the whole world during the Neolithic ages, inferring the idea of a decisive *hizmet* rendered to all of mankind' (Copeaux, 1996: 100–101).

Conclusion

I am not suggesting of course that Christian–Muslim dialogue *per se* is of significance for the self-constitution of Islamist movements. Indeed it is self-evidently not the only influence on Kuzguncuk's group. But is there a way in which this fragment of relationship, this snatch of social life can be valued for both its exceptional and its pedagogic qualities? Firstly the lived experiences of individuals have a validity, if only in terms of themselves, that we neglect at our peril. And secondly, could it not be that similar local interactions and contingencies are in part constitutive of all Islamist groups, so that general explanations for the increase in Islamist vitality need to be supplemented by the study of their production *in situ* on the ground? It may be true that Islam provides a 'common idiom for the deprived to express their social discontent' (Saktanber 1997: 147), or even that 'unemployment among the educated is undoubtedly the main resource of the Islamist movements' (Roy 1994: 51). But the fact remains that even the majority of the deprived or educated unemployed do not find in Islam a meaningful vocabulary of resistance,[17] while those that do are not all Islamist in the same way. For this reason we need to be alert to Islamisms, which are constituted simultaneously with the production of localities as contested practices, as well as in relation to the prior efface-ment of earlier imagined communities by nationalist regimes. We will see this particularly clearly in our analysis of Kurdish Islamism (Part III), which is dealing with a very different set of political considerations.

Let us now at long last walk the brisk five minutes from Kuzguncuk to Fetih Paşa Korusu (forest), to the tea garden and restaurant redeveloped by the Refah Party after their victory in the 1994 election for the Munici-pality of Greater Istanbul. Here we can witness the practices of a different civil society, one made possible by a complementary project of state formation by Islamist elites. In the chapters ahead we will consider whether Refah has indeed created an 'Islamized space' in its restoration of Ahmed Fetih Paşa's residence in the forest. If so, what relation does it have to the Republic's interpolating of its citizens through its construction of public buildings and secular place? And what, we may ask, will it share in common with the Islamism of Kuzguncuk's group? Like blazed trees, we will keep these questions to the fore to prevent us getting lost in the forest.

17. The Refah Party, in its best-ever result, won 22 per cent of the vote in the general election of 1996.

−3−

Civilizing Islam and Uncivil Laicism

Fetih Paşa Korusu

The forest on the south-eastern side of Kuzguncuk was bequeathed to the Istanbul 'Municipality' in 1854 by Ahmet Fetih Paşa, founder of modern museum science in the Ottoman empire.[1] This was the year in which Istanbul, under the inspiration of similar sanitary regimes in European capitals, organized its first major reforms in urban administration and services. The city was divided into 14 districts with the intention to 'embellish and regularize the city as a whole by strict control of building methods, regularization of the roads and the quays, and construction of water and sewage lines' (Çelik 1986: 47). The Asian shore of the Bosphorus, centred around Üsküdar, was then, as always, less densely populated than the European side: 'villages were separated by vacant areas and *yali* (mansions) lined the waterfront' (1986: 41). 'On condition that it would be opened up to the public and that no buildings should be erected on it' (Bektaş 1996a: 143) one of these areas was given to the city by Ahmed Fetih Paşa, a large tract of land that reared up steeply from the old goat track skirting the Bosphorus and joining the *gayri müslüman* (non-Muslim) village of Kuzguncuk to the town of Üsküdar (the ancient Scutari).

Laced throughout with trails, Fetih Paşa Korusu (Forest) is still thickly wooded and sweetly-scented, with elms, chestnuts, willows, firs, laurels, pine and plane trees growing familiarly side by side and on top of each other on the park's fierce slopes. Rising to a flattened plateau at its crown, the forest falls away rapidly on the park's back side, where Kuzguncuk has scrambled around the walls to meet it. The views over the busy sea lanes (where the trees permit) are spectacular, tramp steamers ploughing their way past Ahmet Fetih Paşa's historic *yalı* on the Bosphorus, once

---

1. All information regarding Ahmet Fetih Paşa is taken from Bektaş (1996a: 142ff.). Çelik (1986) shows that there was no unified greater city Municipality at that time: the park was possibly left to the Ministry of Public Works.

said to be among the most beautiful waterfront residences in Istanbul. In the summer the park is heavily patronized, picnickers crowding its open spaces for impromptu barbecues, lovers sidling along its paths, a sports court in its heart echoing to the twang of lipped-out basketballs. In the shade of the mature trees the ground is strewn with the debris of past festivities, among them the dried olive seeds that unwary local people might mistake for pine nuts. Wandering street-sellers and soldiers on weekend passes are legion: a boy sells conscripts-on-leave the opportunity to impress by shooting up balloons strung like coloured globes between two trees.

Fetih Paşa Korusu was given a major facelift in Bedrettin Dalan's mayoralty (1987–9), when the central government, on its return to civilian hands, passed two pieces of legislation that had significant effects on the urban landscape of Istanbul. The first resulted in a massive increase in the proportion of national tax revenues flowing to local councils. In the space of one year alone (1983–4) metropolitan governments' share of tax receipts rose from 6.4 per cent to 10.1 per cent. This meant, as Keyder and Öncü note, that 'for the first time in over two decades, the increase in Istanbul's revenue base outstripped current expenditures necessary for the maintenance of a municipal bureaucracy and basic services to allow for major infrastructural investments' (1994: 400). The second reform involved the streamlining and centralization of local administrative power under the authority of the metropolitan mayors of the three largest cities (Istanbul, Izmir, Ankara). In Istanbul this entailed, coincidentally, a return to the same number of district municipalities (14) as suggested by the 1855 Commission for the Order of the City (*Intizam-i Şehir Komisyonu*): the new law abolished 40 or more smaller councils, and devolved a number of services to the 14 new municipalities, including rubbish collection, street repairs and supervision of building regulations.

One consequence, then, of the Greater Istanbul Municipality's new-found wealth and mobility was an upgrade of the city's parks and gardens,[2] including in Kuzguncuk the designing of two small new parks on the shore of the Bosphorus. Fetih Paşa Korusu too was beautified in this period – its winding paths were paved or straightened, large ornamental lamp-posts appeared beside them and the forest itself was tidied up. The small tea garden and ornamental pool on the crest of the park were likewise cleaned and expanded.

---

2. Part of this programme included the environmental clean-up of the historic Golden Horn, the project capturing the imagination of the press in Dalan's oft-quoted promise 'to make its waters as blue as my eyes'.

The victory of the Refah Party in the 1994 local election led to a new burst of activity in the park. Though the land's original deed specified that there should be no further building activity, there were two rundown but large *yalı* inside the boundaries of the forest, one the sometime residence of Ahmet Fetih Paşa himself. Refah immediately began to restore these buildings (and extend them), turning the larger one into a restaurant with indoor and outdoor tables, and the other into a split-level tea garden. Refah has taken over (better, redeveloped) at least three other 'showpiece' sites in Istanbul as well: Çamlıca Restaurant, Hıdiv Kasrı (the former mansion of the Ottoman governor of Egypt) and Emirgan Park Restaurant, though these have all had long and varying histories as public places. If, as noted earlier, municipalities are dependent for the bulk of their revenue on central state financing (though they do have rights to tax some economic activities), it is probably true that their main influence on urban politics is 'through [their] ownership and control of various public buildings, parks and social spaces' (Çınar 1997: 30).[3] But this is no mean power: in the production of local and civic identities one office of interior designers is worth a busload of riot police, as Napoleon might have said, under other circumstances. Refah's interventions in public space should be read, then, as empirical presentations of an imagined social order even as they constitute it.

Fetih Paşa Korusu and Islamized Public Space

In short, the Refah Party's self-conception is on show in Fetih Paşa Korusu, as is its vision of the citizenry it hopes to civilize through their consumption of the facility. Has Refah attempted to create in the forest an 'Islamized space', a utopian place in which Islamic social relations (however defined) dominate, a liberated zone somewhat similar to the homes of Ahmet *agabey* and his friends in Kuzguncuk? Olivier Roy claims this is the distinguishing feature of Islamism once its revolutionary zeal is exhausted or frustrated: a drift into neo-fundamentalism and grassroots activism, in which pockets of Islamized space become bridgeheads 'with the idea of later spreading the principles on which [they are] founded to the whole of society' (Roy 1994: 80).

---

3. Keyder and Öncü note that in the immediate aftermath of the Motherland Party's Municipality reform bills, and in the return of Istanbul as a corporate borrower to the foreign credit markets, the Mayoralty of Istanbul became an influential position indeed. But Dalan's successors have not been as flamboyant or prodigal as he, nor has the whiff of financial scandal surrounded City Hall to the same degree.

What are such Islamized spaces characterized by? Certainly by a stress on head-covering for women, but also by the banning of alcohol, and by the organizing of work relations to render conformity to Islamic obligations (separation of genders, daily prayer, fasting during Ramazan etc.) more convenient. So cafés or restaurants might be closed on Friday afternoons to allow employees to attend the mosque, or a small prayer-room (*mescit*) provided inside or next to factories and entertainment complexes for the same reason.

Has Refah attempted to create such an Islamized space? The first thing to note in proposing a more specific answer is the setting of the tea garden and restaurant – within a forest that, though cleared of dead trees and litter by the municipality, is not made to conform to a park master plan (unlike a Botanical Garden, which maps the whereabouts and species of every shrub), but grows free within the confines of its redbrick walls. For as Bauman notes, there has been a long association between the civility of the self and the formality of the garden. 'Courtesy was an act of adjustment and survival which made the jungle of Versailles inhabitable' (Bauman 1985: 7). The courtiers were as carefully cultivated as the hedges were groomed. Civilizing society was akin to ordering the wilderness: both needed a paternal but firm hand to transform the state of nature. Kemalism's civilizing project too required a bedding-down and an uprooting – modern society and ordered parks imply each other, metaphorically and in practice. So Bozdoğan writes that

> Largely unexplored by critical studies of architectural history is the trans-
> formation of provincial towns under the modernizing agenda of the young
> republic, the construction of public buildings symbolic of the administrative
> and ideological apparata [*sic*] of the new regime . . . complete with the formal
> square (*Hükümet meydanı*) and the municipal park (belediye parkı) with their
> inevitable Atatürk statues . . . (Bozdoğan 1994: 39 – my emphasis).

Forests, unlike parks, are prone to anarchy: Refah's choice of a forest setting is revealing of a certain modesty, even self-doubt surrounding the nature of its *mission civilisatrice*.

Upon approaching the tea garden and restaurant from the Bosphorus side of the forest the first thing you encounter is the large (and probably illegal) car park. Though the park is within easy walking distance of Üsküdar, and on countless bus and minibus routes, the expectation that patrons will arrive in cars both assumes a certain prosperity, and coronates a particular lifestyle. Of course Istanbul's urban structure is increasingly determined by the motor car. But the car park casts into relief the way notions of the nuclear family and its sphere of privacy and conviviality are taken for granted by Refah's architects. By way of contrast, the provision of free buses for poor families to attend weekend summer picnics at green spots on the outskirts of the city by the I.E.T.T. (Istanbul Electric Public Transport, also under the authority of the Greater Istanbul Municipality) shows Refah's cognizance of the class differences separating its possible supporters. It gives a clue, too, to Refah's targeted users for Fetih Paşa Korusu.

The restaurant and tea garden themselves are bordered with flowerbeds, while the blazing white timber walls of Ahmet Fetih Paşa's old residence are immaculately maintained. On entering the restaurant the diner is greeted by a formally dressed waiter (black tie, white shirt, black trousers) and ushered to a vacant table in one of the wooden-floored rooms, where couples, families, even single diners may be eating. Thus there is no organized separation of the genders, and no family salon either, though the mansion has many rooms, enough to set aside such a place. The restaurant does not serve alcohol, but they do fill the large wine glasses on the tables with water. European visitors should feel at home, for the interior furnishings are basically French, with high-backed chairs, ornate chandeliers, and cream-coloured serviettes shaken out by the waiters: a religious friend once remarked that the only Islamic thing here was the customers.

The music piping softly though the speakers, however, is non-Western – Turkish Art music (*Türk Sanat Musiği*) with a dash of Sufi (*tasavvuf*) orchestration, though Vassili assured me that the origin of Turkish Art music was the Byzantine court. This theory, though I am not sure if Vassili was aware of it, was first propagated by Ziya Gökalp, a leading ideologue of the early Republican period, in his 1923 *Principles of Turkism*. Here, according to Tekellioğlu, Gökalp made a distinction between Eastern music, taken from the Byzantines, and folk melodies, the tradition of ancient Turkish music (Tekellioğlu 1996). Music in fact was harnessed to the civilizing project. 'Turkish' Art music, and religious music, were even banned from the radio in the 1930s for a period, as the state sponsored the teaching of Western polyphony in the new conservatoria of music. According to the official position, Turkish folk-music alone represented the genius of the nation, and was notated, scored in accordance with Western harmony and recorded in the 1920s and 1930s, a decade or so after Vaughan Williams was 'retrieving' the lost traces of ploughmen's songs and shepherds' tunes in pre-Great War Britain. Bela Bartok too was part of this great upsurge of interest in folk-music as the bearer of national identity, although his collecting of folk-tunes with Zoltan Kodaly in places as far afield as Algeria and the Edirne region of Turkey suggests a different political logic at work (Kahn 1995). Turkish folk-music, as collected and classified by the Turkish State Radio researchers, was in fact often Kurdish – but this of course was contrary to reality as announced by the state.

How significant this choice of music is, I'm not sure. The rehabilitation of Turkish Art music in the 1950s, indeed its rise and rise to being a staple feature of state television, reveals its incorporation within the changing cultural policies of the regime. Its playing in the restaurant promotes, then, a certain refinement and seriousness. Yet perhaps the absence of folk (*halk*) music, with its more recent appropriation by leftist and Alevi politics, is telling as well. In this case the restaurant's construction of an indigeneity against the West (no rock or Turkish pop music here) excludes in the same clef other potential localities – in this instance the possibility that an unorthodox Muslim creed like Alevism and the music claimed as constituting it could be made to represent Turkey 'in the competition of civilizations' (words of Refah's Istanbul mayor, Recep Tayyip Erdoğan, at the opening of Çamlıca Restaurant).

Fifty metres away in the tea garden a similar style of music (probably the identical cassette) flows from the speakers tied to its trees. The beautifully restored building, furnished in the same simple yet luxurious manner as the restaurant, is surrounded by 30 or more small tables. The long embroidered drapes upstairs are tied back from the windows to ensure that the view through the trees and over the Bosphorus remains open. The main difference resides in the back room – there the floor has been torn up and replaced with concentrically ordered black and white pebbles, while its wall has become an artificial cliff-face, wetted at its base by a clattering waterfall. Its chatter all but drowns out the soothings of the *ney* (a type of wooden flute). There is nothing particularly 'Islamic' about this simulacrum of nature, with its patches of greenery, uneven rock surface and splashing water. *Huzur Islamdadır* (In Islam is Tranquillity) is a slogan often seen around the Islamist traps – perhaps the haven in the forest, and this room in particular, where one can drink and eat in the midst of millions to the sounds not of car horns but burbling water, is meant as an embodiment of such a claim. But similar havens and rooms all over the world suggest a more global dialectic is at work, a dialectic in which the felt need for 'nature' as a refuge, a getaway is understood not as a reaction to the global destruction of a sense of home but as an aspect of its reconstruction. As with the choice of music, the important problems revolve around the clash of 'interests served by strategies of what [we may] call glocalization' (Robertson 1995: 28). Refah's adoption of some sort of 'international' style for its back room may indeed project an air of universalism against other (suddenly) parochial presences. Strategic submission to 'imperialism's culture' can be as politically self-interested, then, as strategic essentialism.

What beverages do the tea garden and restaurant at Fetih Paşa Korusu serve? Interestingly, both offer Coca-Cola, which has been publicly removed from the menu by Refah at another of its sites, Çamlıca Restaurant. There the Municipality has taken an opposite tack: the mayor of Istanbul, in his speech at its opening ceremony stated that 'The Çamlıca premises have been renovated in accordance with the principles of national identity, national culture and national personality. No foreign beverages will be served here, whether alcoholic or non-alcoholic. Our people will enjoy Turkish beverages and Turkish meals' (Çınar 1997: 31). Çamlıca, however, has not been as successful in exorcizing foreign substances from its kitchen as the mayor would have liked. As Çınar points out, the thirsty punter can still order 'Nescafe' (the generic name for instant coffee) – and this in a country famed for its Turkish coffee! Nescafe is available at Fetih Paşa Korusu too, as is *biftek* (beef-steak) and *krem karamel*. 'Nationality' obviously does not carry so much weight here. We can probably speak therefore of a genre of renovated public places (Fetih Paşa, Çamlıca, Hıdiv Kasrı, Emirgan etc.) in which gradations of 'authenticity' are exhibited, both before the tourist gaze (the construction of particularity *vis-à-vis* the West) and the gaze of Istanbul's own residents (the construction of universality *vis-à-vis* the local). 'Glocalization' equates then with an obvious hybridity of public space, as socio-political movements selectively indigenize global flows in the context of the struggle for locality.

Who consumes Fetih Paşa Korusu? Low prices, especially at the tea garden, make it accessible to most people, and the restaurant too is good value: a grilled fish at Kuzguncuk's renowned Ismet Baba tavern costs twice as much as in the forest. In summer, especially at weekends, the facilities are well patronized, reservations being necessary for the restaurant on Saturday nights. Probably the majority of diners are 'religious' – family parties of *sıkma baş* (veiled) women wearing long coats, and men with *çember sakal* (rounded beards). In contrast the café is a haunt for young couples, Islamist or otherwise, older people during the day and groups of covered girls in the late afternoon. Non-religious people too are well represented, the complex being non-discriminatory on grounds of 'civility'.

Islamist Spaces in the Domain of the Republic

Refah's work in Fetih Paşa Korusu, then, clearly involves the opening up of public space to both Islamist and non-Islamist subjects, unlike interventions inspired by official Kemalist discourse, which takes special care to exclude unauthorized expressions of Islam from the public domain. This can be seen not only in the key reproductive sites of republicanism (the university, concert hall, Palace of Justice, hospital, even the stadium)[4] but also in the 'pristine secularism' of the 'official-ceremonial' zone of state television.

Yet secularization, like Islamization, is a process, not a state. It is always being achieved. Analysis of the threat of an activist Islamism, growing (like a cancer) often portrays the secular order as in passive crisis, its once-and-for-all reforms rapidly being wound back, its original energies atrophying over time. But similar research should be devoted to the equally productive practices of secularism and the making of contemporary secular subjects. This, first, would be informed by a history of consumption, of the consumption by the cultivated palate of republicanism in the form of its theatre and music, sculpture and galleries. It would be a subjective history also, a history of the construction of taste, a history of the ways people and families 'civilize' themselves, sometimes in contradistinction to 'Islamic' values, sometimes by mummifying them, freezing them in the collecting of tiles and carpets, miniatures, Ottoman furniture or calligraphed Korans.[5]

But secularism is not always achieved by the state (theatre, orchestra, exhibitions). In Istanbul, for example, there has been in the last few years an explosion of rock bars, where skilful and loud punk, metal, and grunge bands (including some all-women groups) play to an appreciative and knowledgeable sub-culture. Criticized as a purveyor of cultural imperialism (by a Marxist friend, and no doubt also by Islamists) local rock music enters an arena (i.e. music) historically of intense interest to the state and its new elites. Yet rock music is an aesthetic of ambiguous meaning, both as a global 'trans-culture', and in its articulation with the politics of national identity. Is the popularity of the rock scene in Istanbul related, I wonder, to both the rigid conventions of self-presentation and the political pressure on 'culture' always to signify in either laicist or religious terms? For rock bars seem a space, restricted as it is, for 'ugly ducklings' to swim in, a cultural space that transgresses some of the symbolic markers of class, religion, respectability (and gender?) that dominate civil life. Rock bars,

4. Sporting events too are grist for the nationalist mill. So Fenerbahçe (one of Istanbul's most famous football teams) carried a banner around the field before its match against Ankaragücü proclaiming *Atam Her Zaman Izindeyiz* ('My Atatürk, we are always in your footsteps') (reported in *Yeni Yüzyil,* 8 October 1996).

5. Deniz Kandiyoti notes some of the historical research written on the changing habits of socialiability in Istanbul's upper and middle classes, including Ekrem Isin's work on nineteenth century modernization and daily life in *Tanzimattan Cumhuriyete Türkiye Ansiklopedisi* [From Tanzimat to the Republic Encyclopaedia]. And there is Duben and Bahar's 1991 study, *Istanbul Households: Marriage, Family and Fertility, 1889–1940.* But Kandiyoti makes the point that ethnographies of the modern (and hence of secularity) that 'deal with the full complexity of the contemporary cultural landscape are long overdue' (1997: 113).

with their studied lack of interest in politics, are secular spaces seeking relief from the state's over-politicization of culture. On the other hand, the SHP (Social People's Party), where once it would have organized a folk-music concert, hired a rock band for its election campaign meeting in Kadiköy, 1996.

Secularism from above, however, is concerned to educate. Islam on the 'official-ceremonial' zone of state television is carefully stage-managed, presented more as an historical artefact than a contested and hence living 'faith'. How lovingly the camera pans over the fineness of the ceramic tiles glittering with tulip bulbs, sonorous flute music in the air. Or passes slowly over the façade of the Ottoman Baroque mosque, one more trace of civilization alongside the glorious ruins of Byzantine and Seljuk buildings witnessing to the richness of the cultural heritage of Turkey. On the homogeneous world of state television, living Islam means laic Islam: 'Every Friday evening, during a 15-minute "religious hour" the talking head of State Religious Affairs appeared to deliver an edifying message on the virtues of charity, honesty or humility befitting a good Muslim, speaking in standardized Turkish and dressed in secular garb' (Öncü 1995: 25). Yet the manicuring of Islam for orderly consumption conjures up at the same time another Islam, deviant, unkempt and unlettered, an Islam from the boondocks that refuses to be put in its place. '[L]urking in the interstices of everyday life and practices . . . the other, dark face of Islam has thus been as familiar for Turkish audiences as its visible "civilized" face' (1995: 24). This Islam is the more to be feared for its inability to be properly enunciated.

With the declaration of Fetih Paşa Korusu as neutral ground by both Islamist and laic subjects however, the 'dark' and 'civilized' faces of Islam sip tea, drop crumbs and fill ashtrays side by side, sometimes even at the same table.[6] This encounter is transgressive of the strict codes of conduct constituting the utopian orders of both secular modernist and Islamist worlds. So the Constitutional Court has ruled in a recent decision that the wearing of headscarfs to university is contrary to the principles of the Constitution. As the court affirmed, higher education students should be people who

6. One extraordinary incident I witnessed occurred while sitting in Fetih Paşa Korusu tea garden with a covered woman, translating another foreigner's questions about the way women are thought of in Islamist circles. A total stranger from the adjacent table interrupted our conversation to ask about polygamy in Islam. The woman, not wearing Islamist clothes or headscarf, said her husband (who was not religious) was having an affair and was justifying it in the name of Islam. She wanted to know the conditions under which the taking of a second wife was acceptable. My Islamist friend quickly disabused her of the belief that the Koran legtitimized her husband's behaviour.

firstly and above all else adopt as their own Atatürk's reforms and principles and prove these principles correct in their own behaviour . . . Students who don the turban or veil, who wear clothes that carry religious connotations, who are opposed to contemporary appearances and fashion are behaving contrary to Atatürk's reforms and principles. Such students should act according to the duties incumbent upon them [as educated people], in order that their trustworthiness and sincerity are not to be doubted (*Yeni Şafak*, 31 October 1996 – my translation).

The policing of the public domain from the side of utopian Islamists is just as determined:

women should not see any men outside the legitimate categories. They should definitely not deal with the water delivery man, milkman or street sellers. They should not become accustomed to going to the market or local milkbar. Shopping should be left to the husband; women should be grateful for whatever he brings home. Lazy husbands load the work of going to the market on to their wives: this is an unforgivable sin. Muslim women should not accede to such a request and should protect their husband from falling into this mistake. Women should go out, then, only at their husband's side and only when absolutely necessary. In the street women should cover their heads and bodies with loose and full-length clothing. Muslim women should not visit crowded places, nor spend time with non-religious neighbours and acquaintances. Before going out they should first obtain permission from their husband, and should not overstay the arranged hour. When receiving or giving hospitality they should not wear expensive, luxurious clothes that may encourage wasteful or envious desires in other women. They should not adorn themselves with jewellery nor go to the meetings of women who do. They should not indulge in gossip or dwell in their speech on topics of a material or worldly nature. When visiting as a family men and women should definitely sit apart from each other. They should not be deceived by Western or foreign influences like other lost and miserable Muslims (Düzdağ 1995: 46–7 – my translation).[7]

7. I have chosen Düzdağ's book because it is published by *Iz Yayınevi*, one of the biggest Islamist publishing houses in Turkey, who also bring out the most intellectual and liberal of the Islamist newspapers, *Yeni Şafak*. Their simultaneous printing of material implicitly or explicitly critiquing Düzdağ's interpretation indicates just how multifaceted Islamist positions on gender are. *Tarikat* Islam (religious communities gathered around a teacher or mullah, whose authority is commonly inherited) is often far more restrictive *vis-à-vis* the opportunities given to women than are political Islamists, who ascribe a more activist role to women in the struggle against secularist regimes. Olivier Roy, helpfully in my opinion, labels this difference as one between neo-fundamentalism and Islamism, though one should be sensitive to the slippage between the two, as well as to some of their shared assumptions. See Açar (1991) for a comparison between the space made available to women in the discourse of three different Islamist journals.

Düzdağ goes on to argue quite logically that veiled Muslim women should even leave the political struggle over their exclusion from the university to the men. He recommends that students take precautionary note of an (unnamed) sociologist's claim that protesting Islamist female students are not merely criticizing the State's policies when they march in the streets, but are also challenging the dogmas and commands of Islam at the same time. University education is a two-edged sword, and to prevent it cutting both ways the Muslim woman's field of *cihat* (holy war), he concludes, is in the home (1995: 51).

We see, then, that both the state and this particular variety of the Islamist movement concur in the attempt to drive Islamist women out of the public sphere altogether. Likewise neither of them is backward in formulating a project of control over women's bodies. The 'private' sphere in which Islamist women would be corralled, however, is in both Republican and Islamist discourse constituted and recruited as a key ally in the political struggle for the public domain. Private habits should be redolent of public virtues, and women are vested with the responsibility of ensuring that the imagined communities of nation or *ummah* are discovered sheltering in the benevolent environment of the home.

Liberal Islamism and Olive Branch Architecture

In Fetih Paşa Korusu by contrast there is a democratic opening up of space to sections of civil society previously excluded by the evolution of Turkish modernity. In this process Refah has found itself unable to promote the assumed eternal hostility of Islamist and Republican visions of the good society. But neither have the tea garden's visitors. Veiled girls flicking cigarette ash into the wind, bearded men toting mobile phones, the conspicuous consumption seen in high heels, fashion accessories, silk scarves and new cars – new Islamists for new Islamist spaces. The Islamist clothes designer and *Tekbir* fashion-house owner Cafer Karaduman answers the critics of his cakewalk shows blandly by saying, 'Am I defending them to you by doubting their unlawful (*haram*) character? I know that it is a sin for women models to take their place in the fashion-parades. I am unable to give an explanation. But today there are many things that Muslims do that are difficult to explain' (Çayır 1997). Fashion parades and high-quality glocal restaurants are just some of the activities that deconstruct, for those with eyes to see, the 'dark' face of Islam. But they deconstruct too the claims of other Islamists that appropriate this very 'dark' face as authentic Islam. Refah's work in Fetih Paşa Korusu is simultaneously then a competing aestheticization of Islam to the one presented on State television, and a civilizing project aimed towards itself, i.e. an internal reform movement. Çayır concludes his article by saying, 'I would still probably describe myself as an Islamist (*Islamcı*). But certainly not an 80's Islamist . . . My modern profession blends into my identity . . . And I must confess. I am a mongrel (*ilişmiş*) Muslim sociologist. One who does not use the word 'and' . . . to separate existence into two great worlds, modern and Islamic (*mahrem*)' (ibid.).

To return at last to our original query, should Refah's tea garden and restaurant in the forest be analysed as an 'Islamized space'? Not, I think, in the sense mapped out by Roy, despite the appearance of several tell-tale features indicating such a process. True, the facility does not serve alcohol, and the municipality has built a small prayer-room (*mescit*) next to the restaurant. And Çınar for one argues that the Greater Istanbul Municipality's prohibition of alcohol in places under its jurisdiction is the single policy that may indeed be thought of as an expression of Islamization. But she goes on to note that Refah's restrictions are made, not in the name of Koranic stipulations, but as part of a policy combating discrimination, to enable access to public places for people whose beliefs do not allow them to attend functions where alcohol is served. Refah's objection problematizes of course the assumed neutral character of the public sphere. And the same logic could be employed by an Islamist Municipality to regulate, say, the length of dresses, mini skirts being able to be inscribed as an obstacle to the ability of pious Muslim males to enjoy public places. This has not happened. Indeed, it is the state that enforces a dress code for both its male and female employees. Accordingly the Republic has long been accused of de-sexualizing the women it emancipated. 'Kemalist women', says Ayse Kadıoğlu, 'were expected to relegate their sexuality to an insignificant realm and focus on their public visibility as emblems of modernization' (Kadıoğlu 1994: 659). State feminism, then, could be seen as a form of gender 'syndicalism', made subservient to the greater good of the nation. The wearing of suits (and the abolition of the fez) were part of the state's production of masculinity – gender syndicalism applied to the making of 'national man' too. The display of Atatürk's clothes, his suits, top hats and tails, is prominent in the museum next to his tomb.

But in no other aspect does Fetih Paşa Korusu conform to Roy's model (deduced mainly from the actions of the Algerian FIS, upon their winning the mayoralties of the large cities). So there is no discrimination against uncovered women, no attempt to encourage women to wear veils or to enforce a 'modest' dress code. Sex apartheid is non-existent (the tea garden even had a unisex toilet when it was first opened), and the restaurant and tea garden open for lunch in the month of Ramazan. Friday trading, too, is unrestricted. Lastly Roy makes the point that Islamized zones are puritanical spaces, often involving the closing down of cafés: 'neo-fundamentalism entails a shrinking of the public space to the family and the mosque' (Roy 1994: 83). Certainly Fetih Paşa Korusu does not fit this bill.

Yet if we accept Roy's claim that the Algerian Islamists' puritanical rejection of all worldly diversions is in fact a far cry from a certain *joie de vivre* of 'traditional' Islam, Islamization as a process should be defined not by its return to some original Islamic essence but by its relationship to the real relations of power in which it is historically enmeshed. It will thus appear in many forms according to the political context in which it emerges. On these grounds Fetih Paşa Korusu restaurant and tea garden *is* an Islamized space, different of course from the 'liberated zones' created by the Islamisms of urban Algeria or the warriors tribesmen of Afghanistan, but equally an amalgam of different sources and influences and their spiralling future trajectories. Much of the drama of national politics resides in the historic, but mutually constitutive, polarization of secularist and Islamist identities in Turkish modernity. Refah's pronouncement of a cease-fire in the Fetih Paşa Korusu site, its flourishing of an olive branch, is of great importance in creating a demilitarized civil zone. No more (nor less) hybrid than public spaces symbolizing the two other warring parties, the restaurant and tea garden (along with the Municipality's other restorations) proffer a third way, a way wooing the constituents of the Islamist movement itself. If, as Çınar concludes, Çamlıca restaurant's valorization of 'indigenous' culture signifies the 'rejection of the West within' (1997: 25), then Fetih Paşa rejects the inner East with equal measure.

Islamist Populism, Social Distinction and Class

Jean-Paul Sartre tells a story somewhere about a man sitting on a park bench, half-way up a hill. The man looks over the scene, at the ducks swimming in the pond, the dog straining at the leash, the strolling lovers. The sun warm on his back, God in his heaven, the gentle breeze; and the world below him all his, object of his gaze, its activities given a meaning by his presence. The park is centred, granted perspective from where he sits. The man yawns, stretches, glances casually up behind him. He freezes, aghast. There higher up the hill sits a man on a park bench, surveying the scene . . .

A year or so after Refah's restaurant and tea garden were opened for business in Fetih Paşa Korusu, a huge hole appeared almost overnight in the crown of the park. Concrete was poured, the steel struts of columns pushed into the air, and soon an imposing new structure was lurking over the rooftops of Kuzguncuk and beyond, able to be seen even from the waters of the Bosphorus. A small campaign initiated in Kuzguncuk (by Cengiz Bektaş among others) to stop the construction work was carried on by the Istanbul branch of the Chamber of Architects. The lorries and jackhammers were stilled for a period as the Greater Istanbul Municipality suspended operations to investigate the project. Yet by hook or by crook, and despite the obvious breach of the conditions under which the Forest was bequeathed to the City, building activity resumed some time later, until a bigger and better, luxurious restaurant/function-centre graced the scene. 'It took dominion everywhere,' as Wallace Stevens said of the jar in Tennessee[1] (Stevens 1990: 76).

---

1. I placed a jar in Tennessee,/And round it was, upon a hill./It made the slovenly wilderness/Surround that hill. //The wilderness rose up to it,/And sprawled around, no longer wild./The jar was round upon the ground/And tall and of a port in air. //It took dominion everywhere./The jar was gray and bare./It did not give of bird or bush,/Like nothing else in Tennessee ('Anecdote of the Jar').

Bourgeois Islamism and Dilruba Restaurant

Like the man in Sartre's fable, Refah's enterprise has been trumped by the Dilruba Restaurant, reducing its ability to control the production of its own meaning as unique. Put less negatively, Dilruba has clarified the range of possible interpretations able to be sustained in any reading of the new site, now understood as encompassing the two areas. At a passing glance Dilruba and Fetih Paşa Korusu restaurants share a family resemblance. Both have been designed as repositories of 'localness', and both are political practices assaulting secularist assumptions that repress open or unofficial expressions of Islam in a de-Islamized public domain. But Dilruba's organizing of some of the same signifiers to construct a rival presentation of national culture for diners to savour along with their food is more explicitly an intervention of class power: Dilruba is concerned to spice the cuisine produced in its 'authentic' Ottoman kitchen with a taste or civility that will enable patrons to separate themselves off from those who cannot appreciate such pleasures. This is not just performed through the restaurant's decorations, atmosphere and musical genres: the prices alone are intimidating to the poor. To sup from the groaning tables of the smorgasbord breakfast provided on Sunday mornings would cost a small family US $40, while main courses are three times more expensive (and exotic) than at Fetih Paşa Korusu. For the extra money diners listen live to the same style of Sufi music that crackles out of the speakers down the hill. Like a rich uncle, Dilruba is what it is only in relation to its poor relatives.

In the process of constituting themselves as a more exclusive (Islamist?) middle class, what do consumers of Dilruba's locality experience? Unlike the black trousers and bow ties of the waiters at Fetih Paşa Korusu, Dilruba's waiters wear 'genuine' Ottoman uniforms, the designs being copied, according to the chief steward, from the dress of people in old photographs. 'Ottoman' in this sense denotes late eigtheenth- or early nineteenth-century Ottomanism, an Ottomanism already impregnated for three or more generations with 'Westernization'.[2] Interestingly, only the waiters wear the orange blouses and red sashes wound tightly around their waists; the man cooking the pizzas beside the blue Iznik-tiled open-oven in a corner of the room is draped in a white apron. The function room too is expressive of an Ottoman nostalgia, its ceiling embellished by geometrically-precise cream squares, its centrepiece a painting of a flower arrangement on one of the wooden panels.

2. Ottoman modernization (*Tanzimat*) is usually dated from 1839, the year of the Imperial Rescript of Gülhane [Park].

The owner has also appropriated public land in order to build beside the restaurant a biggish *mescit* (prayer-room) with separate entrances for men and women. Like the restaurant, the *mescit* too is topped with somewhat angular-looking cupolas (*kubbe*), similar to the roofs of many mosques. Though there is no gender segregation in the restaurant, the complex does provide it for those who ask – one wedding I noted had the groom and the male company seated in the restaurant and the bride and the women in the function room.

Rather incongruously, a large nomad's tent has been erected on the complex's lowest garden, complete with wooden stools woven from straw and round metal trays for the waiter to place the food brought out from the kitchen. Next to the tent in a prominent position on the grassy knoll is a village *ayran*-maker, a cigar-shaped steel-banded barrel hanging on two chains connected to a metal tripod. The barrel historically was swung back and forth to make a salty drink from yogurt and water. Like the pots and pans swaying above the public brazier (*ocak başı*) inside the restaurant, these signs of rural life are more works of art (sculpture) than functional implements. By contrast with what is enacted at Çamlıca, where *köylu* (village) women make and sell *gözleme* (savoury pancakes) in the garden, diners at Dilruba do not need to interact with any flesh and blood nomads while waiting for their food.

Dilruba's ambience is created, then, by the site's invocation of, and gesturing towards, three different discursive formations: Ottomanism, Islamism and Anatolianism. Constituted by their particular ordering of a network of signifiers, none of these three political visions is so settled that its signifiers are not liable to be broken off and grafted on to another discourse as a key sign. Indeed, the symbols constituting the discourse of Turkish-Ottomanism are prone to appropriation by Islamist reinterpretation, and vice versa. Signifiers are always polysemic; it is their very indeterminacy that makes them useful as footsoldiers in the production of identity. An *ayran* barrel perched on the lawns of a five-star restaurant in Istanbul carries a different meaning than would its display on the cover of an *Alevi* journal. In the same way a rearrangement of the importance of the various signifiers constituting a discursive formation allows for the multiplication of the political interventions made in its name. Anatolianism (*anadoluculuk*), for example, may be split between Turkist and multiculturalist tendencies that privilege different signs in a similar chain of signifiers. Disputed discourses can themselves become shorthand signifiers in competing projects of state or civil society formation.

Dilruba's genius consists in its harnessing together representatives of three different (but related) imagined communities to legitimize not merely its squatting on public property, but to de-politicize each of their universal claims. By re-inscribing them within the context of Dilruba's production of a class to whom nothing, once commodified, is foreign, the site is re-constituting a class difference bridged for a period by Refah's populism in Fetih Paşa Korusu. In contrast to Fetih Paşa Korusu's and Çamlıca's opening up of public space, and the corresponding widening of the bounds of citizenship to encompass groups historically unwelcome to the prime sites of modernity, Dilruba entails a closing-off of such possibilities. The restaurant owner Abdurrahman Iraz admitted as much in an interview in the paper:

> We want to enlarge the restaurant from one cupola to four. To the increase in diners we will give the answer of a larger kitchen. This will be the type of kitchen that the customer will be able to enter and inspect. Unlike at Çamlıca, we want this to be a place where those [donkeys] who have just slipped their tether [i.e. peasant riffraff] are unable to come (*Burası da Çamlıca gibi ipini koparanın gelemeyeceği bir yer olsun istiyoruz*) (*Cumhuriyet*, 3 May 1996 – my translation).

In this process the pursuit of profit, according to Abdurrahman Iraz, is of little importance. The aim of the restaurant was to 'win' for Turkey its most modern and best-decorated (*donanımlı*) kitchen. For this reason (presumably) the people who opposed the development were described by Iraz as 'traitors' (*vatan haini*). This of course is a nice irony, as Iraz had already made it clear that Dilruba's aim was to provide a 'cultural service' (ibid.) for an elite: are the interests of the nation and those of its elite so synonymous that to oppose one is to betray the other?

Last we should note Iraz's claim that he intends to turn the existing garden next to the restaurant into a Botanical Park, where swans will swim among newly planted water-lilies inside the ornamental pool paved with special stone quarried at Antalya. The reference to botanical gardens reminds us of civilizing processes, processes pursued, like the planning of a botanical park, in the light and name of science and rationality, complete with balanced representations of flora from all the varied eco-niches of a particular environment. Outside – a Botanical Park, and inside – a Cultural Garden, Dilruba Restaurant has selected and displayed the finest examples of 'tradition' from different civilizations for the gaze of the connoisseur. Civilizing processes remind us too of the Turkish nation-state, which has long been the driving force in introducing a selective 'civilizing' (Westernizing) of Turkish society. Dilruba reveals both a 'de-etatisation (Göle 1996: 34) of the civilizing project (as it is appropriated by civil society), and a widening of, and struggle over its aesthetic characteristics – fashion *alla franca* (in the European way) is no longer unquestionably accepted as the sole criterion of civility. That is, in the struggle for the accumulation of symbolic capital, Islamic, Ottoman and Anatolian discursive signifiers are aestheticized in Dilruba to produce an Islamist counter-elite. Islamism in this sense 'is the formation of the Muslim subject and agency which has been excluded from modernist [Western] definitions of civilization and history-making' (Göle 1996: 26). Dilruba is in short the expression of a civilizing will migrated to civil society, a civilizing will that disputes that mastery of Western culture is the only legitimate basis for a social distinction that it too is coveting.

Islamist Caste Versus Social Class?

In attempting to attract the Islamist elite that once patronized Fetih Paşa Korusu, Dilruba not only acknowledges the internal differentiation making up the Islamist movement, it also contributes to its realization. If by default it facilitates the erosion of the presumed unity of the Islamist *ummet* (universal community of believers), it expresses too the increasing hetero-geneity of civil society. True, Islamist subjects have probably always struggled to harmonize in a single social movement a rich pot-pourri of concerns and interests.[3] Yet Dilruba shows how increasingly difficult the project to construct an Islamist counter-culture is, one held together as much by its alienation from a presumed homogeneous Westernized elite as by being structured according to shared discursive ideals. Dilruba is symbolic, then, of one of a growing number of tensions within the Islamist movement itself – in this case between a *molla* (mullah) Islamism with close links to *tarikats* (Sufi orders) and the inhabitants of the *gecekondu/apartkondu* slums of the big cities on the one hand, and a more educated Islamist elite less prepared to countenance the constraints of a communi-tarian Islamist monoculture on the other.[4]

3. Olivier Roy for example describes Islamist movements as 'oscillating between two poles: a revolutionary pole, for whom the Islamization of the society occurs through state power; and a reformist pole, for whom social and political action aims primarily to re-Islamize the society from the bottom up, bringing about, *ipso facto*, the advent of an Islamic State' (Roy 1994: 24).

4. One of Turkey's largest and most luxurious five-star holiday villages has recently opened for business on the Aegean, run by an Islamist consortium and advertising itself as Turkey's most 'honourable' (*namuslu*) holiday place. With separate beaches and pools for men and women who want them (and shared beaches for those who don't), and a bar stocked to bursting with exotic fruit juices, it was criticized by Ali Bulaç, one of Turkey's most prominent Islamist intellectuals, as demonstrating once again Turkish Muslims' genius for legitimizing the illegitimate.

The special breakfast smorgasbord prepared for Sunday – not Friday – mornings at Dilruba attracts, like the Hotel and village, both wealthy Islamist and laic families to graze its laden tables at their leisure.

These tensions are reflective too of differing postures taken towards modernity, over different ways the modern and the Western are conflated or separated in the oppositionary practices and rhetoric of Islamist groups. So one of my friends told me about her time attending an illegal *Mahmud Efendi*[5] Koran course in the poor and oddly-named Üsküdar suburb of *Selamsız* (Without Greetings) in the late 1980s. She lived there for a year with twenty other twelve- to fourteen-year-old girls in a small bare apartment, eating from the same pot and sitting on cushions on the floor (having one's own plate, like furniture, was considered unIslamic), sleeping in the same room, being instructed about proper conduct in the most mundane areas of life.[6] For example the girls were taught to dab, like *Hazreti Muhammad*, a pinch of salt on the tongue before eating, were instructed in which order to cut their fingernails (not one after the other, but the middle finger first), in which direction to lean while squatting above the toilet and which prayers to say upon entering and leaving the cubicle (the prayers were printed on the back of the toilet door), in which order to dress, how to cut their hair, what to do while menstruating (underpants and bras were forbidden as they were made by male hands), how to eat (it was forbidden to use forks, or to cut bread – only breaking the bread in your two hands was considered lawful), and what to wear (black *çarşaf* (full length dress) for women and *sarık* (turban) with *şalvar* (baggy trousers) for men were compulsory). Here modernity and the West are constructed as synonymous, and by contrast Islamist practice is understood as a return to the example of the Prophet.

Such return to the *sünnet* is at the same time a creative construction of a retrieved, and hence rhetorically justified 'authentic', separatist Islamist

5. Mahmud Efendi is the leader of the *Ismail Ağa Cemaati* (community), an independent branch of the *Nakşibendi tarikat*. Mahmud Efendi's followers are very strong in Üsküdar, but the *tarikat*'s centre is in the Çarşamba district of Fatih, Istanbul where it has set up one of the biggest Koran course and student accommodation services in Turkey. Rusen Çakır argues that the logical result of Mahmud Efendi *cemaat's* anti-modernist insistence on the need to return to the *sünnet* (a following of the personal example of *Hazreti* Muhammad) is Islamic ghettoization. He notes too that its obsession with the smallest details of its members' daily life is justified in the name of the *fıkıh* (jurisprudence) of Imam-I Azam Ebu Hanife (Çakır 1990: 62).

6. In the civilizing of the Turks by the state, even table manners and service were a focus of specific stricture. As Atatürk himself said, 'Gentleman, setting a table, serving at table are really serious matters. It is one of our most important needs . . . We simply have to order these matters *like civilized people* in our homes, our restaurants, and our hotels' (Atatürk 1989: 232 – my emphasis). It is in this context that anti-modernist Islamist claims to a return to an 'authentic' Muslim lifestyle are made. See Al-Azmeh for a critique of Islamist revivalism as a form of modernist romanticism (1993).

lifestyle in the heart of cosmopolitan Istanbul. But many of those who seek to pursue it are also rather financially weak and educationally disadvantaged – i.e. in terms of Marxian political economy are simultaneously members of either the proletarian, the petit bourgeois or the lumpen-proletariat classes. This quest is problematized, however, once we note competing Islamist identities being manufactured by subjects living more middle-class lives. This is not to argue that varying class and Islamist cultures are reducible to epiphenomena of one or the other's logic – indeed they are self-evidently not false expressions veiling individuals' true status, despite the claims of some Marxists and Islamists.[7] Nor are different Islamisms self-serving expressions of class interests and solidarities, though obviously they are not unrelated to each other. True, one may wish to argue that in some circumstances the stressing of Islamist identity (especially by rich Muslims) is indeed a ruse, that is, a manipulation of emotive vertical ties that fractures the unity of the working class (but that, being a ruse, does not take in the bourgeoisie themselves who perpetrate it). However, the pursuing of the common interests of the working class (especially by Turkish nationalists) may just as easily be a ruse as well – a populism in the name of horizontal ties that fractures the unity of the *ümmet* or the subaltern nation or ethnic group, for example the Kurds (but that, also being a ruse, does not take in the dominant ethnic or religious group of the working class who perpetrate it either).

If the military in the wake of the 1980 coup seemed to follow the first course (by introducing compulsory religious lessons in schools, for example), the Turkish Workers (*Işçi*) Party appears to follow the second (by subordinating the problem of state racism against Kurds to the struggle against imperialism). Of course, if one accepts the claim made by Paul Willis that the 'working class is the only class in the capitalist social formation which does not have a structurally based vested interest in mystifying itself' (cited in Marcus 1986: 181), then the position of the Workers Party is in the last analysis defensible. For the working class as the universal class achieves in its own liberation the liberation of society as a whole. But working-class formation as a cultural form related to its dynamic resistance to other similarly self-constituting classes in a capitalist political economy is not the only culture of resistance in Turkey. Cultural forms forged in the conflict over the economy of nation, the economy of gender, and the economy of civility inform the sensibilities of participants who

7. If for Gilbert and Sullivan everyone born alive is born either a little Liberal or a little 'Conservat-*ive*', for Islamists everyone is born a Muslim until proven otherwise.

make themselves subjects in the context of political struggle. Indeed, it is in the peculiar interactions of these four fields of social relations that the particularity of Turkish modernity resides. Granted, who could deny that a bitter class conflict is in process in Turkey today? Cross-cutting this process, however, sometimes coinciding with it, sometimes contradicting its solidarities, is a bundle of other conflicts, which are simultaneously co-opted into the class struggle, escape its imperatives, and complicate its alliances. Because people are discriminated against not only in economic terms, non-capitalist relations of power make the jaws of oppression in Turkey many-fanged.

Nilufer Göle reminds us of this in her claim that the antagonism between Islamist and secularist alternatives in Turkey resembles the tensions of a dual 'caste' system, a bipolar vertical split in which the cultural domain of lifestyle and symbolic self-presentation becomes the focus of struggle between groups. Behind the hardening of the Islamist and laic coalitions lies a conflict over the equivalence established by the modernist elite between lack of civilization and Islam. In rejecting this equation

> the untouchables have abandoned their own places and entered the zones –
> university, media, urban spaces – forbidden to them. The breaking of this
> taboo lies at the root of the headscarf problem. No one feels perturbed at a
> traditionally covered 'pious grandmother' or a woman from the *gecekondu*
> with a covered head. Whereas headscarves in the university or black cloaks
> (*çarşaf*) in the urban [boulevards] give rise to feelings of loathing. For when
> the bodies of the other caste share the same space, the purity of those spaces
> is polluted (Göle 1994: 15 – my translation).

With their presence ritually fouling the areas once off bounds to them, Islamist untouchables also blacken the script 'Western, thus modern', scribbling in its margins the message 'Islamic, yet modern'.[8] This vision of two great camps, opposed not on class but on cultural/civil grounds, is a useful corrective to the vulgar economism of many of the most common arguments used to explain Islamism. So Refah for example is often held to be the party of middle-sized business unable to expand because of the market monopoly of big business: Islamist revitalization in this case is read off the intra-class struggle of the bourgeoisie. Yet why such a conflict should utilize or necessitate an Islamist political grammar in particular is unclear. Further, political discourses constitute interests as much as express them – they do not just describe or veil objective structural 'reality'. In

---

8. Göle, adopting the terms of Afsaneh Najmabadi, writes that Islamist politics has forced a shift in the discourse on women, nationalism and chastity, from 'modern, yet modest' to 'Islamic, thus modest' (Göle, 1996, 24).

short, listing the apparent causes of the breakdown of the political order
in the Muslim world does not in itself constitute an explanation for why
resistance takes the form of Islamist projects.[9]

Yet in providing a corrective to an overly ambitious economism, the
caste metaphor tempts us to take the rhetoric of the Islamists too much
for granted, to draw the white and black lines in Turkey rather too tightly.[10]
Fetih Paşa Korusu, Dilruba, and the Koran course for girls of the *Ismail
Aga Cemaati* illustrate the differences within the Islamist movement. The
idealization of the *Pax Ottomana* illustrates the similarities between Islamists
and secularists. Political tensions are above all relational: the Islamist
movement, whilst challenging the terms of the caste split, may itself split
over its own internal divisions. So an alliance between Göle's opposing
castes against a common enemy (let us say the legitimacy of Kurdish
political subjectivity) raises the question, for example, of Islamism's
sympathy with certain aspects of Kemalism. Here I remember a friend's
sister who was studying at the local *Imam-Hatip* (Teaching/Preaching)
high school recounting to me that her religion teacher told the class how
the slain guerrillas of the PKK (Kurdish Workers Party) were all uncir-
cumcised – that is, *kafir* (non-Muslims or infidels), perhaps even Armenian.[11]

In short, while being sensitive to the struggle over the norms of civility
between Islamists and secularists, we should speak of the plurality of
Islamist and laicist identities in formation. For the professed unity and
mutual hostility of the two protagonists become political projects as much
as they are current realities. That is, the production of Islamist and laicist
subjects is dogged by shadows from at least two other directions: on the
one hand by the culture of class, constituted through resistance to economic
exploitation and the aspirations of an emerging Islamist elite; and on the
other by the assimilationist project of the nation-state, with its continued
stimulating of both Turkish and Kurdish identities. These 'add value' to
the complexity of agents' identity and political interests.

The reducing of Turkish modernity to any one single historical logic
is then a political choice and strategy. In doing so, interpretative traditions
or formations attempt to constitute political subjects. Instead of emphasizing

---

9. Sayyid notes that the most common sociological reasons given for Islamist movements are the failure of nationalist secular elites, the lack of political participation, the
contraction of the petty bourgeoisie, the flow of petro-dollars with their accompanying
uneven development, and the effects of cultural erosion (Sayyid 1997).

10. 'We are Turkey's Negroes,' said Emine Şenlikoğlu, the well-known Islamist novelist
and writer, in a newspaper interview in 1994 (Göle 1994: 18).

11. With the arrest of Abdullah Ocalan in 1999 the armed struggle of the PKK has
ceased, opening the way perhaps to new political initiatives to reassess the Kurdish policies
of the state.

the Republic's will to Westernize cultural practices, gender relations or education, which elevates the Muslim subject into both the chief target and the major hope for transforming the present, the experiences of history might as validly be highlighted in class terms. In such a narrative, the newly constituted 'national-popular regime',[12] by nurturing its own bourgeoisie (and proletariat), sets the stage for the class actors to emerge and clash, in response and reaction to changes in the world economy.[13] Islamist movements would be analysed then as a dependent variable in the context of economic struggles.

But if such perspectives overestimate the autonomy of the economy, neither does Islamism leave much room for multiple or hybrid Muslim subject positions in its construction of a Muslim political subjectivity. By defining Muslims as a despised majority in Republican history and thereby positing in response the unity of all persecuted Muslims, it refuses to give credence (for example) to the possibility of the disunity of Muslims as workers and employers. That is, just as the advent of communism in Russia meant that class struggle was no longer possible (since class politics was illegitimate, the ground for it having by definition been removed), so Islamism as a utopia envisions the ending of politics (whether of class, gender, or ethnicity) in the name of the posited unity of the community of believers (*ummah*).

Here the division of labour and gender differences become de-politicized (i.e. withdrawn from the realm of power) and functionalized, so that 'natural' differences (between male and female, workers and owners) are utilized in the name of service to the community as a whole. Rather like St Paul's vision of the charismatic church in his first letter to the Corinthians – 'if the whole body were an eye, where would be the hearing?' (1 Cor. 12:17) – difference is relegated to the pre-political level and then regulated, instead of being traced to its site of production. Thus the distribution of wealth is the locus of concern (*vis-à-vis* the institution of *zekat*, the giving to the poor of a tithe from one's profit) rather than the source of that wealth in production, as is the ordering of roles between the sexes rather than their prior structuring by power.

The claim, then, that 'the stage is set for a possible alliance between reformist elites and moderate Muslims' (Göle 1996: 43) is also an admission of the possibility of an ideological role for Islamist discourse – ideology

---

12. Touraine uses this term to describe the developmentalist regimes that have dominated Latin American countries for most of this century (Touraine 1994b).

13. See for example Çağlar Keyder's lucid interpretation (1987).

in this sense referring not to systems of thought or philosophies *per se* (Marxism, Kemalism, Thatcherism), but to their application in the social arena. Thompson's definition of ideology is particularly useful here: 'Ideology can be used to refer to the ways in which meaning serves, in particular circumstances, to establish and sustain relations of power which are systematically asymmetrical – [i.e.] relations of domination. Ideology, broadly speaking, is meaning in the service of power' (Thompson 1990: 7). Meaning in the service of power also involves the struggle to exclude other possible ways by which these same subjects could constitute themselves. Ideology, then, disaggregates potential resistance. (But does not meaning in the service of resistance simultaneously disperse power?) That Islamist discourse is being used in this dual ideological sense is well perceived, I maintain, by participants in the movement itself.

Kuzguncuk's Islamists and Fetih Paşa Korusu: The Ideology of Islamism

Zeynep, the woman who as a girl attended the *Mahmud Efendi* Koran course, has in the last few years slowly withdrawn from the Islamic movement and stopped reading its women's magazines, *Aile ve Kadın* (Family and Women), and *Mektup* (Letter), because she claims they give a false idea about the equality of Islamic relationships. Despite growing up in a religious family (her mother is a teacher of the Koran) and though a reader of Arabic herself (she earns extra money by reading the Koran to different groups of women during *Ramazan*), Zeynep is very sensitive to nuances of power manifest in religious events, especially those concerning women and men. She uses the word *bencillik* (selfishness) to characterize the predominant Islamist male interpretation of women's and men's roles in Islam. Here Zeynep, 24 years old but unmarried and living with her family in Kuzguncuk, is not criticizing the position of women in Islam but the way the Islamist movement fails to educate women to be independent enough to take up the rights given them in the Koran. For example, she says that the great value given to women in Islam and their being consequently entrusted to men for their own security (*emanet*) is usually interpreted by Islamist males as a right to control rather than as an obligation to develop this precious gift.

Zeynep in my opinion is quite capable of seeing the ways in which her interests are infringed by the religious values structuring the relationships in her family. She shows great skill in outwardly conforming to the expectations and desires of others while living and thinking according to her own. For her the Islamist movement's practice of Islam is not gender-equal but prone to subversion by individuals or groups in the process of fulfilling their own desires. She claims to know of Islamist men who have deliberately taken a *cahil* (ignorant) girl from a village and made her 'religious' in order to marry a second wife illegally (in a religious ceremony) once their financial situation improves. For Zeynep applied Islam is perceived in Thompson's sense as ideological, and her insights derive from her own struggle to maintain a position of relative autonomy *vis-à-vis* her mother, her *ağabey* (older brother), and the circumscribing of her possibilities in the environment in which she moves.

Or we may think of Ahmet *ağabey*, who shuns the beautifully restored restaurant and tea garden in Fetih Paşa Korusu (not to mention Dilruba), despite the self-presentation of both as Islamist-friendly public spaces and their refusal to sell alcohol. Neither do the members of his small Kuzguncuk Islamist group spend any time there, not even in the height of summer, when a cool breeze skips across the Bosphorus and ruffles the tassels of the floral umbrellas spread over the tables. Bus drivers, factory workers, shopkeepers, taxi chauffeurs, or self-employed by day, Kuzguncuk's Islamists see Refah as the most statist party of them all, designed to suck up all those Islamist groups attempting to bring in and live the *şeriat* and thus neutralize them – in the name of Islam. For Ahmet *ağabey*, Refah's acceptance of the Western-inspired electoral rules is symptomatic of its mainstream status: by contrast 'In Islam', he maintains, 'there is no synthesizing'. He means, of course, that there can be no Islamic socialism either; yet he envisions a society where everyone would be free to live under the legal system of their own choosing, including socialists ['The judge would ask the socialist lawyers, "What is the punishment in socialism for this crime?"'].

Ahmet *ağabey* is suspicious, then, of Fetih Paşa Korusu's Islamist credentials – his critique of Refah and boycott of Fetih Paşa Korusu (and Dilruba) reveals his fear that the Islamist movement is constructing new relations of domination in the name of a populist Islam. Ahmet *ağabey*'s Islamism is class-nourished, not class-conscious; but this does not mean there is a neat fit on the one hand between 'conscious' (*şuurlu*) Muslims radically rejecting all compromise with the system, and on the other hand socially mobile Muslims and 'participatory' politics. Instead, we need to pay attention to people's class and gender positionings to catch the myriad meanings in their words and actions. For Ahmet *ağabey* class differences within the *ummah* should be ameliorated by the giving of alms – not that class structuration is conceived as an insurmountable problem, as the political and economic spheres of life in his ideal Islamist society would be separated in practice. The most pious, the most religious/knowledgeable would have the right to become leaders of the community, rather than the richest (or their parliamentary representatives). For Ahmet *ağabey* and his small but active *cemaat* (congregation) in Kuzguncuk, the Refah Party and its cadres are obstacles to an Islamic society, not its harbingers. Refah is self-serving.

Unlike Ahmet *ağabey* (and his wife), however, Zeynep does go to Fetih Paşa Korusu tea garden, does acknowledge that its presence has offered her, as an Islamist woman, a legitimate place to sit and socialize. This obviously because Fetih Paşa Korusu presents Zeynep with something new – an Islamized public space that condones her straying from the private, but as we have seen, intensely politicized domain of the home. Concurrent, then, with its deconstruction of the 'Westernness' of Turkish modernity's public spaces, Refah's opening of social space to Muslims in Fetih Paşa Korusu (its 'spatialization of politics') has unanticipated consequences for its own practice of gender. In contrast Dilruba's exclusivity bars poorer Islamist women (like Zeynep) from appreciating, and hence benefiting from, its Islamist aestheticism.

By contrast with Refah's liberality in the forest, Ahmet *ağabey*'s ideal Islamist society, like his desired Islamist city, would be made up of self-contained, self-identifying communities, all living according to their own preferences. Democracy would operate in the framework of a plurality of legal systems. Individuals would be free to join the group of their choice, though after choosing they would naturally be 'forced' to live according to its dictates, and the unity of the group would thus override the interests of factions or individuals (let us say Zeynep) within it. Difference then, or the 'other' would be truly accepted as the 'other', not merely tolerated – as long as there was no 'other' (or 'hybrid') amongst the Muslims themselves.

Yet Ahmet *ağabey* sketches his pure Islamist city as he sips tea under a coloured street awning sitting next to Vassili. Would he truly be happy in a city whose lifestyle apartheid ensured such 'unprincipled' urban spaces and encounters could not occur? Conscientiously denying what he most enjoys, Ahmet *ağabey* is as schizophrenic as the modernizing Ottoman bureaucrat in Refik Halit Koray's story 'The Peach Garden', who 'on stifling summer days abandoned starched collar, cravat, riding coat, and intolerant legalism for the delights of night-gowns worn at dusk in the peach garden of the small town to which he was assigned' (in Mardin 1997: 70).

Like that reformist bureaucrat, Ahmet *ağabey*'s approach smells faintly of ideology too. His vision of a society structured along the lines of autonomous, self-defining groups in whose living arrangements the state would not interfere implies in one way an ethnicizing of religion and politics. One chooses to be socialist or Christian or Kemalist, concepts that are then stripped of any universal or rational content and rendered as mere lifestyles. Being a Muslim in this sense becomes one identity among many others: but in this model there is ambiguity, since the society organized on these principles is at the same time called Islamic. The whole society is imagined as if it were a string of prayer beads: self-contained units held together by the murmured words of the *Lailahe illallah* ('There is no God but Allah').

Simultaneously in this model we see a religious colouring of ethnicity: Turkish and Kurdish Christians would be understood firstly as Christians and secondly as members of an ethnic group, as would Kurdish and Turkish Muslims. Indeed, to choose to be ethnic (whatever this would entail) would be difficult to conceive: Turks or Kurds (who by definition are Muslim according to some Islamist positions)[14] could choose only to be either secular or religious. The political Islam of Ahmet *ağabey*, then, understood as both a cultural and a religious identity, lives uneasily with other forms of political subjectivity, and Kurds who choose to be both secular (or Islamist) and ethnically assertive are placing themselves in an unacceptable position for such Islamism.

Islamist believers in Kuzguncuk, then, in attempting to create a local community polemically situated in opposition to elite sovereignty (both secular and Islamist) in the cultural field, find themselves in an ambiguous position *vis-à-vis* Turkish nationalism. For in Islamizing the rhetoric of anti-colonial discourse (those oppressed by the forces of Western imperialism are no longer merely the masses but the Muslim masses), the ascription of an essential but estranged Muslimness to the people leads to the continual imputation of self-hatred and alienation against anyone who wishes not to be Islamist. Correspondingly, Ahmet *ağabey*'s politics excludes, in theory at least, the pursuit of interests in anything other than its own discursive terms. Kurdish Muslims then are encouraged to bracket their ethnic identity within an Islamist one, leading to Kurdish accusations of a new assimilation – in the name of Islam – mirroring Turkish nationalist strategies. But more on this in Part III.

14. 'Turks who are not Muslim have lost their Turkishness, such as Finns, Hungarians and Bulgarians' (Hakimcioğlu, 1992, 22).

Conclusion

We must admit, in summing up, that Dilruba, historically, aesthetically and politically, is dependent upon Fetih Paşa Korusu's prior existence. Firstly it was completed a year after Refah officially opened its tea garden and restaurant in the forest. Secondly it shares many of the same stylistic tics and partakes of the same strategy of glocalization (the construction of particularity *vis-à-vis* the 'West', and the construction of universality *vis-à-vis* the 'local'). And thirdly it re-opens the wound of a class distinction damped down for a time in the clinking of the tulip-shaped tea glasses and the soothing tones of the *ney* by Refah's populism. If Fetih Paşa Korusu is Refah's answer to the Dr Jekyll of the state's official Islam and its antithetical Mr Hyde in the 'dark' face of the Islamist movement, its civilizing intent is directed towards modifying the extremes of both. Dilruba, however, is not exercised to educate recalcitrant Islamists. Indeed it would, quite openly, prefer the Ahmet *ağabeys* of this world to stay away. Unashamedly elitist in reply to the self-regard of Istanbul's secularist elite, Dilruba's hope is to prove Islam fit to enter the stakes in the competition for high culture.

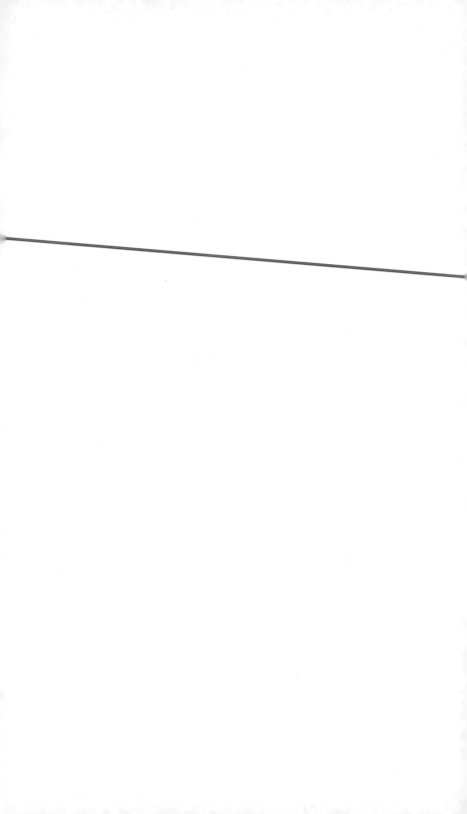

–5–

Carnival and the Staging of History

Less than a kilometre away during the month of Ramazan, the Refah-controlled Üsküdar Municipality puts up every year a huge circus-size tent in Democracy Square (*Demokrasi Meydanı*), where it provides a free *iftar* meal (breaking of the fast) for whoever rolls up. The line of hungry people (which begins at the tent's entrance not far from the corner where the unemployed men queue in the morning hoping to be hired as day labourers) snakes between the benches and around the fountain, interrupted at regular intervals by the metal tubes of the waiting fireworks, which will be set off some time before the evening's entertainment commences in the tent. Here the bourgeois Islamism of Dilruba, and the liberal Islamism of Fetih Paşa Korusu are both supplemented and contradicted by the third string in the bow of the Islamist social movement, the carnival Islamism of rallies, festivals and spectacles.

Carnival Islamism

If liberal Islamism is concerned to stress the shared interests of subjects constructed as enemies by official and 'untouchable' Islam respectively, and bourgeois Islamism seeks to demonstrate its good taste in the struggle for symbolic capital, carnival Islamism celebrates its own impropriety and revels in its own marked difference. Characterized by its temporary but total occupation of public space, either in mass political rallies, fairs or exhibitions, carnival Islamism makes its presence felt like a series of rolling strikes. For a paradigmatic moment an Islamist order, chaotic, boisterous and emboldened by both its contrariness and sheer weight of numbers, descends upon a place and turns it into a parable, a preview or foretaste of paradise; a football stadium, where a mass outbreak of ritual prayer substitutes for the frenzy of a goal, the crowd at an odd angle to the grandstand so as to face Mecca. But sooner or later, in a night or in a week, the space returns to 'normal' – the caravan moves on, and carnival Islamism, by its disinclination to put down roots and confront the possibility of its own compromise, reinforces the polarized categories that constitute both itself as transgressive and public space as secular. So Refah holds its political rallies in sporting venues or in parks, which its banners, music and supporters transform into provisional Islamized spaces. Yet their very ephemerality as festive events militates against any puritanical tendencies – these are not Islamized spaces in the Olivier Roy sense, despite their oft-attempted segregation of the sexes.

What is carnival Islamism composed of? What does it do? In the Ramazan tent at Üsküdar for example, where different entrances facilitated the separate seating of men and women, and where admission to the entertainment was free, an excited crowd was in attendance every night. Each evening spectators were appealed to by the 'speaker of the day' (*günün konuşmacısı*), who addressed the crowd for 20 or 30 minutes on a number of topics. So in the Ramazan of 1996 the Refah mayors of the Üsküdar and Beyoğlu municipalities spoke, as well as two Refah Party national parliamentarians, the heads of two local Islamist radio stations, the custodian of the Aziz Mahmud Hudai tomb, the old preacher of the mosque next to Ayasofya Church/Mosque (now a museum) and various Islamist journalists (though one attacked the audience for enjoying such frivolous fare when Muslims in Bosnia and Chechnya were dying). The entertainment during those same evenings consisted of Turkish Art and Sufi music, Turkish folk-music (Black Sea region), theatre, a children's night, a 'Sale of the Century'-type game (on Islamic topics), a Koran-reading competition, a call-to-prayer chanting competition, poetry-reading, and a human rights night. On two occasions during the month there were also midday programmes prepared especially for women, presumably with women speakers. At all other times women were mere spectators in the tent – there were no women performers, singers, musicians, comperes, contestants or speakers.[1] This contrasts starkly with the 'Brain Storm' (*Beyin Fırtınası*) series organized by the Refah-controlled Beyoğlu Council in the town hall, for example; here a series of symposiums on different topics (for example Modernity and Democracy, Women in the Public Sphere, Laicism and Cultural Difference) featured both men and women, Islamist and laicist academics appearing side by side in the same sessions. Once again we see liberal Islamism's concern to accommodate the cultural norms of

---

1. There has long been a debate in the Islamist movement over whether a woman's voice is 'private/shameful' (*avret*) or not. Channel 7, Refah's television channel, works around this problem by having women presenters for programmes directed at women, though there is no way of censoring who watches which programme, of course. Whether lawful (*caiz*) or not, the ban on women speaking in the public presence of [male] strangers is one of the lines in the sand that has come to symbolize the 'dark' face of Islam.

secularists, and carnival Islamism's distinguishing of itself by its refusal to do so.

The day Ramazan finished the tent was gone, the puddles on the exposed pavement recaptured the reflected sky, and the square regained its status as a thoroughfare to the bus stop on its far side. But only for a while – the Üsküdar Council and the Islamist publishing company Timas organized the 3rd Üsküdar Culture and Arts Festival a few months later, which took over the square again and turned it into a vast Islamist book fair. As part of the Festival the Council provided horse and carriage rides, a football tournament, tight-rope walkers, concerts, theatre, free soup and special rice. They paid too for a large number of circumcisions for boys and the pre-wedding celebrations (*kına gecesi*) for many brides. Doubtless the Refah Party has shored up its vote for the next election: but can carnival Islamism transcend its strategy of winning temporary control of urban space, even if such activities are repeated on an annual basis? For resistance through carnivalization is possible only against a previously bedded-down normalization (hegemony) of particular moral practices – power operates then through the routinization of a particular social imaginary, in this case through the very habitual banality of secularism. Carnival as scandal can only offend in the context of an artfully-wrought common sense.

Carnival Republicanism

Yet though public spaces and facilities are at the same time secular spaces already, other political movements still feel the need to 'carnivalize' themselves in those very same spaces. Presumably then, the interpolating of subjects by architecture alone is felt by them to be insufficient, as needing reinforcement in the shoring up of power. Bozdoğan notes that architecture is an unreliable ally as an instrument of regime:

> if we agree that public space is an ambiguous territory upon which power and dissent contest each other, the architectural and urban design of the early republic is yet to be studied in terms of a politics of design – in terms of the ways in which design lends itself to a democratic versus authoritarian project rather than being either totally autonomous or the unambiguous expression of one or the other (Bozdoğan 1994: 40).

Further, architecture needs to be read, as Fetih Paşa Korusu shows, by reference to its expropriation (consumption or use) by the populace – see here, for example, the unintended 'afterlife' of Brasilia in the study by Holston (1989).

In the light of its temporary 'decoration' of public amenities or spaces accepted, even constituted, in this very process as politically neutral, Carnival Islamism does not propose to tear down and replace the urban landscape of contemporary capitalist space with a romantic pre-modern Islamic city of classic orientalist proportion. Yet in an interesting article in *Yeni Şafak* by Mustafa Demirci entitled 'Our Cities' Metaphysical Foundations' an argument is made for the particularity of Islamic cities, which are 'created in an environment of knowledge, in the name of revealed authority and with the intention of controlling evil, whose character reflects naturally and without strain the modesty and piety, compassion and mercy of Allah, a complex that in short realizes the ideals of *şeriat*' (*Yeni Şafak*, 31 July 1996 – my translation). The writer refrains from calling for a re-Islamification of the city's design, but his inclinations are clear.[2]

Football stadiums, indoor basketball halls, conference centres etc., though interpreted by some Islamist writers as hindering the execution of the Muslim's religious duties, have thus been partly removed from the sphere of political controversy. There is, though, a certain prejudice against the playing of sport in some 'anti-modernist' Islamist circles, although

2. Indeed there is an extensive debate around the concept 'Islamic City': the Islamic city is defined as structured around centres of worship, with the city's various quarters divided along ethnic lines (i.e. ethnic segregation); by their lack of a regular street pattern (i.e. lots of dead-end streets) thus allowing a semi-public space for women to appear; by their lack of spatial division according to wealth; and by the ubiquity of men's and women's sections in the design of the domestic house (*haremlik-selamlık*). Yet as all these characteristics have been noted in pre-Islamic cities [as well as in medieval Europe, according to Braudel], one wonders whether there has been a mere slippage in discourse from oriental to Islamic City? In Istanbul the dichotomy between the Islamic and European city is often visualized, according to Zeynep Enlil, as the difference between Beyoğlu and the historic peninsula. Enlil argues that Istanbul however has never conformed to the Islamic City pattern (whose theoretical pedigree is traced to Islamic Andalusia, Syrian and North African cities, and is caught up in complicated debates over the transformative and re-constructive role of French colonialism in Algeria and Morocco), as in Istanbul Muslims and non-Muslims often lived side by side, even selling property to each other in defiance of Sultanic law. She points out that according to an 1810 Istanbul water-works plan there were very few *çıkmaz sokaklar* (dead-end streets) in Istanbul, compared to their frequency of occurrence by the late nineteenth century, over the very period of Ottoman modernization/Westernization (Enlil, in discussion). Interestingly one of the first city planning acts of the Kemalist government was a law proscribing *çıkmaz sokaklar*.

revealingly not against the learning of martial arts.[3] Yet judo or taekwan-do are obviously as alien to Islamic traditions as blue jeans and rock bars. This is not hypocrisy: Turkish society has not been reconstituted in the name of Asian civilization. The learning of martial arts does however illustrate the dialogical imperative at work in the construction of authenticity – authenticity is defined dualistically against the rhetorically constituted difference of the oppressing other.

Sporting arenas have become backdrops to the main drama, whose various actors fill and empty the theatre, bringing their own props with them. İnönü Stadium for example is not only hired out by Islamist groups. The state too takes advantage of its size to organize rallies on the Republic's official holidays, rallies as carefully choreographed as Refah's at the same venue. 'In order for traditions today to serve to legitimize those who con-structed or appropriated them, *they must be staged*' says Canclini (1995: 109 – my emphasis). In this way commemorations become public retorts to one another, insults traded across time and in the political litter left behind, physically and metaphorically, after each event. Organizers take pains to graffiti over the political claims of the other by ensuring their motifs contradict the motifs of their opponents.

One big carnival I went to was put on by the state for Youth Day (*Gençlik Bayramı*), 19th May (*On-dokuz Mayıs Günü*), when nationalist historiography celebrates Mustafa Kemal's leaving of Istanbul and his landing at Samsun to begin the struggle that would result in the founding of the Turkish Republic. The actors were the youth themselves, as were the immediate audience – the show was performed by the students of a number of schools, whose non-active classmates participated in the stands by their enthusiastic cheering of certain spectacular manoeuvres, as well as by their joining in with the songs. The pageant was tightly synchronized, each group being passed by its replacement as it sprinted from the field. The basic narrative of the rally was the re-telling, through ordered calis-thenics, running, leaping and much simultaneous flag waving, of the Republic's emergence from the darkness of the Ottoman empire. Here

---

3. A friend explained the injunction against football as deriving from the cutting off of the head of a prophet and its kicking around by his enemies. When I asked where he learnt this story he replied from a *tarikat* member, who had heard it from his *hoca* (teacher). Through just such byways is profane (unofficial hence unendorsed) knowledge disseminated. David Phelps makes the fascinating point that the story resembles events celebrated in the Shiite feast of Muharram, when the carrying off to Kufa of the head of the Imam Hussein is remembered (personal correspondence).

the state has 'society present itself with a scene of its origin' (Canclini 1995: 109). Simplified extracts from Atatürk's speeches, many of them exhortations to the youth to fulfil the future left in their trust, were interspersed with 'good' orientalism: folk dancing with girls prancing in national costume, boys clapping in a circle on the outside and *saz* (a type of lute) music. The orbiting rings and whirling spheres of the performers in their different colours complemented the commentary and the music – Rodrigo's guitar concerto (jazzed up) and for the climax the choral movement from Beethoven's 9th Symphony. 'We are Atatürk youth' (*Biz Atatürk gençleriyiz*) boomed the speakers, 'We are the Turkish nation' (*Biz Türk milletiyiz*). Bach's organ fugue completed the frenzied finale. 'Music', as Stokes says, 'is one of the less innocent ways dominant categories are enforced and resisted' (1994a: 8).

This, however, was merely the prolegomenon to the main declaration, made fittingly by the true guardians of the Kemalist legacy – the military – this through one of Istanbul's elite schools, Kuleli Lisesi (Military High School). Scarcely had the last excited teenager run off before in paraded Kuleli's cadet corps to the stirring music of its military bands, rifles on shoulders, followed by the gymnast-clad body of the whole school, in different-coloured but matching singlets and white pants, then the black-belted judo group and a final squadron of marching school soldiers. Thus commenced a highly impressive performance, singlets falling and rising symbolically with the music, heroic talk of the Independence War, the recounting of sacrifices, the recital of epic poetry and snatches from Ataturk's addresses to the youth. All the time the choreography continued, with elaborate human sculptures, a memorable one evoking the statue in Taksim Square around which wreaths are placed on national days, kneeling figures pointing to the gun-toting, flag-waving figure towering in its centre above the heads of boys already high up on shoulders. *Toprak senin. Gök senin* ('The earth is yours. The sky is yours') wrote the singlets, as the shape of Turkey was formed around the edge of the soccer pitch. *Vatan asla bölünmez* ('The Motherland will never be divided'). *Bu memleket Türklerindir* ('This country is for the Turks'). In the foreground the judo and gymnastic teams smashed bricks and jumped through burning hoops, and a party of students dressed in battle fatigues swung down dangerously on ropes from the edge of the grandstand's overhanging roof. The event finished with the human sculpture of the Turkish flag to the strains of the national anthem.

Certainly the display presents the idealization of the military's desired cultural order. Here the productive disciplining of the masculine body is functionally directed towards the denial of social difference and the maintenance of a unified hierarchy. The youth are summoned, put on a war-footing, but the enemy is never named – to do so would be to concede an insubordination that becomes the more legitimate the more the state is forced to mobilize against it. Acknowledging protest disrupts the facade of unanimity such displays project. Thus the celebration's chief target, the Kurdish rebellion and its military protagonists the PKK, are present only in euphemisms, constructed in the reiteration of a set of implied understandings. More real, however, are the ever-watching clouds of *şehitler* (military martyrs), those who have run their race with distinction and now cheer the new generation on as they strive to grasp the prize for which their predecessors gave their lives. For if, despite their efforts, they have not yet received their reward it is only with and because of today's youth that they should be made perfect. And not just through those who are completing with perseverance their turn on the track, but the spectators too, who may also be called to involvement. The eulogies from Inönü Stadium were broadcast live to the nation on the state television channels. The rituals of power are exhibited as much to inspire an already sympathetic audience as to overawe the opposition. For who else would watch them? 'Elites are also consumers of their own performance' says Scott (1990: 49), as on the giant page of the football field they draw up an inventory of their own postulated contributions and qualities.

The Dramatization of Difference

For all that, the hit-and-run tactics of carnival Islamism are not random – they too are organized around narrativized events remembered and signi-fied as important according to a particular and alternative valuation of the past. Carnival Islamism sometimes holds celebrations according to the Islamic calendar (for example an evening rally on the *Kandil* (feast) when Muhammad's birth is commemorated), sometimes in protest at or in memory of current struggles (e.g. a Chechnya or Jerusalem solidarity night).[4] Sometimes the two are made to coincide.

---

4. Sometimes celebrations are held on evenings that have become important to the laic community. So New Year's Eve (31st December) has become the focus of Islamist censure in the shape of rival events such as solidarity nights or campaign meetings. Or again, *Sevgili Günü* (St Valentine's Day) has become a *cause célèbre*, inciting protests outside florists' shops.

A few weeks after the *Gençlik Bayramı* carnival at İnönü Stadium, the Greater Istanbul Municipality and *Milli Gençlik Vakfı*[5] (National Youth Foundation) held a large retaliatory rally in Gülhane Park. As a venue Gülhane Park is an ambiguous site *par excellence*. Situated directly beneath the walls of the *Saray* (the *Seraglio*, the Sultan's Palace, now Topkapı Museum) on the historic peninsula, the park has for 80 years been the domain of the people, a carnivalesque place in distinction to the excessive formality and meticulously displayed etiquette documented in the museum's various palace courtyards high above it.[6] Famous in the 1980s for its hosting of concerts featuring all the big *arabesk* music stars (Orhan Gencebey, Ferdi Tayfur, Emrah, Mahsun Kırmızıgül, Ibo etc.) the park itself is a constituent part of any performance.[7] The few sad animals that make up what passes for Istanbul's zoo, the fairground rides and blaring Turkish pop-music, the myriad religious and nationalist book-stalls, the temporary exhibition sites with their lurid photographs of massacred bodies and ruined burning villages in Chechnya, the food tents, street-sellers, and trinket-hawkers, the proletarian and peasant throng that on weekends dots its slopes with picnics and jostles its way through the top gate to flow out at the bottom – Gülhane Park too is an arabesque song.

The rally was held in the park's amphitheatre, ostensibly for *Hicri Yılbaşı*, the festival commemorating Hz. Muhammad's flight to Medina and heralding, in countries that conform to the Islamic calendar, the beginning of the Muslim new year. As in the nationalists' day out at İnönü, the reciting of epic poetry and the judicious use of music [at one stage even the same music! – Rodrigo's guitar concerto wafted out of the P.A. in both İnönü Stadium and Gülhane Park as companion to a dramatic

---

5. *Milli Gençlik Vakfı* is often said to be the Refah Party's youth wing, but according to its president, Nevzat Laleli, it does not have any 'organic' link with Refah. Laleli, who stood unsuccessfully for Ankara as a Refah candidate at the last election, explains the relationship thus: 'Refah Party, which is always searching for clean (*temiz*) people to enter politics, is happy that MGV is able to meet this need' (*Radikal*, 31 October 1996: 8 – my translation). The foundation has 350,000 members, 1,800 branches in all of Turkey's provinces (Şırnak, Tunceli, and Igdir, which are all under martial law in the Kurdish areas, excepted), provides free accommodation to 16,000 students in 125 hostels and distributes a monthly allowance to another 20,000 students (ibid.).

6. The moving of the Imperial Household to *Dolmabahçe Saray* (palace) away from *Topkapı Saray* occurred in 1856. According to Zeynep Çelik, the first public park introduced in Istanbul was in 1869, when Taksim Park was designed; it immediately became the 'promenade favorite of the Pera community' (Çelik 1986: 69). The gardens of Topkapı Palace were opened as a park some fifty years later, under the auspices of the Young Turk government in 1916 (1986: 70).

7. True to form however, Gülhane Park was host to a number of other concerts as well, featuring Turkish pop and Turkish Art music stars.

poem] were vital ingredients in the ritual of resistance that creates and sustains the existence of any contrary community. At the same time different musical genres accompany and hence are posited as culturally constitutive by particular groups: so the religious songs sung in Arabic are notated as essential expressions of an Islamist culture that rejects the civility of the secularists. As in the Ramazan tent at Üsküdar, there was a reading too from the Koran by the young champion of the MGV's Koran-reading competition. (In the nationalists' ceremony there was a reading from a poem about Atatürk. The Turkish of his speeches, like the Arabic of the Koran, is no longer intelligible to present generations.)

The highlight of the evening was the fiery speech by one of the stars of the Islamist circuit, the Refah mayor of Rize. In it he threw the usual symbolic scraps to the crowd: a demand that *Aya Sophia* be opened up for *namaz* (ritual prayer); a complaint about the unjust gaoling of a Muslim who burst upon the memorial ceremony at Atatürk's tomb clutching a Koran in his hand; the condemning of the West over Bosnia and Chechnya; news that American Blacks were converting *en masse* to Islam.

The Mayor of Istanbul, Tayyip Erdoğan, gave a more measured address (but still managed to claim Mehmet Akif, the writer of the national anthem, for Islamism); in it he promised to bring clean water to Istanbul. He recommended too Greater Istanbul Municipality's special Chechnya tent-display in the park, with its photos and posters of damaged buildings, wounded/dead bodies, and grim-faced guerrillas. There was no mention nor display of the equally distressing situation in the Kurdish areas of Turkey; one suspects because, like the civil war in Afghanistan, it is not so easily amenable to analysis stressing Christian/Western enmity towards Islam as its source and the onset of a new crusade. (But these omissions from the roll-call of sufferings are noticed by religious and irreligious Kurds alike, and work to disenchant them from the spell of carnival.)

Hicret Gecesi (The Flight to Medina) is just one example then of a whole series of rallies, meetings, commemorations, protests, entertainment and exhibitions that carnival Islamism organizes to assert its legitimacy as an alternative order to the present regime. Carnival Islamism is not concerned to present reasoned political programmes nor policy to revellers, but to heighten believers' sense of difference from the secular norm. Yet ironically the more carnival Islamism dramatizes its radical difference the more such differentiation appears to be the result only of the theatre itself: carnival Islamism seems caught up in a shadow boxing match of 'mere' burlesque proportions. Red dressing-gowned carnival Republicanism, trumpeting slogans, parades its boy-soldiers around Inönü Stadium – and in reply green-trunked carnival Islamism, shouting 'Muhammad's army!,'

'Allah's soldiers!', runs its youth in battle fatigues up and down *Abdi Ipekci* indoor arena. Carnival Islamism organizes at a Refah election rally a mock funeral rite, carrying a coffin around the basketball court with the words *Taklitci* ('Imitator') [of the West] *Çiller* written on it – and a month or two later goes into a coalition with Tansu Çiller and her party. The very success of carnival Islamism as a spectacle renders it too good to be true. (But if all the world's a stage, does it matter?) Not only does carnival Islamism bring its props with it to the performance; the players themselves arrive in their costumes. Carnival Islamism's effect, paradoxically, is to strip bare these extras of their Islamist gestures and affectations in their everyday lives. Carnival Islamism is not content to put on a show for whoever comes; in demanding that the comers themselves become the show carnival Islamism makes carnival Islamists. Yet in creating the possibility for revellers to become in non-show time caricatures of the characters on exhibition at the show, carnival Islamism causes the carnival Islamists whom it engenders to be stripped of their ability to be convincing, by disclosing its own artifice.[8]

In the lighting-up of selected historical events, carnival Islamism and state festivals cast shadows that sometimes obscure their structural similarities. If *Hicret Gecesi* re-lives the migration of Hz. Muhammad from Mecca to Medina and the anticipated triumph of his victorious return, *Gençlik Bayrami* remembers Ataturk's fleeing from occupied Istanbul to Samsun and the beginning of his successful campaign to establish a nationalist state. If *Hicret Gecesi* enables Muslims to conceive of themselves as a group in exile, bound together by the oppression of their foes, *Gençlik Bayram* reminds Turks that they too are a nation under threat, that the might of internal and external enemies is ranged against them and seeks to divide up their land according to their great hostility. Carnival convinces each (Muslim and Turk) that they are living in hard times. But it assures them too that the persecuted will be vindicated. So Sevki Yilmaz (mayor of Rize) can say to the roisterers at Gülhane Park:

> Those people who are advertising the virtues of the West should examine the event of the exile. Today Hz. Muhammed is not introduced in the universities. If he were, there would be no more Bosnias. There is a need for a new flight

---

8. Of course, in the eyes of many of my interviewees, carnival Nationalism suffers from the same weakness. Having been told about the distinctive moustaches of the cadres of the extreme nationalist *Milli Hareket Partisi* (National Movement Party) I was still disturbed the first time I encountered, in a street buffet not far from the main police centre where I was renewing my visa, a gaggle of moustached civil police, greeting each other not with a kiss but by knocking foreheads together. There was no lack of authenticity, though, in the handguns stuck in trouser belts revealed by the gusting wind.

[*Hicret*] and a new conquest [*Fetih*]. With your commitment this new *Hicret* will be realized in the shortest possible time, and here the order of Mecca will be established, an order in which no principles other than Allah's principles will apply (*Sabah*, 2 June 1995 – my translation).

This is little different, I suppose, from the state's oft-asserted promise that the Kurdish rebellion will be crushed forthwith – *ya bitecek, ya bitecek* ('It will finish, or it will finish'). Carnival Nationalism, in theatrically staging for society the renewed commitment of youth to the Republic, makes the defeat of a regime producing such disciplined and single-minded athletes/ performers literally unimaginable.

Retaliatory Historiography

For the Tappers, anthropologists commenting on their fieldwork in the provincial town of Eğirdir in the early 1980s (i.e. just after the military coup), Turkish Islam and Republicanism are best seen as 'expressions of a single underlying ideology of social control' (Tapper and Tapper 1991: 80). In Eğirdir, according to the Tappers, Atatürk and Muhammad respectively – one the founder of the Republic, the other of Islam – become guides to the realms of this life and the life beyond. Though there may be a handful of 'fanatics' in the town less inclined to consent to this well-ordered and complementary division of material and spiritual labour, bureaucratized official Islam is accepted 'without question by virtually all Eğirdir towns-people' (1991: 78). Eğirdir in short is prefigured towards a Turk–Islam synthesis, 'in which ideas about Turkey as a nation-state and ideas about Islam are mutually reinforcing' (1991: 60).

The carnival Islamism of Istanbul (and Ankara) has, in contrast, effected a separation of the laicist and Islamic strands of this discourse. It embodies a rival investing of meaning in the past, in which the polemical 'symbolic control of urban space through graffiti, flags, the language of signs and colour coding' is instrumental (Stokes 1994a: 8).[9] That this symbolic control of urban spaces, or resistance to it, is taken seriously by all parties in the struggle is shown nicely by a small report printed in the leftist newspaper *Demokrasi*. A Kurdish man in Adana who had given an order to a small company manufacturing pullovers was beaten and arrested by civil police in the street after picking up his goods. The man had ordered three jumpers, one for each of his children, in red, gold and green.

9. Green for Islamist, blue for DSP (Democratic Left Party), yellow for Anavatan (Motherland Party), red for the Turkish nation, gold/green/red for the banned Kurdish flag.

The newspaper report adds that the man had pleaded that his wife was blind in both eyes (*Demokrasi*, 5 February 1996).

As in the bloodily suppressed (until co-opted by the state in 1996) *Newroz* celebrations for Kurdish new year at the end of winter, alternative historical narratives divide and inscribe the past as moral in different ways. Though it seems difficult to gain precise knowledge about when the state instituted its annual round of civic rituals, according to the historian Öztürkmen (in discussion), *Cumhuriyet Günü* (Republic Day) was made a national holiday in 1933 to mark the tenth anniversary of the Republic's founding. Until then *Lozan Günü*, the day celebrating the Treaty of Lausanne, signed by the nationalists and the Western powers in 1923, was more important. Carnival Islamism has on the other hand been creating and commemorating its own fictions concomitantly with the rise of electoral Islam.

The popularity of an alternative series of festivals would suggest that the official ceremonies have lost some of their power for a significant proportion of the people. The open deconstruction of certain aspects of republicanism reveals a deep legitimation crisis: here the 'public transcript of domination' is not challenged merely in the 'hidden transcript of resistance' (to use Scott's terms) but boldly, in the display of insubordination. Even so, there is a certain deference, a prudent concession to the symbols of the laic state that reduces the risk of such protests being interpretable as the desire for the total annihilation of the ruling order. So Refah is careful to start all its rallies with the national anthem, whilst at another Islamist celebration I went to the organizers asked that no flags but Refah's and the national be waved. Challengers are concerned to ensure that their protests are seen as conforming to the 'legitimate' boundaries of reform, so as not to be interpreted as being politically beyond the pale.

State Islam and Carnival Islamism

These Islamist carnivals, in open competition with the civic rituals of republicanism, exist in somewhat uneasy tension, however, with the traditional religious festivals simultaneously presided over by state (laic) Islam. For example the *Kandil gecesi* (when minarets are illuminated) celebrations in Kuzguncuk always filled the mosque, with crowds of men sitting on carpets outside in the courtyard. At times the excitement was palpable, especially when the mosque took its turn to host some of the holy relics controlled by the Directorate of Religious Affairs. So one year for *Kadir Gecesi* (the night celebrating the first revelation of the Koran to the Prophet) the *hoca*, standing on a chair, held up a jar after the prayers had been performed. The men, bunched shoulder to shoulder like a victorious football team, singing as they passed, craned their necks to see a tuft of the beard of the Prophet.

At the same time bureaucratized Islam retains, to varying degrees, the loyalty of large numbers of people through its 'pastoral care' function (though not of course of Ahmet *ağabey* and his friends, who refuse to join in common prayer at the mosque, even on *Kandil* nights and *Ramazan*). The role of the state-paid religious functionary is important in leading the prayers at many funerals, as well as in conducting the *mevlüt* (poem reciting the birth and life of the Prophet), particularly at rite-of-passage ceremonies like weddings and circumcisions, which often take place in people's private homes.[10] Thus one *mevlüt* I went to, ironically at the house of a local Üsküdar *hoca* in celebration for the circumcision of his son, was sung by two other state *hoca*s, as well as by the father. Most of the guests were neighbours and, though men and women sat in separate rooms, including husbands and wives, sex segregation was not strictly enforced. Indeed the boy was resting in a cot in the lounge-room where the women were gathered, and which I had to enter to pin some money to his shirt. This was definitely not a meeting of political Islam. State television too (as well as some of the private channels) always shows a

10. The legitimacy and authority of the state-trained religious personnel varies from region to region, and over time as well. Tapper and Tapper report that since the coming of the Republic 'many of the town's [Eğirdir's] shrines have gone, and . . . the complex sacred geography of the town has now altered and become very mosque-centred' (1991: 64). This accords with the official position of the Turkish Republic, which posits religion to be a matter of conscience between God and the believer, mediated not by dervishes or saints but by the state. By contrast in the demographically Kurdish-dominated Hakkari province the ministry-appointed outsider is 'most often identified with the "religion of the state", and treated accordingly. Together with the school teacher, they would usually be expected to mediate when necessary between villagers and state officials and the military' (Yalçin-Heckmann 1991: 111). This is akin to what Yalman found in a much earlier study, where the 'official' Islam propagated by the state was virtually ignored by the people of 'Eastern Turkey', in favour of the unofficial Islam of the region's unorthodox and clandestine *medrese* (Islamic schools) and local traditional religious authorities (Yalman, ibid. p. 118). Since 1994 the Hakkari region has been at the centre of the state's 'hamletting' policy, whereby villages in remote areas are forcibly evacuated by the military. So in May 1996 the 'Emergency Region Governor reported that 2,297 settlements had been evacuated' (Amnesty International 1996: 127), while *Mazlumder*, an Islamist human rights group, estimated that by the end of 1995 the number was nearer 3,000 (*Mazlumder* 1995). What effect this has had on religious life in the provinces now under martial law is difficult to say, but one doubts that state Islam is any more popular. Indeed the massive influx of migrants to the region's big cities (i.e. Diyarbakır, Urfa, Adana) has meant that civil society has broken down in the Kurdish areas, and is being re-constituted in the new slums and settlements of these urban centres.

nationally-broadcast *mevlüt* on the days of the religious festivals. (Women's religiosity is much less mosque-centred, and the reciting of *mevlüt* readings in the home of the deceased as part of funeral and mourning rituals, and for the birth of a new baby, is mainly their work.)

On the other hand, the 'pastoral-care' work of the mosque's local *hoca* is offset by the populace's general contempt for the pronouncements of the *hoca*s in the *Diyanet Bakanlığı* (Religious Affairs Directorate) on the ordering or regularization of daily life. So during my fieldwork the Directorate ruled after much deliberation that the eating of prawns was now *caiz* (lawful). This did not ensure, if they were not already eating them, a sudden supplementation of prawns in the diet of my non-Islamist friends – though it may have led Islamists to stop eating them, on the grounds that if the *Diyanet Bakanlığı* had legitimized the consumption of prawns it must be wrong. Or again, the Directorate made a ruling about wedding dresses – they were not to be transparent or figure-hugging, and brides should cover their heads (although how this was to be done was left to the bride). But immediately a professor from an Ankara university theology department contradicted the claim. 'Let it be according to the desires of the people marrying,' he said (*Yeni Yüzyil*, 24 September 1996).

Finally, the competing theatricalization of the historical patrimony staged in Islamist and Republican carnivals should not obscure what the two rivals have in common. For in de-coupling the link Laic/Turk, carnival Islamism should not be thought to downplay the state's production of Turkish nationals. It advocates, in contrast, a different insertion of Islam into Turkish identity. Accordingly the Mayor of Istanbul, Refah's Tayyip Erdoğan, can claim (at that same *Hicri Yılbaşı* rally) that the national anthem, the *Istiklal Marşı* (Independence March), constitutes the soul of the Refah Party, despite its culturally excluding reference to the *kahraman ırk'* (heroic race) in one of its verses. Carnival Islamism is not so much anti-nationalist as 'new nationalist', incorporating elements that the 'ideological' Republic, in constituting itself, had once excluded. It is ironic that the state itself, in its post-1980s 'restoration', partly cleared the ground for carnival Islamism to bloom, both by its introduction of compulsory religious instruction in schools, and by its use of Islamic rhetoric against opponents.[11]

11. Yalçin-Heckmann writes that during her fieldwork in Hakkari, the government appealed for 'Islamic unity and brotherhood against the "infidel" Kurdish guerrillas of Marxist-Leninist orientation. The military distributed leaflets in Hakkari in 1987, calling local people to support the government's measures against the guerrillas . . . [who were] accused of co-operation with the "infidel" Armenians and Greeks' (Yalçin-Heckmann 1991: 116). Or again, a friend told me that during his military service the officers had told his platoon that the village below them, which they had been ordered to clear, was an Armenian village. Yet upon entering the houses, he had come across the Koran.

New nationalist or old, not once, in all the rallies and protests and solidarity nights that I attended, did I hear a stage whisper about the 'Kurdish problem'.

Kuzguncuk and the Production of Localities

Alev Çınar, in her article on Refah's administration of the Greater Istanbul Municipality, writes

> [p]olitical Islam, far from being a unified social movement, is a fragmented, multi-faceted phenomenon which cannot, therefore, be adequately understood through singular categories . . . In relation to each of [society's] discursive domains, Islam gains a different meaning and a different significance, appearing as a progressive movement in some contexts and as reactionary in others, as a radical-militant position in certain instances and democratic at other times (Çınar 1997: 23).

Liberal, bourgeois and carnival Islamism share in this same tangle of contrary intentions. Islamism as a social movement is at once compromised, and yet strengthened, by its political vacillation: its intervention into the political arena is hesitant and contradictory. If it hits hard with its jabs, it pulls its punches. Its left and right hooks do not swing in telling combinations. It sometimes beats itself around the head. So carnival Islamism, like a prize fighter, stalks the ring of the public domain and intimidates secular securities by its defiant 'otherness'. In doing so it provokes the state in turn to re-orient its display of the historical patrimony to parry carnival Islamism's attack on Republican culture. At the same time liberal Islamism seeks to mediate between the intransigence of 'black and white' (or green and red) Turkey by constructing a hybrid third space, a space that sidesteps neatly the braying one-upmanship of the carnivals. And bourgeois Islamism is exercised to challenge the aesthetic of Republicanism by embroidering it with orientalist tokens. But its rebuke of the state's exclusion of Islam from 'public' space is tempered by its concern to build an intra-elite or cross-cultural (i.e. Islamist and laicist) coalition, a coalition founded explicitly on the denial of the cross-class Muslim solidarity of carnival Islamism.

In short, if liberal and bourgeois Islamism is to prosper, carnival Islamism too must remain strong. And the same holds true for Republicanism: the invitation of liberal Islamism (or should we call it liberal Republicanism?), in the shape of Fetih Paşa Korusu, to the discontents of carnival Republicanism is political only in relation to the continued construction of a polemic secularist civility over and against Islam. And does not the bourgeois Islamism of Dilruba restaurant, from the perspective of its laicist consumers, facilitate the emergence of an 'Islamist republicanism', a rival, Islam-friendly bourgeoisie wearied and disadvantaged by the state's continual production of Islamist–secularist tensions in the theatricalization of its own constituting narrative? Liberal, bourgeois and carnival Islamism create their own constituencies and meet their own echoes (and vice versa) in liberal, bourgeois and carnival Republicanism at the very same sites.

Where does Kuzguncuk fit in all of this? Liberal, bourgeois and carnival Islamism flourish brilliantly on its immediate edges, but Kuzguncuk's own Islamists remain unconvinced. In their steadfast refusal to attend the carnivals of either the state or the Refah Party, or to support by their consumption the architectural olive branch proffered by liberal and bourgeois Islamism to secular citizens, Kuzguncuk's Islamists restrict their activities to building a committed, and hence a diasporic, community in Kuzguncuk alone. We might, as Rowan Ireland has done for Brazil, situate their endeavours somewhere uneasily, then, between the 'politics of the state (the politics between projects in state formation in which political elites are the main players) and the politics of civil society (the confrontation between modes of civil society construction) . . . [in which] projects seek and find constituencies in one or other of the emergent formations in civil society' (Ireland 1994: 82). Uneasily, because despite the attempts of the political professionals of Refah to construct just such affinities, in Kuzguncuk they have not been particularly successful in capturing the energies or even the vote of the local Islamist social movement.

In like fashion we should note that despite the dominating role of the 'state within the state' (the National Security Council) in determining social and political policy, it too has had difficulties, at least *vis-à-vis* the alternative Kuzguncuk of Cengiz Bektaş and his friends, in inspiring agents to work as its representatives in the suburb. So one of the more influential social centres of Kuzguncuk, the *Çınaraltı Café* ('Under the Plane Tree'), squatting with its back to the Bosphorus on the T-junction of the main street with the major shoreline road, is a popular meeting-place for the suburb's leftists and intellectuals. Here in the winter presides the famous poet Can Yücel, for example, son of a former Kemalist Education Minister, or Tektaş Ağaoğlu (my upper-floor neighbour), whose grandfather was one of the leaders of the first government experiment in controlled 'democracy', the official opposition of the short-lived 1930 Independent Republican or Free Party. Both have been gaoled and beaten often enough in their long careers to know how bloody-minded the regime is. Socialist Kuzguncuk too does not share the same images of an ideal Turkey propagated by its nationalist and military elites.

Conclusion

Kuzguncuk's production of its own various localities is ambiguously related, then, to the project of the nation-state, in which neighbourhoods are 'designed to be instances and exemplars of a generalized mode of belonging to a wider territorial imaginary' (Appadurai 1995: 215). They are also ambiguously related to the political and economic elites of the Refah Party. [12] How significant is it, then, that Kuzguncuk's 'self-instituting' capability remains strong, and that its various localisms are differentially related to elite national projects of state formation and re-production? Is this a consequence (and proof) of the oft-proclaimed uniqueness of Kuzguncuk, its ability to defer the casting out of its inhabitants from Istanbul's last heaven to wander the mean streets of the global city? Or do all localities produce themselves as plural, even if in pale opposition to the administrative and regional boundaries, regularly 'reformed', that desire to reconfigure their loyalties and identities? Do even the *gecekondu* suburbs imagine themselves as different, skew-whiff to the designs of the political elites, if only we had the eyes to see?[13]

Robertson is undoubtedly right when he argues that 'globalization has involved and increasingly involves the creation and incorporation of locality' (1995: 40). But in our starry-eyed pairing of those sexy lovers (the local and the global) we may overlook their constant chaperoning by the ever-attentive national. Of course the way local, national and global elements are related vary. But Kuzguncuk makes a case for a more careful inclusion of the politics of the national arena and its selective appropriation

12. The Islamic 'Independent Industrialists & Businessmen's Association' (MUSIAD) has 2,500 members, a monthly budget of some Aust. $1.5 million, and has since its founding in 1990 established tens of profitable enterprises (*Yeni Yüzyil*, interview with MUSIAD President, 4 August 1996). Nicknamed the Refah Party's 'shadow cabinet', MUSIAD members were key associates of Prime Minister Erbakan on his first overseas visit to Iran, Pakistan, Malaysia and Indonesia, and have prepared numerous reports for the (then) Government to consider.

13. Sometimes fiction may provide us best with those very 'eyes to see': the character Dilek, when talking about a newly established illegal Istanbul slum, says, 'Emre's suburb has a miraculous air to it. People's lives rise like buildings. Every thought a thin red brick. Dreams and visions mixed with cement. Children multiplying like new floors and plastered with language. Emotions waiting beside unloaded furniture, grudges stagnating like mould in basements. Hopes running wires into half-finished rooms. Ninety thousand people and a year ago pasture. I love standing on the roof seeing stretching away from me the rooms lit up by heroes' (Houston, unpublished manuscript, 1994: 83).

and manipulation by local groups in the making of their own life projects. So we would see no neat correlation between a supposed global discourse of political Islam on the one hand and its particular embodiment in local contexts on the other. Globalization may indeed facilitate the construction of niche-Islams for local consumption, but only while at the same time it faithlessly facilitates a niche-Islam for Kurdish Muslims, bringing Islamist particularity into collision course with itself. The globalization of Istanbul, through which global flows rip like power surges, does not involve the cancelling out of more place-based struggles but adds another dimension to them, activating, disempowering, or advantaging a host of social actors and groups already actively involved in contesting the micro-politics of the metropolis.

To what extent, then, does Kuzguncuk function as a conduit for the nation-state's work of producing citizen-subjects? Certainly not unequivocally, as the activities of both alternative and Islamist Kuzguncuk reveal. Furthermore, competing tendencies in the Islamist movement itself call forth 'elective affinities' within Republicanism (and vice versa), disaggregating to an extent the projects of state actors into diverse 'ensembles of political practice' (Ireland 1994: 88). And nor are the localities produced by Kuzguncuk simply echoes reflecting the fury of these rival projects of state formation. The 'modes of localization' (Appadurai 1995: 215) employed by the state are confronted, then, with Kuzguncuk's own attempts at locality-producing, multiple as they are. Kuzguncuk may not be independent, but neither is the nationalization of neighbourliness by the nation-state the sole way the experiences of its locals are categorized and periodized.

Part II

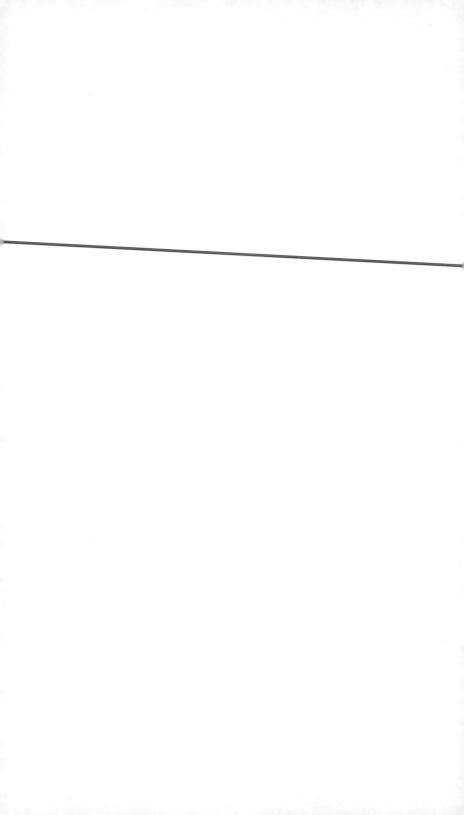

– 6 –

Turkish Republicanism and its Islamist Interrogator

Introduction

In Parts II and III of this study I would like to widen the terms of reference for analysing the 'alternative' modernity represented by the social imaginary institution of the Turkish Republic. In the first five chapters constituting Part I, I focused on Islamist responses to the republicanism of the state, surveying in particular the political – and urban – landscapes fashioned by the effort to enforce a civilizational shift in Turkey in which Islam is removed from the public domain and incorporated (re-inscribed) under the control of the *Diyanet İşleri Bakanlığı* (Directorate of Religious Affairs). Here Islam is re-politicized to support the state's nation-building project – a classic Hobbesian solution that immediately restricts the possibility of constructing civil society. Islam, in this sense, truly becomes an official (state) religion, although we can discern some differences in state policies between the single-party period, the rule of the populist parties, and the period after the 1980 military coup.[1]

In Parts II and III of the book I want to redirect attention to the nationalism of the state, in particular to the way Islam, when brought under the state's aegis, is peculiarly politicized and compromised by the dual nature of Kemalist politics: its republican–civil and monocultural aspects. It should be added that this dualism is not unique to the Turkish experience; every nationalist discourse is to some degree constituted by these two elements, the civil and the ethnic, which are combined in various, often-contradictory, ways to bring nascent subjects under its spell. Again, in looking at the nationalism of the state, I will examine, as in Part I, not so

1. Erik Jan Zürcher in his book *Modernleşen Türkiye'nin Tarihi* ('History of Turkish Modernization') controversially dates the founding of the Young Turk government in 1908 as the beginning of a political regime that lasted to 1950, encompassing the Independence War, the instituting of the Republic and the single-party period (1923–1945) – controversially because the Republic marks its own establishment as the defining break in Turkish history.

much the nationalism of state Islam, but its interrogator and interlocutor the Islamist movement, which though desiring one way or the other to replace Atatürk's *şeriat* with Allah's, is ambivalently situated *vis-à-vis* other political identities provoked by Turkish nationalism.

There is, however, a dissenting view that argues that a fundamental distinction should be made between the autonomous character of nationalities of Western modernity, and the 'derivative' nature of non-Western postcolonial nationalist discourse (see Kadıoğlu (1996) for an application of this argument to Turkey). Derivative nationalisms are marked by a historical dilemma that is part of a much wider problem,

> the problem of the bourgeois-rationalist conception of knowledge, established in the post-Enlightenment period of European intellectual history, as the moral and epistemic foundation of thought which perpetuates, in a real and not merely metaphorical sense, a colonial domination. It is a framework of knowledge that proclaims its own universality; its validity, it pronounces, is independent of cultures. Nationalist thought, in agreeing to become 'modern', accepts the claim to universality of this 'modern' framework of knowledge. Yet it also asserts the autonomous identity of a national culture. It thus simultaneously rejects and accepts the dominance, both epistemic and moral, of an alien culture (Chatterjee 1986: 11).

In other words, the paradox of nationalism as a derivative discourse of Western modernity derives from the adoption of the modern as the universal (in an unreflective genuflection to modernization's own claims), whilst at the same time constructing a unique, homogeneous and 'national' culture that the new nation-state is then empowered to represent. Yet this disarmingly flexible strategy obviously allows the state wide room to manoeuvre in its constitution and defence of a simultaneously modern (civilized)-cum-national society.

Sometimes this distinction is reconfigured to argue for an essential, at times orientalist, difference between Western and Eastern nationalisms respectively, whereby liberal Western nationalism becomes normative, and Eastern deviant. In this regard the TOBB (Union of Turkish Chambers of Commerce and Commodity Exchanges) report into the Kurdish question, published in 1995, makes the common-sense criticism that the Turkish Republic has 'ethnicized' citizenship, which should on the contrary be 'based on a social contract of consent signed by the citizens with the state' (Sakallıoğlu 1996: 5). That is, it posits not only as possible, but as desirable, the 'de-ethnicizing' of the public (political) domain, and the liberal regulation of it by impersonal, modern rules of conduct. The report petitions, then, for a decoupling of politics and culture. In Chatterjee's terms, the report's solution to the dilemma of derivative nationalist discourse is a more rigorous application of the principles of modernity. But wherein, then, would reside the legitimacy of the state, as protector of the particular genius of the people–nation?

Typologies of Western and Eastern nationalism should be reconsidered, not merely because of the increasing multiculturalism of Western societies, but also because the institution of citizenship by Western liberal states entailed in practice both the production, and discipline/management of difference (regional, racial, gendered, sexual) in the name of the national universal. In important ways, and without wanting to dispute the significance of the category of alternative modernities, opposition to 'bourgeois-rationalist' thought and its pretensions to universality is the grit stimulating social movements in the West, as well as the subalterns. Nationalism in the colonial world may be a derivative discourse, but the strategies it pursues to stabilize its production of identity are not peculiar to the post-colony. For implicit in the liberal notion of democracy (as the sovereignty of a self-governing community) is the assumption that that community shares a common national culture. Otherwise how could it represent itself/ be represented (without giving itself over to a Leviathan?) In his defence Chatterjee is seeking to problematize the modernist assumption of the inevitability and normativeness of Western-style nationalism, once the universal process of industrialization is sufficiently developed to tame the irrational and regressive aspects of post-colonial (Eastern) nationalism.

For analytical purposes bureaucratic (state) Islam and 'radical' Islamism can be presented as polarized discursive or ideal-types. Yet in the messiness of everyday interactions their constituents and programmes tend to shade into each other. Perhaps the best way of illustrating this is by describing a ceremonial event that I attended, organized to commemorate the death of thirty-three villagers, massacred by unknown assailants (the PKK? contraguerillas?) in the province of Erzincan. The event was advertised in one of the Islamist newspapers as follows:

> Invitation to a remembrance of a massacre. *Ey Müslümanlar!* (O Muslims!) This massacre was not perpetrated in Palestine, or Bosnia but in Başbağlar, Turkey. On the night of 5th July, 1993 traitorous and treacherous infidels slaughtered the people in this village, in the same way that Jews and Serbs do. 700 years of continuous habitation was wiped from history . . . and Turkey's administrators just watched (*Yeni Şafak*, 5 July 1996 – my translation).

The meeting had all the hallmarks of an Islamist gathering: men and women seated in different sections, chanting of slogans and readings from the Koran, banners hanging from the walls proclaiming 'Palestine, Bosnia,

Başbağlar, Chechnya: you're next in line, Muslim.' And yet, as the evening wore on, the intent of the meeting became clearer: the stage was decorated with the slogan 'to national unity and indivisibility'; there was a live tele-phone hook-up with the Governor of Erzincan, addresses by state officials, announcements of telegrams from parliamentarians (including one from the then Interior Minister, Mehmet Ağar, an extreme Turkish nationalist) and finally a rabble-rousing speech from a bearded (Islamist) speaker, condemning the legal Kurdish party and promising that those 'who strike my police, my army, my flag will be finished – their atheism will cease' (Houston 1997: 5–6). Here we see that Islam's long cohabitation with the state does not make for quick repudiations, and that there is much free trade between Islamist and nationalist identities.

This will best be explored through the lens of the Kurdish 'question', Kurdish Muslims in particular being faced with a state that still refuses to grant Kurds collectively certain elementary human rights, while con-tinuing the historic project of assimilating diverse populations within the gamut of Turkish nationalism. For in the process of resisting the civility of the state Islamists are faced with the problem of reconciling those differences politicized, or even constructed, by the regime that the move-ment seeks to combat. The unifying of religious Kurds and Turks within Islamist discourse in the very context of the production of such identities leads to many compromises. In Part III of this study Islamist responses to the Kurdish problem will be examined, in particular the concerns of the Kurdish elements within it, to render, in Bourdieu's felicitous phrase, 'the probable deviations predictable and therefore more difficult' (1990: 2). But first the historical precedents of the Kurdish problem need to be sketched out.

The Turkish Enlightenment

Turkish modernity, in its Republican moment, arrogated to itself enlighten-ment values of rationality, progress and universality. So, for example, the 1931 statutes of the Republican People's Party (the only party in the parliament)[2] stated that 'The party has accepted the principle that all laws,

---

2. Multi-party elections occurred for the first time in 1950. Until then the political structure of the state resembled the fascist system in Italy – the Minister of the Interior and the Secretary-General of the Party were the one and same person. By 1936 all state officials in the bureaucracy had become local party officials, and 'full congruency' was declared between the Republican People's Party and the state administration. See Keyder 1987: 100.

regulations and procedures used in the administration of the state should be prepared and implemented . . . in accordance with the foundations of and the forms of science and technology in modern times' (Mardin 1993: 365). In its bid to create civilization, and in its corresponding attack on religion and the memory of religious constructions of identity, the state took upon itself the task of liberating the people from tradition. In the name of rationality and the abolition of privilege, the Republic accorded equality to all before the law; this included enfranchising women. The unity of the people was reconceived then, away from holistic visions of society and hierarchy towards the freedom of citizenship. Republican discourse enabled prospective citizens to be caught up in those 'most heroic of the images of the democratic tradition, those of popular revolutions mobilizing against internal [reactionary] and external [imperialistic] enemies' (Touraine 1994a: 6), while making themselves modern. Hence the Republic became the great storyteller of the nation, sponsoring the grand narratives of nationalism, independence and secularism. In this story both Islamic and Kurdish discourses are cast as villains, the first characterized as backward primitivism, the second as parochial particularism. Beside this sorry pair, the universalism of the Republic exists as a sharp rebuke.

Yet within Kemalist universalism lies its own particularistic antithesis: ethnic Turkish singularity, with its concomitant refusal to recognize other ethnic groups as possible joint heirs of modernity, particularly the Kurds. This 'contradictory' symbiosis partly explains the existence of the incoherent claims of the Turkish 'history-thesis' (cf. page 33) and the 'sun-language' theory: because the Kemalist revolution was the embodiment of enlightenment progress, the Turks (in essence) were its cultural carriers, even if the overlay of Islam had slowed down, or threatened the inevitability of their fusion. The Republic's laicism was merely a coming home to history.[3] To refuse to be Turkish in this case was wilfully to step outside the march of history. In this uneasy coalition between the a-ethnicity of Republicanism and the supra-ethnicity of Turkism, Kurdish existence, for example, when acknowledged, was contrasted unfavourably with the universal significance of Turkishness as being tribal, backward, custombound, ignorant, fanatically-religious etc. And since the discourse of Turkish Republicanism is presented not as interpreting history but rather as being constituted by it as history (i.e. its narrative device is to 'de-narrativize' itself, so that the very origin of the nation becomes inseparable from the

---

3. There was, for example, no new mosque erected in Ankara, the centre of the new Republic, until after Atatürk's death.

story of the nation's origin), to be Kurdish (or anti-secular Muslim) is immediately inscribed as being anti-progress and hence morally, i.e. ontologically, deficient.

Bureaucratized Islam, then, having submitted to the requirements of unitary state-building, is pressed into service for constructing (among other things) a regime-friendly Turkish-Islamic identity, especially against other potential identities. For secularism is not a process that de-politicizes Islam. Rather, it removes it from its political role in the old system and disenfranchises those empowered by this role, whilst quickening Islam in new ways to support the project of the new regime. Clearly perceiving itself as imbued with the task of constructing a civil Islam paralleling the civil strand of Kemalism, official Islam is in fact unable to criticize Turkish nationalism's ethnic preference without simultaneously de-legitimizing its own existence. For bureaucratized Islam is integral to the Kemalist project of subordinating notions of identity derived from Islam to ones derived from the nation. Thus, far from challenging the state's cultural policies – the forced and undemocratic assimilation of non-Turkish elements – Islam in its official capacity acts to hasten this process by conflating the universal/modern with a particular ethnic culture. Perhaps the most striking recent example of this is seen in a new translation into Turkish of a historical work by one Mevlana Halid-i Bağdaşı (an influential Kurdish Nakşibendi leader from the last century) by Marmara University's Theology Faculty member Dr Yakup Çiçek. According to a recent series of articles in the newspaper *Yeni Şafak*, the new edition was published with all textual references to Kurds and the land of the Kurds expunged.[4] This despite the official Ottoman maps of the time designating the south-east regions of present-day Turkey as 'Kurdistan'.

Islamist Interrogation of Republicanism

In disputing the privatization of Islam and the self-portrait of the Republic as the bearer of modernity, is the Islamist movement inclined to reject the ethnic preference of official Islam as well? For those living in Turkey, what does its aim of producing an 'Islamic' identity and not a laic one actually entail? For the Islamist project is double-edged: to carve off from the body-politic the flab and fat of one hundred and fifty years of Westernization, and to sculpt the newly-freed, slimmed-down Muslim self into

---

4. See Müfid Yüksel's articles in *Yeni Şafak*, 3–7 November 1995.

its natural and authentic Islamic shape. In rejecting the secular structure of the state, the Islamist movement also questions the whole trajectory of the post-1923 Republic and its modernizing Ottoman bureaucratic predecessors. Secularism is seen as just one component, though a particularly illustrative one, of its Jacobin programme. Islamist analysis of Turkey's problems is grounded in the conviction that the Westernization/ modernization of the Ottoman Empire (and the usage of these terms is highly variable among different groups, as the imitative piety of the *Mahmut Efendi tarikat* testifies) signalled its departure from its Islamic parameters, however imperfectly they may have been adhered to. At a moral level this signifies the abandonment of a just law for a law imposed by the ruling elites of the time serving their own interests: Turkey is no longer a legal state but a state of regulation (*hukuklu Devlet değil; kanunlu Devlettir*). On a cultural level the Republican elite, particularly in the single-party period, is attacked as suffering from an inferiority complex, imposing an alien ideology on Muslims, imitating the West in an act of cultural conspiracy against the customs and habits of the people in the name of someone else's 'civilization'.

This de-islamification is viewed as having been accomplished socially by the importation of nationalisms in such a way that the Ottoman Empire's ethnic minorities and finally its Arab provinces were encouraged by the imperialistic powers to break away from the centre in the name of their cultural/national specificities. Here the famed Islamic tolerance for the relative cultural autonomy of different ethnic groups was replaced by the foreign and regressive doctrine of ethnically homogeneous national states, eroding the unity of the Islamic *ummah* (community of believers). Nationalism in Islamist discourse is vilified as a non-Islamic innovation, a Western process stirring up the worst passions of the minorities, especially ingratitude (*nankörlük*); but it is not often criticized with equal ferocity for its simultaneous privileging of Turks.

In short, the common Islamist critique of the post-1923 regime centres around the deconstruction of the Republic's civilizing mission. Here the modernization of the rump of the Ottoman Empire undertaken in the name of the universality of Western civilization (with the immediate conferring of provincial and parochial status upon Islam) is problematized, as Islamist discourse converges with other postmodern critiques in proclaiming the exhaustion or crisis of modernity as an emancipatory project. Islamist politics then celebrates the return of the Muslim actor and identity, and Islamism can be described as the 'formation of the Muslim subject and agency which has been excluded from modernist definitions of civilization and history-making' (Göle 1996: 26).

And yet the Islamist interpretation of the Kemalist revolution[5] as primarily a forced Westernization by bureaucratic/military elites is simultaneously an occidentalizing and hence an essentializing strategy – and means analysis will be less inclined to ascribe a major role to Kemalism's nationalizing project. Thus the Muslim subject in the act of self-consolidation posits the Western 'other' as his/her antithesis (as represented by the secularist elites), and is theoretically anaesthetized to forget that this Westernized elite also found it necessary to reify one ethnic group above all others in the nation-building process. The Muslim actor then analyses the Kemalist reforms as de-legitimizing Islamic identity in the name of a false universalism, but is blinded by a newly found confidence from noting its compensatory legitimizing of Turkish identity, also in the name of a false universalism. The difficulty for the radical and self-authenticating [Turkish] Muslim subject is this: how to struggle with a discourse that empowers you in one way but not in the other? Of course, in setting up the battle lines between a homogeneous Occident and Islam – as seen in the claim that the only choice is that between Western civilization and Islam – there is no space for difference within this Islamist identity itself, though in fact Muslim cultural homogeneity is a political project, not an existing reality.

The Islamist movement, by dwelling on the cultural colonialism of the Westernizing/secularizing state, is not activating, then, a 'natural' category (the Muslim) but [re-]constructing political subjects (the Muslim

---

5. A friend told me that after the 1980 military coup, the word *devrim* (revolution) was banned by the generals: *Atatürk devrimleri* (Atatürk's revolutions) were now to be spoken of as *Atatürk inkılapları*. *Inkılap* is the Arabic word for 'reform'. It is ironic that Atatürk's famous language policy (which entailed the purging of non-Turkish words, especially Arabic, from the language) was reversed in certain cases by the military leaders of the *müdahale* (intervention), all in the name of Atatürk. Unfortunately for the generals, an almost identical word, *inkilap* (with a dot on the second *i*) means 'to become a dog'. When read out by unwitting television and radio announcers, *Atatürk inkilaplari* described Atatürk as 'becoming a dog'. Worse still, 'Atatürk (and his friends) are becoming dogs', 'Atatürk's becoming a dog is the basis of our programme,' the spokesmen insisted. (I cannot say whether this story is apocryphal or not.)
The generals also banned the word *darbe* (coup), describing their suspending of the parliament and declaration of martial law as a *müdahale*.

actor).[6] This struggle necessarily involves the struggle to exclude other possible ways by which these same actors could define themselves. This is not to say that the Islamist movement is deceiving its followers. Rather the movement consists of the self-creation of individuals as they reinterpret their own discourses. Self-definition is always a dialogical event, and Turkish-Republican discourse, and the elites who constitute themselves as such by their adherence to it, do not just devalue the Muslim 'other' in their self-institution. Republicans against Muslims, Turkish against Kurds, the Kurdish Muslim actor is confronted not just with the civilizing project of the state, but with its Turkifying one as well.

6. The Muslim subject ('someone who places her or his Muslim identity at the centre of her or his political practice' Sayyid 1997: 17) is also a modern institution, as is the scripturalist tendency (misrepresented as a 'return to the Koran') in nearly all Islamist movements. Literacy, state Islam and Islamism have led, as the Tappers found in the town of Eğirdir, to a decrease in the practices of saint worship, healing, sufism and 'superstition', as well as to an increase in orthodoxy. Mardin reports a young officer's experiences in training conscripts from Anatolia during the First World War:

> When I asked, 'What is our religion?' . . . I expected that I would receive the answer, 'Thanks be to God, we are Muslims.' But I didn't receive this answer. Some said, 'We are of the religion of Imam Azami.' Others, 'We are of the party of the prophet Ali.' A few couldn't give an answer to the question. True, several men said they were Muslims; but when I asked 'Who is our prophet?', things became even more confused. No-one could have imagined the names of the prophets that were mentioned. Someone said, 'Our prophet is Enver Pasha.' And when those few who knew who our prophet was were asked 'Is our prophet alive or has he departed from us?', the problem became unsolvable. Half the men were convinced he was still living, half that he had died . . . (Mardin 1993: 55).

–7–

The Kurdish Problem: Assimilation as a Legislative Practice and Narrative Ideal

Introduction

Before moving on to investigate more specifically Islamist analysis of, and responses to the Kurdish problem, we should understand what this problem is, grasp why it is that the Kurdish majority areas of south-east Turkey have been for decades, indeed ever since the proclamation of the Republic, in almost constant upheaval. Yet delimiting the Kurdish problem is no straightforward matter. Different perspectives compete to define, and hence proffer remedies for it, though the denial of its very existence is also a common claim.[1] Sometimes the problem smells as rank by any other name – the 'Eastern question' is often puzzled over, as is the curse of 'regional under-development', with its concomitant condemnations of the area's 'feudal' social structure, insufficiently transformed by a modernization that 'whetted the appetite of the Kurdish population without destroying the traditional order . . .' (TOBB Report – Union of Turkish Chambers of Commerce and Commodity Exchanges, cited in Sakallıoğlu 1996: 12).

The problem can also be approached according to its intimate relationships with other aspects of Turkish political life – for example as the most important key to the flood of human rights violations occuring in the country, or as a vital influence on the consistently tense relations between Turkey and its immediate neighbours, or as an element in the policies of the US and the European states towards Iraq and the Middle East as a whole. The south-east region can be charted too by its various economic indices,

---

1. Alparslan Türkeş, General Secretary of the nationalist MHP (National Action Party) said in an interview after the 1996 election that 'the Kurds are our people, they are all of Turkish stock. They are Turks that have become Kurds (*Kürtleşmiştir*) only through neglect. Turkey is not a cultural mosaic, everyone in Turkey is a Turk' (*Yeni Yüzyil*, 26 December 1996).

which document the level of unequal development at least partly responsible for its rapid out-migration, as well as the increasing importance of the GAP (South-Eastern Anatolian Project) programme with its planned 22 dams on the Euphrates and Tigris and large-scale irrigation and electricity schemes.

But the human rights situation is probably the most succinct indication of the chaos to which the south-eastern provinces in particular have fallen prey. Indeed, awareness of the extent of human rights abuses must be the most difficult aspect of fieldwork to cope with, let alone imagine and incorporate into one's research. In the two years I lived in Istanbul the regular reports, even the escalation, of torture, beatings, disappearances, extra-judicial killings, deaths in custody, indiscriminate or arbitrary murders, detentions and arrests depressed me greatly. Some events, neither particularly exceptional nor unusually appalling, stand out in my memory: the riots in Gazi Osman Paşa, which resulted in more than 20 deaths, most with a single bullet wound in the heart; the beating to death by police of the journalist Metin Göktepe; and the bombing of the office of the Kurdish newspaper, *Özgür Ülke*. These all occurred in Istanbul. Conditions in the ten Kurdish provinces under the State of Emergency are of course far worse, where conservative accounts estimate that 2,200 villages have been partially or completely destroyed (Interior Minister Nahit Menteşe mentioned this figure in his report to Parliament in 1995). A Kurdish man visiting an Istanbul friend from Diyarbakır, the biggest city in the south-east and massively swollen with refugees fleeing the fighting between the military and the PKK, asked me to put in my book the fact that Istanbul was a 'human rights heaven' compared to Diyarbakır. David McDowall claims that since 1992 almost 3 million people have been rendered homeless, and that the Turkish military have nearly 300,000 troops stationed in the provinces under Emergency Rule (Mc Dowall 1997: 32).

The suspension of normal legal procedures opens the door to another problem: the probable role of both the PKK and state functionaries (Special Forces, police, village guards etc.) in the heroin trade into Europe. The profits are so vast that the effects on already creaking state structures need to be analysed. In this regard the legacy of ten years of martial law in many of the south-eastern provinces and the total breakdown of civil society in these regions have brought a form of immunity for paramilitary and other forces to conduct well-organized smuggling enterprises. The development of a war economy and the emergence of groups committed to the conflict's continuation take the notion of a *rentier* economy to new heights. Research into the dimensions introduced by such factors poses a problem indeed. At the very least, knowledge of the state's brutality (and/or involvement) casts a sheen of unreality over many of its statements, let alone its various initiatives to 'strengthen civil society', or parade its status as a socially responsible citizen of the international community (while I was there the 2nd UN 'Habitat' conference was hosted in Istanbul). The temptation is to become as simplistic in one's analysis: to conclude that the political order is as fascist and/or mafia-ized, as the state is ruthless in its defence of it.[2]

The Problem of the Kurds or the Kurds' Problem?

But grasping in a nutshell the dimensions of the Kurdish problem is no help in understanding it. Taking a cue from Castoriadis, I want to unweave the tangled skeins of the Kurdish problem into two separate but intimately related threads. In an article entitled 'Anthropology, Philosophy, Politics', Castoriadis notes the enigma of knowledge concerning humanity: 'this knowledge of man [*sic*] (in the objective genitive, knowledge about man) is also a knowledge of man (in the subjective and possessive genitive) – therefore . . . man is at once the object and subject of this knowledge' (1997b: 99).

It might be useful to apply this distinction to the Kurdish problem. The problem is approachable firstly as a problem focused on the Kurds. What do we know of the Kurds? How can the problem they pose be solved? How shall they be managed? In this frame the problem of the Kurds is someone else's problem – the Turkish state's (or Syria's, Iraq's, Iran's), the military's, the functionaries' and representatives' of the 'civilizing' agencies (teachers, doctors, health workers, judges, lawyers etc.), the intellectuals', the political parties', concerned citizens', human rights campaigners' etc. Such different groups or institutions will understand the particularity of the Kurdish problem according to the values that inform their *modus operandi*.

So for the state the Kurds are a problem to its guardianship of the cultural homogeneity of the nation. For the armed forces the Kurdish guerrilla resistance presents a threat to their instituted aim of defending the country's territorial and national integrity. For the civilizing bureaucracies Kurds constitute an enormous challenge to the efficient carrying out of their duties (language problems, problems of access, of cultural difference)

---

2. See for example Amnesty International's disturbing report *Turkey: No Security without Human Rights* (1996), or the Human Rights Watch Project's 1995 publication, *Savaş ve İnsan: Türkiye ye Silah Transferleri ve Savaş Yasaları İhlalleri* (Weapons Transfers and Violations of the Laws of War in Turkey).

and post-PKK to their very presence in the region). For intellectuals, especially those employed at the state universities, the Kurdish problem represents an uncomfortable taboo that picks away at the scab formed over the post-coup reorganization of the tertiary education sector and the self-aggrandizing discourse of the independence of science and research. For the political parties, pulling in the vote (by local candidates, patron–client ties, populist policies, lentil crop price-rises, religious manipulation, circumcision ceremonies, etc.) subsumes their interest in the Kurdish problem. For conscientious citizens the effects of the Kurdish situation (and the state's reactions to it) on the very checks and balances meant to safeguard democracy in the Republic as a whole must dominate their concerns. For human rights workers the Kurdish problem translates as a bottomless well of human suffering.

But the Kurdish problem is not just a problem for national security, for democracy or peace or the rule of law, or even for the Turkishness of the nation. The problem of the Kurds is at the same time the Kurds' problem. The Kurds have become a problem unto themselves. The Kurdish question is not merely a question then over what to do about the Kurds; it is also a question which the Kurds address to themselves, a question directed at the very nature of their subjectivity.

Separated in this way, these two skeins are complementary, yet irreducible to each other. And yet in being untangled they still double back upon each other. Here the question, according to Castoriadis, becomes not a vicious circle but a circle of reflection (1997b: 100). We are talking, in other words, about the problem of identity, and whether merely showing how the ethnic subject is constituted in discursive structures – summoned, disciplined, produced, and regulated etc. – is adequate if we wish to understand the self-production of the subject at the same time. The Kurdish problem is the sum then of the 'objective' and 'subjective' knowledge of the Kurds, and of the interplay between these two.

The Problem of Kurdish Existence

How is the Kurdish problem represented then? In which discursive categories is the problem to be 'objectively' explained? In the first place the problem is identified as residing in the very fact of Kurdish existence. If there were no Kurds, according to this logic, there would be no problem. So a new book on Kurdish nationalism for example describes (in its blurb) the Kurdish movement in the Middle East as a 'powder-keg waiting to explode', as though their mere ethnic specificity (as well as their sheer weight of numbers) explains in itself the Kurdish nationalist movement.

For after all, they are the largest ethnic group in the Middle East 'without a country of their own' (Olson 1996). It is no coincidence, however, that it is with precisely this presumption that the Republican state has often treated those Kurds living within its sovereign domain: that is, as a fifth column needing to be closely supervised for recidivist separatist tendencies. According to Jeremy Seal (1996: 238) on the very day the Republic abolished the Caliphate (3 March 1924) it also published a decree banning all Kurdish schools, associations and publications. This a year before the first 'Kurdish' uprising in the territory of the new regime, the Sheik Said rebellion (February 1925), with its mixture of Islamist and nationalist sympathies. Like a jealous husband, nation-state paranoia often excites the very thing it fears.

Historic state suspicion of the Kurds is of course related to the nation-building project, where the newly formalized national culture is presented as expressing an abiding ethnic essence. But if the Turks have existed as a proto-nation since the dawn of time (as Turkish nationalist discourse insists) then the possibility is also raised that so have the Kurds. Ironically, the naturalization of the Turkish self as the political sovereign in the new state naturalizes in the same breath the suddenly threatening essential Kurdish self (obscuring the actual mechanics of the construction of Turkish and Kurdish identity). Essentialist presentations of the Turks (for whom the new state was founded) are mirrored then in the fear of the essentialist existence of the Kurds (as potential inhabitants of a rival nationalist historiography). On the other hand, if the Kurds could be proved to be Turks all along the fear would be allayed. Accordingly state policies towards the Kurds have pursued both these strategies. Alongside the state's determination to forbid any form of Kurdish political organization, any Kurdish societies, any Kurdish cultural or language associations (even to the extent of prohibiting the speaking of Kurdish, or the giving of Kurdish names to children)[3] there has also been extensive ethnographic and linguistic research undertaken to demonstrate that the Kurds are Turkish anyway. A good recent example of this is the 1997 book *Etnik Sosyoloji* (Ethnic Sociology) by Istanbul Professor Dr Orhan Türkdoğan. In a chapter entitled 'Ethnic Structure and the South-East' he writes:

> in 1856 the Czar's Erzurum consul Alexander Jaba, on instructions from the Petersburg Science Academy, conducted an examination of the vocabulary of the tribes in Erzurum and its environs. The study was published in 1860 in

---

3. The ban was partially lifted in 1991, when the legalizing of Kurdish for private communication was agreed to (Gürbey 1996: 14).

St Petersburg with the title *Récueil de Notices et Recits Kourds* [Notes on the History and Tales of the Kurds]. The book was translated into Turkish by Dr Fritsche in 1918 under the heading *History and Social Life of the Kurds*. In the work Alexander Jaba reveals that of the 8,307 Kurdish words he found, 3,080 were of Turkmen origin, 2,640 of ancient Persian origin and 2,000 from modern Arabic. Only the 300 words left over were truly Kurdish. Yet if it is considered that these 300 words were found in the proto-Turkish regions it will be seen that they are of Turkish origin. Jaba's research however did not grasp this. According to the famous German researcher de Groot, 'on the *Yenisey* inscriptions the word Kurd appears; but one of *Oğuz Han's* 24 grandchildren was named Kurd. On the *Orkun* gravestones no present-day Turkish words are found, but from today's spoken Kurdish 532 words can be seen. This shows that the Kurds are a branch of the Turks and that they came to Anatolia in ancient times from Asia.' The 300 words that Jaba found have their root here. It will be understood then that because of its composition from three languages Kurdish cannot be an independent language. For this reason, as has been proven since Ziya Gökalp, Kurdish is not a language but a dialect. As is well known, the Kurdish of the Kurds that live in Iran is heavily influenced by Persian; that in Iraq by Arabic; and the Kurdish in Turkey by Turkish. This shows us that Kurdish is a border dialect of Turkish (Türkdoğan 1997: 119–20 – my translation).

Türkdoğan concludes by stating:

> there is no such thing as the Kurdish people or nation. They are merely carriers of Turkish culture and habits. The imagined region proposed as the new Kurdistan is the region that was settled by the *proto-Turks* [my italics]. The Sumerians and Scythians come immediately to mind. The Eastern problem as it is some-times called shows itself to be solely the game of the imperialists, played when it suits with the Armenians, when it suits with the Iranians (1997: 134 – my translation).

Professor Türkdoğan's endeavours should not be thought of as revealing some idiosyncratic personal prejudice but as being part of a state enter-prise, as a quick glance at the list of professorial colleagues cited in his sources demonstrates. As Türkdoğan's text shows, Turkish nationalist discourse, and the politics of the state, have not been concerned so much with emphasizing the difference and inferiority of the Kurds, but with forcibly integrating them into the 'larger community of Turks' (Sakallıoğlu 1996: 6). Of course, proving the non-existence of Kurds is only half the problem; proving the existence, and defining the specificity of that same larger community of Turks needs to be elucidated as well. For this reason Turkdoğan's very next chapter is entitled 'On the Identity of the Turks' which concludes with his bemoaning the fact that from a sociological view, the Turkish community has not yet achieved rendezvous with its national identity . . . This nationalization process should be realized. Intellectuals and political party members should not be given permission to threaten the social structure with separatist and fragmented perspectives informed by unscientific sociology and anthropology . . . Turkish history should be written. Turkish thought's evolutionary pattern, its understanding of state and government, and the main principles of the Turkish family structure should be publicized. Turkey's regional socio-cultural investigations should be approached in a systematic manner. To do this, those who work in the areas of anthropology, ethnographic sociology and culture should develop in a scientific way a culture map of Turkey (1997: 148) (my translation).

As an illustration of the sort of research he has in mind he cites a recent finding of the Turkish Historical Society's president, Professor Dr Yusuf Halaçoğlu. His research on the land-title deeds drawn up in Sultan Suleyman's reign argues that the large majority of tribes registering themselves as Kurdish were in fact Turkish, hoping to strengthen their claim to grazing rights, etc. According to Halaçoğlu, 'this research will contribute to the solving of the Kurdish problem' (*Yeni Şafak*, 2 August 1996), because 'the records show that the Kurds were not a separate ethnic group from the Turks' (Türkdoğan 1997: 148).

Kurdish Identity and State Assimilation

More positivist scholarly works too often mirror the self-justification of the Turkish nation-state (a state for the people called Turks) in their proclivity to take as given the very processes one would wish to problematize – nations, nationalism, ethnicity, subjectivity, identity, etc. Thus the debate over the exact number of Kurds in Turkey (8 million, 10 million, 15 million?) is seen as originating in the confusion caused by the historic reluctance of the state to collect census data on ethnic background (for fear of encouraging that which it denies), rather than in any theoretical hesitations over the fluidity of the making of identity. (The censuses for their part show the same contradictory impulses as official policy: in the four conducted between 1945 and 1965, for example, there was a question on mother tongue but none on ethnicity (Türkdoğan 1997: 106) – hinting at a similar concern to police the activities of an officially non-existent minority).

And yet a long interview with one of the ex-leaders of the MHP (*Milli Hareket Partisi*, the Turkish nationalist/fascist party) is a revealing window into the complexities of the process of making identities, into the problematic relationship between discursive practices and self-constitution.

Mehmet Pamak is asked: 'We know that your family was exiled from the Van region [Eastern Turkey] to Çanakkale [Western Turkey]. How did it happen that, although you came from a Kurdish family, you worked for years in the Turkish nationalist movement and even became one of its leaders?' In reply he says:

> Because I was born in Çanakkale, my national identity [*kavmi kimliği*] was generally perceived as Turkish. Over time however the rumour that I was actually Kurdish was passed secretly from ear to ear. And when I was forced to concede that it was so, those who learnt of my Kurdish identity began to doubt me . . . Yes, at last I am admitting, I am the child of a Kurdish family. As you explained, our family was exiled from Erciş to Çanakkale. My family was one of the survivors of the infamous 'Zilan' massacre. The fighting started with the [government's] claim that they wanted *şeriat*, that they don't wear hats [*sic*], and concluded with the herding of the villagers into the Zilan valley, thousands of people, men, women, children, and the aged, and their massacre by machine-gun fire. My grandfather told me that blood flowed out of that valley for days. My grandfather, father and several others fled to Iran to save their lives, but my aunt who was just a baby and my 80-years-old great-grandmother were bayoneted to death when the soldiers came back to the villages . . . When events had calmed down those of my family who survived returned and were immediately exiled to Çanakkale. My family was met with great hostility in the village in which they were settled. I can well remember us being derided as 'Kurds with Tails' [*Kuyruklu Kürtler*] or the threat that 'you came from the east wearing one shoe and we will drive you from this village in the same state' . . . Despite all this torture, my family never embraced Kurdish nationalism [*Kürtçülük şuuru*]. My grandfather only said, 'We were attacked by the soldiers because we wanted *şeriat*' . . . In fact, forget Kurdishness, we tried to prove that Kurds were Turks, we even became Turkish nationalists. My family became leading lights in the Çanakkale Nationalist movement . . . Even so, the whole time that I was a Turkish nationalist I was desperately unhappy . . . For example, at one of the administrative meetings a name of someone from the east was put forward. When one of the other committee members said, 'Forget him, he's a Kurd,' I felt incredibly upset. 'Hey, aren't the Kurds Turks? We're not against Kurds but against Kurdish nationalism,' I protested (although we thought that Turkish nationalism was legitimate) . . . Through examples like these I slowly understood just how wrong, divisive and destructive Turkish nationalism, all nationalism (racism) is. The crisis I was in was only healed by the embrace of Islam. Anyway finally I can announce that I am a member of a Kurdish family that was exiled to Çanakkale from Van for wanting *şeriat*. From this time on everyone should understand that I am first and foremost a Muslim, who has suffered for Islam like Selmani Farisi, Süheybi Rumi and Bilali Habesi. But for those who want to know me, let it be acknowledged that I am Kurdish too (Pamak 1992: 330–3 – my translation).

The reticence of Pamak's family to 'remember' being Kurdish, their grief, fear and horror at the ruthlessness of the state, their shelter in the half-way house of Islam, even their self-protection in the cloak of Turkish nationalism are all alluded to in Pamak's answer. This being the case, a related debate could be held over the exact number of Turks in Turkey, for allied to the state's project of constructing Turks is a similar determination to deconstruct Kurds. Neither, then, are self-evident categories, despite the conceit of census-takers. For would a snapshot of ethnic affiliation at any one time tell us anything of the process of assimilation as a legislative practice and a narrative ideal, not to speak of its morality?

Yet the ongoing need felt by the state to both narrate and legislate Kurdish identity out of existence attests to a continual refusal by Kurds to become 'docile bodies'. For even the claim that there is no such being as a Kurd opens up a discursive space for a negative or 'anti'-identity: henceforth 'Kurds' are those who refuse to become Turks. But the self-production of Kurdish identity is more than this. In disputing the 'objective' knowledge claimed by others, subjects constitute themselves as self-knowing Kurds in a different way. The 'subjective' knowledge of Kurds themselves incorporates the 'objective' knowledge of others to create contemporary Kurdish identity. To the extent that this 'objective' knowledge is itself made up of contradictory, often antagonistic discourses (which are also in a constant process of transformation), contemporary Kurdish identity too is hardly unified but subject to competing claims over its constitution. Yet ironically, Kurdish identity in Turkey is prevented from fragmentation, even pulled towards a unified centre by the negative role ascribed to it in the newly constructed uniform Turkish national identity. Mesut Yeğen (1996) argues that the Kurdish question as enunciated in Turkish state discourse was constituted in the re-inscribing and problematizing of Islam ('reactionary' politics and the fury over the abolition of the Caliphate), tradition (tribal resistance and banditry), and the periphery (regional backwardness, smuggling, and resistance to taxation and military service), which became the social spaces wherein Kurdish identity was constructed.

Yılmaz Güney's brilliant film *Sürü* (The Herd), for example, traces the difficulties of a small group of Kurdish nomads as they make the long journey to Ankara to sell their sheep. Dispassionate in its unromantic portrayal of both nomad and city life, the film manipulates the tropes that constitute Kurdishness, while critiquing both the modernity of the capital of Republican Turkey and the rule of the tribal patriarch. The daughter-in-law he never accepted dies in the room of another Kurdish family who have already made the move to Ankara; the camera draws away to reveal it to be the third-storey glass-less window of an unfinished apartment in a new *site* that the merely caretaking family will never inhabit.

But what of those who accept the 'nature' of Kurdishness as it is represented/constituted in Turkish state discourse, and hence do not wish to be Kurdish? Are they successfully 'assimilated'? My dentist in Kuzguncuk, for example, was born in Bingöl (a town in the south-east that has been the scene of heavy fighting over the last few years), but moved to Ankara when he was a baby. For him Kurdishness equates with ignorance, incivility, superstitiousness (religiousness) and backwardness, and he has no interest in Kurdish politics. Yet could he not in his own person put to the sword the 'truth' that to be Kurdish is to be ignorant and uncivilized (*medeniyetsiz*), etc., if he wished to be Kurdish? Obviously ethnic identity in Turkey is not that self-willed; the putative social essences that mark difference (and exclusion), that fill up the spaces between the boundaries that maintain distinctions between ethnicities, are not so easily re-negotiated. Giving up a cherished belief about others that similarly defines you as different results firstly in your own self-dissolution, as well as issuing in a challenge to the cultural hierarchies that make up the economy of nation and civility. On the other hand, assimilation or dissimilation only 'works' from the side of the subject if the social essences thought to define the 'other' are not posited in principle as immutable (unlike say a settler colonialism, which may be concerned to separate as racially irreconcilable the cultures of colonists and natives).

Thus the 'inferiority' of Kurds (as represented in their attachment to reactionary politics, their tribal customs, and their regional backwardness) did not exclude their 'perfectibility' as Turks, if only they would submit to the nationalizing process. But as their true identity was Turkish anyway, the cultural genocide mooted by the civilizing process was not one that necessitated their physical destruction (contrary to what transpired in the Armenian massacre in the years before the Republic's founding). Kurds could become Turks by becoming modern (as did my dentist), or change back into Kurds by reinterpreting the history that privileged Turks in that way (as has the ex-Turkish nationalist Mehmet Pamak).

Resistance to Assimilation: The Construction of Kurdish Identity

What then of those who do not accept the 'nature' of Kurdishness as constituted in Turkish-Republican discourse, or who analyse its categories as evidence of state oppression of Kurds? And what of their relationship to one of the key features of contemporary Kurdish experience: the migration from the economic peripheries to the large industrial cities of the country, and the reconstituting of Kurdish identity in the transformed political conditions of the urban centres? For globalizing Istanbul is now the biggest Kurdish city in the world, particularly since the escalation of the war between the state and the PKK (Kirisci and Winrow 1997: 26). Günter Seufert's research on an Alevi-Kurdish 'tribe' (the *Koçgiri*) in Istanbul suggests indeed that Kurdish ethnic identity is gaining a resonance among youth (second-generation Istanbul tribesmen and women) that it does not possess for the first migrants to the city in the mid 1960s. So a friend of his says: 'Unlike me, my father speaks fluent Kurdish but he sees himself first as an Alevi and only second as a Kurd. He names the Sunni Kurds *guro*, which in Kurdish means illiterate and a boor. The Alevi Turks, however, he calls *tirki bireh* and its meaning is Turks who found the way. What a contradiction!' (Seufert 1997: 172).

This 'contradiction' however is only of recent perception. Yet its emergence is revealing of both the revitalization of interest in Alevi identity, and the heterogeneity of narratives attempting to re-imagine and map their own and others' history. For the splitting of Alevi politics along ethnic lines – Turkish-speaking Alevis are now being wooed by the extreme nationalist and anti-communist National Movement Party (MHP) with claims that Alevism represents the embodiment of pure, pre-Islamic Turkishness – is an indication that the historic Sunni–Alevi antagonism is being overlaid, even undermined, by the intense politicization of Turkish and Kurdish identities.[4] In this case tentative steps towards an understanding between religious Kurdish Sunnis and Kurdish Alevis is bitterly opposed not just by nationalist but also by anti-Islamist Turkish Alevis (for different reasons). In a recent article in the liberal Islamist journal *Ülke* Müfid Yüksel argues that historical sources show the veneration of common religious figures by both Anatolian Sunnis and Alevis, and appeals for a united front (in Islam) to prevent the country plunging into the conflagration of ethnic and religious strife sought by the 'atheist elite' (Yüksel 1997).

Seufert's friend binds Alevism and Kurdish identity more tightly together than his father, and as a consequent prises apart a Turkish/Kurdish synonymity in the Alevi subject constituted through its difference from Sunni Islam. This also reveals just one of the possible ways of being Kurdish that Kurdish nationalism must transform if it is to prosper as a social movement and a discursive formation. Yet this transformation can only work with that which is at hand. Given the multiple identities already

---

4. Şener and Ilknur assert that about one in three Kurds in Turkey is Alevi (in Seufert 1997: 175).

instituting the Kurdish subject, new understandings are palimpsests, constructed out of and over the traces of history marking people's lives. So members of the Istanbul tribe of *Koçgiri* imbibe, or even, like Obelix, fall into, the magic potion of a meaningful history from the day they are born. This history tells them, according to Seufert, that they have 'always been in opposition to Sunni Muslim Turkism. [They] were always peripheral and [they] have always been suppressed and outlawed. The entities in which this contrast occurs may have changed from the "Alevi Tribe vs. Sunni Muslim Empire" confrontation to the "Kurdish Socialist vs. Turkish-ruled Capitalist State" confrontation, but the frontier is still the same' (1997: 174).

Yet if the 'frontier' is still the same, this change in entity (from tribal Alevi to socialist Kurd) is by no means insignificant. For with it come new alliances and new enmities, new possibilities for self-constitution through dialogue with, or the rejection/recognition of, others. With this change comes a new forging of solidarities, but also a different exposure to power and the gaze of the state. New ways of being Kurdish in the changed conditions of the global city (see Chapter 1) are not created automatically in response to the universal demands for greater cultural reflexivity allegedly imposed by the processes of postmodernity and globalization. Instead they are forced through the narrowed sandglass of the national imaginary, forged in response to the living out of 'banal nationalism' in the everyday practices of city life – the national flag flapping outside the five-star hotel, the weather report, the Atatürk photo on the masthead of the daily paper, the staging of international sporting events, the organization of the annual film festival. 'Its banalities allow us to forget that we are constantly reminded of the omnipresence and persistence of the nation . . .' (van Loon 1997: 163). For Kurds, then, national culture as a 'daily plebiscite' of affirmation (Renan) translates into an interminable election campaign in which no party ever represents them.

A more convincing explanation for the 'politicization of Kurdish identity on the basis of ethnicity' (Sakallıoğlu 1996: 14) than that proffered by the theories of globalization may be inferred from study of the periodization of official Turkish nationalism. According to her analysis, the conflict between the PKK and the state has burgeoned into a major war since 1984 because

in contrast with the earlier period, when official nationalism denied the existence of a Kurdish entity but implicitly accepted it as a socio-cultural reality, the post-1980 nationalism constructed its own definition of socio-cultural reality . . .

The Kurds: Assimilation as Legislative Practice and Narrative

The military intervention of 1980 presented a watershed in the transformation of Kurdish nationalism as the post-1980 state promoted a new understanding of national identity based on a synthesis between a large dose of Sunni Islam and ethnic Turkishness in reaction to the fragmentation of national unity prior to the army takeover by ideological polarization (1996: 8).

The 1980 military coup is a convenient rupture therefore to mark the onset of the 'globalization' of the Turkish economy, although the similarity of Turkey's import-substitution policies to those of other equivalent late-developing states since the 1930s would suggest that the world economy was not globalized in the late 1970s so much as re-structured.[5] Both the military regime and the Motherland Party after its victory in the 1983 parliamentary elections applied the standard policies limiting state intervention in the operation of the market, receiving in the process a record five consecutive structural adjustment loans from the World Bank. Yet the export drive initiated successfully in the 1980s was in fact partially facilitated by the state, which earmarked export tax-rebates for companies surpassing government-set export targets, leading to a form of rent-seeking (Öniş 1991: 31).[6] The unorthodox nature then, of Turkey's economic liberalization programme is argued by Öniş to herald 'a significant restructuring of the state [and certainly not its retreat], that is, centralization of government as well as a (state-induced) concentration of private power' (1991: 33). In this context the intimate relationship between the business elites and the state testifies to the continuing ambiguity surrounding both the autonomy and the inclusivity of civil society in Turkey. If the globalizing of the world economy forced the post-1980 state to reconstitute an imagined 'socio-cultural reality', so the state sought to shore up its creaking hegemony over society by itself globalizing the economy.

---

5. See Barkey (1990) for an analysis of why import-substitution failed to achieve its goals for political, not economic reasons (not that such a stark separation of spheres is helpful).

6. Boratav, Türel and Yeldan conclude their study on the distribution of income in Turkey since the 1980 liberalization by arguing that 'Far from eliminating rent-generation and rent-seeking, the so-called liberal phase of the 1980s created new forms and patterns thereof . . . Fictitious exports, speculative urban and touristic rents, privatization and stock-exchange manipulations, government tenders, administration of fiscal incentives, bailing-out firms and banks in distress were the most important new areas of rent generation' (1994: 68).

Kurdish Nationalism

If Kurdish nationalism has managed in part to foreclose on other ways of being Kurdish,[7] post-coup Turkish state discourse has in one sense cleared the arena to prepare for Kurdish nationalism's turn before the footlights. For in the process of redefining the Turkish national identity, Kurdish identity too has been re-routed/rooted. In this case we should hardly be surprised if, in its invitation to the nation (as a new community of virtue), Kurdish counter-nationalism shares some of its tropes with Turkish nationalism, including a severe secularizing tendency. Indeed, the enlightenment orientation of Kemalism, with its laicist and evolutionary understanding of history, inspires the discourse of the Kurdish groups in the same way as it does the 'bourgeois' Turkish republic.

We do have the problem, though, of the PKK's Marxist-Leninist programme, which the Turkish Republic has never pursued even in rhetoric: indeed all socialist and communist parties were banned after 1925 and only re-emerged with the adoption of the more liberal 1961 Constitution. Further – though how conclusive this is I am not sure – the PKK's Marxist pedigree is constantly under attack by Turkish communist parties. So in response to the PKK's 1991 pamphlet *Din Sorununa Devrimci Yaklaşım* (A Revolutionary Approach to the Religious Question) an anonymous writer from the *İşçi Partisi* (Workers Party), in a polemic longer than the pamphlet itself, claims:

> This is not the first time it has come to light that the PKK is not Marxist. Its programme and practices since its founding have revealed in many ways the PKK's anti-Marxist identity. However, the PKK's approach to the religious question has shifted from even the position of the progressive bourgeois or the bourgeois democrats . . . Consequently, even if Kurdistan wins its independence, it will not progress far along the road of democracy and socialism (from *'Dine Devrimci Yaklaşım' Mı Kürt-Islam Sentezi Mi?* – A Revolutionary Approach to Religion or a Kurdish–Islamic Synthesis?, 1992, p. 4 – my translation).

7. In an appraisal of the views on Islam and ethnicity expressed by Kurdish people in the extreme south-eastern province of Hakkari (where she carried out her fieldwork) Lale Yalçın-Heckmann makes the prescient suggestion that 'if the "cultivated and shared disposition" ceases to be heterogeneous, that is, if the mixture of strong kinship ideology, tribalism and fluid ethnic identity loses its significance, then the Islamic discourse, because it is so all-encompassing, *or* the nationalist discourse, because of its increased application (by both the Kurds and the Turkish state) may replace the convertible and fluid qualities of these discourses' (Yalçın-Heckmann 1991: 117). City living, to the extent that these alternative sources of identity are re-worked or weakened over time, would seem to confirm her speculation. But whether this leads to a separation of Islamic and nationalist loyalties, in the context of the pressure of state discourse that forces them together, is doubtful. The proper question is to ask how the two are related. But more on that in Part III.

– 108 –

What was it about the pamphlet's approach to Islam that so enraged the critic (and that might give the reader a whiff of the militant anti-religious fundamentalism characterizing much of the modernist Turkish left)? Undoubtedly it was its suggestion that certain traits in Islam might indeed be sympathetic to a struggle against oppression and injustice. In this way the PKK pamphlet, as Sakallıoğlu notes, 'comes very close to Atatürk's advocacy in the early Republic of a "good" Islam to legitimate the secular cultural transformation of Turkey by a religious idiom' (1996: 19) – though the comparison might not be appreciated by either side. Enraged, the communist critique counters by asserting that

> [f]rom any perspective it is impossible to claim that religion, in the age of imperialism, has begun to play a progressive or anti-imperialist role. Religion hasn't changed, neither in its dogma, nor in its function. There is no progressive or revolutionary essence in religion. Religion has no dimensions that can aid in the anti-imperialist struggle. No religion is closer than any other to the people or proletarian movement. All religions are backward. Every religion simply serves the interests of the exploiting classes (ibid. p. 11 – my translation).

Not all communist groups are so hostile, but even those sympathetic to the PKK's politics fear a backsliding from its Leninist programme. For example the group *Ekim* (October), in its third *Conference Proceedings*, argues that although the 'Kurdish people under its revolutionary leadership have claimed national liberation and equality', the movement has reached the limits of its own strength. It will either 'deepen its revolutionary struggle with the support of the Turkish working classes . . . or under the pressure of the oppressive order will use its present gains to force a "political solution". But the weakness of today's class movement and of the Turkish class struggle in general has forced the Kurdish nationalist movement to consider a political solution.' In this case 'a greater influence will be exerted by the Kurdish bourgeoisie on the nationalist struggle. The Kurdish parliament-in-exile is the latest example of this' (Ekim 1995: 16–17 – my translation).

Kurdish nationalist discourse (as ideal-type) does not attempt to unravel the major themes of the state's modernist narrative, but seeks to inscribe itself in an identical way, bar one vital difference – it does not seek a Turkish state but a non-Turkish or even a Kurdish one. Kurdish discourse can be read in the mirror of Turkish-Republicanism, with provision of course for explaining how the struggle against imperialism by the nationalists was subverted into its opposite, with Kurds being betrayed in the process. For this reason, perhaps, the PKK for example portrays its struggle as being for all the oppressed peoples of Mesopotamia, viewing the racist Turkish state since its inception as the handmaid of Western interests.

The founding of the Turkish Republic is however not only interpreted
as a defeat: it empowers by way of negative inspiration – 'one day soon
we Kurds will be able to tell the real story of national liberation'. It follows,
I think, that the discourse of Kurdish nationalism is simultaneously a
greater and a lesser threat to Turkish-republicanism than is Islamic
discourse. Greater, because the more fervently republicanism (modernism)
asserts its values in its struggle against Islam, the higher becomes its
'exchange value' – exchange Kurd for Turk and the drama of national
liberation constantly inserts neophyte characters into its quest. More
insidious also, because to reject the logic of a Kurdish state is to reject
the logic of the Turkish state as well. Racists of course could always argue
that Kurds, for whatever reasons, are culturally incapable of administering
a state of their own – remember Türkdoğan's claim that because of its
alleged composition from three languages Kurdish cannot be an independent language; nor presumably the Kurds an independent nation either.
Still, there is comparatively little theoretical struggle by the state against
Kurdish separatism (bar the labelling of its proponents as terrorists) and
likewise little theoretical critique of the project of Kurdistan. Instead, the
warfare is reduced to mere brutality, in an unwinnable battle between two
constituents of the nation-state narrative. Yet ironically, because this war
can only be fought militarily it is less of a threat to Turkish-republicanism
than Islamic discourse, as even the carving off of an independent Kurdistan
from the rump of Turkey would not de-legitimize the integrity of the
remaining space held together and traversed by republican discourse. That
space would just be smaller.

By contrast, Islamist discourse does not seek to emulate but to assimilate.
Its aim is not to bite off a territorially separate 'Islamistan' but to de-
secularize and islamify everything within the sovereign boundaries of
Turkey. Islamist revisionism is directed, then, towards the republicanism
of the Kemalist polity (Kurdish re-writing focuses of course on its Turkish
elements), and its relationship with Turkish nationalism is problematic. In
this way an Islamist narrative of nation is not the oxymoron it should appear.

Conclusion

Contemporary Kurdish identity resides in sum at the point of an intersection,
the dangerous place where being (de) constituted (assimilated) and
constituting oneself collide. If constituting oneself involves disputation
over how one is constituted (and hence a different knowledge of oneself
and others), life for Kurds in the nation of the Turks is very difficult. For
being 'Kurdish', as a discursive outcome of various narratives defining

the Kurd as problematic or non-existent, is tiring – in Baykan's suggestive phrase (1993: 55) this epistemic violence works to make Kurdish identity burdensome, even questionable, by its 'erasure of biography'. The erasure of biography, however, is never mere abolition. It involves at the same time the bestowing of an alternative life-story and telos, a forced invitation to a replacement biography. Yet the endowing of new [fictive] kin relationships with new peers and invented communities is never accepted without a struggle.

Firstly, as we have seen, the social imaginary of the new stepfamily may be expropriated and used against them. Secondly, not only can the nation-state project be subverted, it can also meet with Kurdish reluctance, even downright refusal to become Turks or Modern in the manner envisioned by members of the new regime. Thirdly, the actual process of biographical erasure/bestowal is in any case unevenly prosecuted and sometimes actively contested even by those authorized to carry it out. Thus although the metropolitan centre may decree that 'those who are not of pure Turkish stock can only have one right in this country, the right to be servants and slaves' (Esat Bozkurt, Minister for Justice in the Kemalist state in the 1930s – in Vali 1996: 45), the agents assigned to actualize such sentiments on the ground may variously be under-resourced, overworked, disloyal, pragmatic, corrupt, confused, vacillating, etc.[8] Tempting as it may be to homogenize state actors, their endeavours purposively to transform the Kurdish areas may be as varied as is resistance to them on the part of Kurds.

---

8. So in the film *Hakkari'de Bir Mevsim* (A Season in Hakkari) the leftist teacher exiled to the isolated Kurdish-speaking village decides in the end that it would be better not to teach the children Turkish.

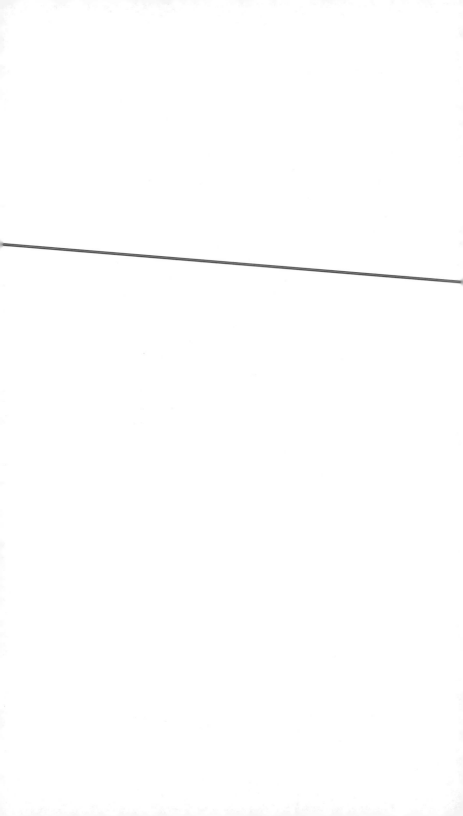

–8–

Profane Knowledge: Kurdish Diaspora in the Turkish City

Introduction

If implementation of the state's project to erase the biography of Kurds has been necessarily patchily executed in the peripheries, we might expect that the reconstitution of Kurdish identity in the metropolis will partly reflect these same processes, but will add to them the peculiar socio-political determinants of the city. Among these, as we have seen in Kuzguncuk, is the ambivalent autonomy won by various groups to self-institute locality even under the influence of the production of neighbourliness by the nation (itself a contested project). But Kuzguncuk, unlike say sections of Gazi Osman Paşa or other outlying and newer suburbs of Istanbul, has not experienced any significant influx of Kurdish migrants.[1] For not only have its zoning regulations been strictly enforced (by an honest *muhtar*), making it impossible to demolish or re-develop its older houses, but the suburb had already been colonized by an earlier wave of rural–urban migration. Obviously research into the production of locality, and with it identity, by Kurdish settlers would need to be pursued in suburbs of significant Kurdish population.

However in order to rescue this discussion from the realm of mere assertion, I propose – briefly and reluctantly – to discuss the family of my best friend in Istanbul, a Kurdish family that migrated to Istanbul in 1984 from the environs of Bitlis, long a region of heavy fighting and a city in which some of the worst assassinations of Kurdish journalists over the last few years have occurred. Briefly, because I want to move on as foreshadowed to the responses by the Islamist movement to the Kurdish problem.

---

1. Yet Kuzguncuk, like other areas of Istanbul, always has an itinerant population of Kurdish workers, living on building sites or in dank cellars, workers who upon finishing a job move on to another area. If such labourers are unlikely to sit in the local coffee-houses, they are nevertheless contributors to the local economy, and no doubt here and there strike up relationships with the people they are working for. Yet the popular image of Kuzguncuk as Istanbul's 'last heaven' or multicultural parable is not usually thought of as incorporating this invisible Kurdish presence. Itinerants may be passing through, but itineracy is permanent.

Reluctantly, because I am only too aware of the temptation to treat as emblematic the experiences and politics of a single family, tailoring them to illustrate the above discussion. And reluctantly, lastly, because, as always in the recounting of someone else's story, the story-teller transforms it into something new, giving it a meaning for others that it never possessed for those who lived it. The truth, we might observe, is not what it used to be.

Notwithstanding such misgivings, and though it might be argued that individuals are best not thought of in terms of their ability sovereignly to transcend their historical situatedness, individual lifestories still have an intrinsic interest. But because individuals only become individuals in particular social, historical and gendered contexts, biographical notes sometimes reveal a commonality shared by any number of lives, lending them at the same time an interest beyond themselves, if only as exceptions that prove the rule. This interest 'beyond themselves' does not need to be based on some presumed ethnic essence common to all Kurds. For Şeyhmus's family, like any family, is particularly placed in a class, a religious and a cultural field – all of which makes its experiences and interpretations not socially universal but peculiarly mediated. Kurdishness, then, is differently lived among Kurds, and only inasmuch as we attempt to take such differences into account can the experiences of Şeyhmus's family be exemplary for elucidating some of the complex processes at work in the partial remaking of identity in the context of an imagined Kurdish diaspora.

Losing the family fortune

Not only the Kurdish provinces as a whole, but Şeyhmus's family in particular have suffered a massive economic impoverishment over the past twenty years.[2] The militarization of the south-eastern provinces has not only severely damaged the regional economy, but has transformed its economic logic – a provisioning for battle (in whatever way) takes precedence over an economics with more civil intent. Here the employment of a civil militia recruited from amongst Kurdish villagers to work as village

2. The Kurdish region, like any region in Turkey, has been undergoing constant change. The escalation of the war between the PKK guerrillas and the Turkish Armed Forces is one further strand in the muddle of loose ends that constitute the social reality; others include the mechanization of agriculture, infrastructural investment, an increase in modern education institutions, improved communication, expansion of market mechanisms, dissolution of 'feudal' social relations etc., etc. Akşit *et al.*'s study of population movements in the South-Eastern Anatolian Project (GAP) region reveals that there has been net out-migration from the region in all of the five-year periods between 1965 and 1985, with higher than the average national rates in the period 1970–85. The 1985–90 census data was not yet available (Akşit *et al.* 1996). The war, then, has clearly collided with processes already in train.

guards (*kurucular*) is a prime example. The ramifications of such developments are difficult to assess, especially as the normal institutional, media
and judicial structures have been suspended in the areas under emergency
rule. Trade and productive activity, requiring a minimum of legitimate
and institutionally predictable legal frameworks to ensure their reproductive
life, are obviously compromised in such circumstances.

Clues perhaps to the exclusion of the south-eastern provinces from
the revised economic development strategy of the 1980s may be seen
indirectly through various indices. For example, in the fourfold increase
in Turkish exports in the wake of the 1980 stabilization programme, Turkey
has moved from being primarily an agricultural goods exporter to an
industrial goods exporter. In 1980, according to Taskin and Yeldan, '57.5
per cent of the total exports were agricultural goods and only 35.9 per
cent were industrial. By the end of the period [1990], the share of industrial
goods had reached 79.4 per cent of the total exports whereas only 18 per
cent of total exports were agricultural goods' (1996: 159). Given the way
more developed areas suck capital and markets away from peripheries,
the export boom has probably pauperized the south-eastern region, whose
economic mainstay has been farming and animal husbandry. The flow of
scarce state resources in the form of tax rebates and high export subsidies
to manufacturing has not aided the south-east, and may even have redistri-
buted funds from east to west. Further, even if we note that agricultural
exports have risen in dollar terms over the same period, regional disparities
would call their representativeness into question. As with tourist revenues,
the south-east region has been drastically disadvantaged. Lastly we might
note that in 1996 the Government was forced for the first time to import
live animals (from as far afield as Australia), since the livestock industry
has been crippled in the south-east.[3]

3. Some idea of the damage caused by the state's policies can be gained from an
open letter sent to the national government by the *Beritan* tribe [a self-ascription] through
the good offices of *Yeni Şafak* newspaper. The letter says:

We are the tribe worst affected by the war, as we make our living by breeding cattle. Because
the state has banned access to pastures we are unable to continue to make our living. In
1995 we owned 650 to 700 thousand cattle and sheep, whereas today that number has
fallen to 25 thousand. With the banning of access to pastures and state oppression, as well
as the closing of Middle Eastern markets, our ability to survive as pastoralists is endangered.
Previously we used to take our herds from Diyarbakir to paddocks in Erzurum, Bingöl
and Muş. Now we are banned from using any of the roads. The road to Elazığ can be used
if we pack the animals into trucks. But some of our families who have tried this have been
detained by the soldiers in the Karakoçan area and have not been given permission to go
on to Erzurum. We Beritan are living on the verge of poverty in tents like refugees. We call
on all of those responsible to do their duty as our endurance in waiting is running out . . . *Yeni
Şafak*, September 1996 – my translation.)

The loss of income (and status) by Şeyhmus's family, then, is a reflection both of personal and regional decline. According to Şeyhmus, when he was growing up his father 'owned' three villages, all inherited from his grandfather, a major landowner and important religious leader (*Şeyh*) in the Bitlis area. Through a combination of circumstances, including the depredations of bad luck, ill-timed legal proceedings, bad decision-making, and family feuding, as well as the outworkings of the political and historical processes alluded to above, Faruk *ağabey* (Şeyhmus's father) has contrived to lose most of his fortune, planting now only the 500 *dönüum* he still controls.[4] Deliberate state discrimination has not helped either. Concerned, for example, that some of the money would make its way to the PKK, the government tobacco monopoly delayed buying the 'Kurdish' tobacco from the Bitlis area for two years in 1994–5, resulting in its gradual drying out in storehouses and subsequent loss of value.[5] Faruk *ağabey* now only plants crops in which non-state buyers are also actively involved.

Şeyhmus and his sister were the first members of the family to leave the village, being sent to Izmir to learn Turkish at primary school. They joined the family in Istanbul when Faruk *ağabey* decided to study journalism in 1984 as a mature-age student. The shift to Istanbul has not resulted, however, in a clean break from the village, for the economic livelihood of the family is still derived from the land in 'Kurdistan', even if the peasants once dependent on Şeyhmus's father have in the recent past gained possession of the fields they labour in. Faruk *ağabey* is obliged to spend about half the year in Bitlis organizing his farming, paying poorer villagers to drive the tractor (also hired – Şeyhmus told me that once they used to own the only tractor in the region), buying fertilizer and negotiating with either state or private concerns to buy the crop. Şeyhmus told me also that his father used to own a purple Chevrolet, perhaps the only one in the country! A passing comment by Yüksel indicates that such conspicuous consumption was not, however, only the strange prerogative of Faruk *ağabey*: 'with the onset of electricity, in the villages where the Kurdish

4. One *dönüm* equals approximately 900 square metres.
5. Hann (1990) makes the interesting observation that Black Sea tea, described by him as the most appropriate symbol of the new Turkish society, was neither well distributed in the south-east nor was its taste particularly popular. Smuggled tea was the preferred brew (p. 99). The Kurds' discriminating palate is symbolic in its turn of the lack of that reciprocal influence between civil society and state in the south-east that Hann argues has developed in Rize. Indeed, Hann's study of the state's successful investment in tea production in Rize and its environs – which has made it one of the richest areas in the country – makes sense of a Kurdish friend's comment that *Rizeliler* (like the ANAP head Mesut Yılmaz) run the country.

Nakşibendi aristocrats dwelt . . . more refrigerators, dishwashing machines, televisions-videos could be encountered than in the villages of middle Anatolia and the Aegean . . . Similarly before the use of automobiles was widespread in many Anatolian regions, in the villages where the Kurdish *şeyhs* lived automobiles were in plentiful supply' (Yüksel 1993a: 108–9).

With one foot in the city and one still in the village, Faruk *ağabey* has become a divided man, unable either to make the transition to capitalist factory-owner in Istanbul or to regain the lands and status he once enjoyed as landlord in Bitlis. His disappointment at his failure to achieve the goals he had hoped for renders him particularly sensitive to slights or any perceived lack of respect from others. This in turn has bedevilled many of his attempts to enter into partnerships with other Kurdish businessmen in Istanbul, leaving him curiously isolated and perhaps overly prone to carping dissatisfaction with the behaviour and choices of his wife and four children. A difficult man in unpropitious times, Faruk *ağabey*'s defeats are not all the state's doings.

Şeyhmus, who like Faruk *ağabey* is a brilliant observer of cultural conceits, claims that in Kurdistan the expectations incumbent on ruling families bring them to a precipice: symbolic/moral domination requires wealth, and one has to give much to earn the respect of people. That is, reckless generosity is a desirable and admirable trait, but reckless generosity runs the risk of exhausting one's reserves, given the constant struggle for the high moral ground. This is one reason why Şeyhmus himself has no intention of ever returning to the village – he has seen at first hand the pressures (impossibility?) of maintaining symbolic dominance with a dwindling supply of capital. But even with the wealthy, public respect and acknowledgment is earned not merely by wealth (though without it high social status is not possible) but also by virtue – so Şeyhmus told me that when Ramazan came around his family, while eating lunch, would draw all the curtains and bolt the doors to avoid public opprobrium during the fast. But if Şeyhmus's father had to give to remain an *ağa* (landlord, master), he would be recompensed in return by political influence (for example, were he to stand for Parliament he would be assured of a block of votes), availability of labour, and symbolic deference (what we might call 'psychological protein'). As these feudal arrangements break down Şeyhmus's family (or Faruk *ağabey*'s children) are in transition to other nodes in the economy. Thus a narrative of decline is intertwined with a narrative of social activism, of fingers activated to plug holes (wider kinship 'fingers'), of bribery and courts, of the educating of children, and of political alignment with the most radical of the Kurdish groups, the PKK.

Fractured Family and 'Legitimate' Domination

One major effect of the family's migration to Istanbul has been the vastly increased independence of the family's daughters, and the tensions this has engendered between Faruk *ağabey*, his oldest son and able but unwilling lieutenant in domestic matters Şeyhmus, and the two girls. For although Şeyhmus claims to have renounced his cultural privilege both of supervising the lives of his mother, brother and sisters, and of telling them what to do to his own advantage, his father's regular absences from the Istanbul house cast him in the role of supervising both the financial and household affairs of the family. The return of Faruk *ağabey* brings further stress, as Şeyhmus may be prevailed upon to find out why his sister has not been working well at university for example, or who she is associating with. The discursive practice of '*ağabey*-ness' (elder brother-ness), as a key element in the ideology of patriarchy, is not of course all bad for the *ağabey*, despite (or maybe because of) the profession of self-sacrifice: the good *ağabey* (elder brother) does not abuse his legitimate authority but rather suffers self-deprivation for the sake of his weaker siblings.[6] Hence *ağabey*-ness is a discourse of power constrained by a discourse of sacrificial obligation – the *ağabey* is strong because the others are weak, which is why the *ağabey* has to be sensitive to their frailty. To put it differently, *ağabey*-ness is an act of domination mediated by acts of refraining from domination. Like many instances of 'legitimate' and ordered inequality, only when exercised tyrannically does it become unbearable. On the other hand constant acts of petty or domestic intransigence demonstrate that the parameters of submission are under permanent review.

Yet if Şeyhmus's sisters are educating themselves (with Faruk *ağabey*'s blessing and full support), Şeyhmus's mother Suheyla *abla* is caught up in another world. Though trained in her father's house in the sciences of Islam (she can speak and read Arabic, and has studied some basic Islamic jurisprudence (*fıkıh*)), Faruk *ağabey*'s militant cynicism towards Islam has de-legitimized her areas of expertise. Faruk *ağabey* would never consider Koran readings in his house nor allow her (even if she wanted) to attend women's meetings for religious/social purposes. And as Şeyhmus's family has no other relatives in the city, the main guests are friends of the children or occasional travellers from the village. These visitors are always treated

---

6. The mother of one of my friends told me that in the Black Sea region of her village, girls who had never had an *ağabey* found it more difficult to marry, the assumption being that they would not have learned to obey, nor have been 'broken in'.

very formally, with special concern given to presenting a picture of family order useful for shoring up political capital back in the village.[7]

Indeed, my own moment of heresy occurred when I went to ask Suheyla *abla* a question while Faruk *ağabey* was hosting a man from the village in the lounge-room. Suheyla *abla* said later that her husband had interpreted it as an affront to his ordering of gender relations in his own home: the villager would have told them back in Bitlis that a *yabancı* (stranger) was familiar with the women, shaming Faruk *ağabey*. According to Suheyla *abla*, this exclusion of the women even from male relatives was considered aristocratic, and not many commoner families could afford to maintain it. *İnşallah* ('God willing') she said, when I asked her if the PKK was working to change such a situation. Şeyhmus, not surprised at his father's offended reaction, commented rather sadly, 'You see what it's like living in an ignorant society.' For though the practice of gender separation serves the needs of the landlord class by emphasizing their superior virtue and difference from the people (and hence, ultimately, their fitness to extract labour from them), its necessary continuing reiteration in the context of declining wealth becomes a burden on the family.

Thus although Şeyhmus is particularly acute in his understanding of village culture, and although Faruk *ağabey*'s critique, or even disregard, of the cultural expectations of Kurdish society is thorough and ongoing, on the subject of the 'honour' of the women non-conformist behaviour is rather less in evidence. Şeyhmus too was careful to ensure appearances were kept up – once when Faruk *ağabey* was away in the village, Şeyhmus made me leave the house early in the day with him because there was an old lady staying there, and he didn't want her to report that a *yabancı* was at home alone with his mother and sister. Having two educated daughters was one way *Şeyh* Faruk could show his freedom from the social conventions of the villagers. His daughters would be, in true Kemalist fashion, modern but modest. Yet if his daughters were to contribute to the struggle for an independent Kurdistan, he would not allow his wife any self-governance, let alone float the possibility of autonomy or independence from his rule. In an echo of Binnaz Toprak's argument that the Republic legally emancipated women (from Islam) but did not liberate them, Faruk *ağabey*'s modernism *vis-à-vis* his daughters is refracted through a more

---

7. Interestingly, the privilege of answering the telephone too was ordered hierarchically. Faruk *ağabey* was the first line of defence: if he was not home Şeyhmus would pick up the earpiece. Only if Şeyhmus or Faruk *ağabey* were away would Suheyla *abla*'s quiet '*efendim?*' interrupt its ringing. The jangle of the telephone then, like a knock on the door, was felt as the outside world's approach to the family, and needed to be met with the appropriate face (or voice), at least until the caller's status was clarified.

important nationalist logic, whereby women as political subjects are constituted as Kurdish before feminist, or as feminist only for the sake of the new society of justice needing to be built.

Profane Knowledge and Kurdish Islam

Suheyla *abla*'s early religious training indicates that her family were self-consciously Muslim. But it would be wrong to conclude that Faruk *ağabey*'s family were any less knowledgeable. In fact Suheyla *abla* and Faruk *ağabey* are first cousins, Suheyla *abla*'s uncle being Faruk *ağabey*'s father. Not only this, but Faruk *ağabey*'s father was a famous *Şeyh* (head of a religious order), whose title has come down to Faruk *ağabey*. Exiled in different towns during his long life, Faruk *ağabey*'s father attracted *müritler* (disciples) wherever he stayed. His tomb near Bitlis has become a place of pilgrimage during *Kurban Bayram* (the Festival of Sacrifice), local villagers and faithful disciples from all over the country gathering to wash his grave and cook the slaughtered animals at the side of the family *mescid* (small mosque). At the end of the day the meat and rice etc. are collected and taken on trucks to be distributed to the outlying villages. According to Suheyla *abla* thousands of people come each year, and Faruk *ağabey* always provides a significant number of the animals for slaughter.

The charismatic and politically loaded nature of such an event contrasts with the slaughter of a steer in the yard of my apartment block in Kuzguncuk, where only the landlord (who lived upstairs), his family, the butcher and two or three helpers witnessed the deed. The landlord, Mevlüt *amca* (uncle), himself a pious man, was unperturbed when the bull was brought to the ground facing the wrong way, but his son reminded everyone it had to be cut facing Mecca. Mevlut *amca* would have let it pass, but someone else took up the cause and the steer was turned over and stationed at the side of the hole nearest Mecca. Mevlüt *amca* next morning gave me a couple of steaks, which I promptly gave to Suheyla *abla*.

Suheyla *abla* lived in Syria herself when a child, as her family too was forced to flee to Damascus during a revolt in the 1950s. When they returned they moved to Diyarbakir, where her father banned them from ever walking across the park in which the leaders of the 1925 Şeyh Said uprising were hanged by the *Istiklal Mahkemesi* (Independence Tribunal) and then buried in an unmarked pit without proper preparatory procedures by their families. Suheyla *abla* said a large Atatürk statue stands somewhere near where the gallows stood. People, like elephants, have long memories, and stories of suffering or injustice are passed down in whispers as ugly rumours and disreputable counterweights to the official transcriptions of history, to the power of state-sponsored sanctuaries for secular pilgrimage (such as parks) that are sometimes built over the very bones of earlier lives.[8]

Poets, however, are not the only ones who fail to conceive that the nation-state itself is the institution that seeks to prevent children guessing that, along with the bones, they are also left with 'what still is the look of things, what we felt at what we saw', and with 'what we said of [the past] became a part of what it is'. For the nation-state is also the great town-crier. It feeds on the corruptibility of both the flesh and the memory to exhume its own heroes, build its monuments, dedicate its fountains and squares and public buildings to right-thinking citizens of its founding era. It organizes cere-monies of public grief for those fallen in its service. It curses its betrayers. (Sometimes they become one and the same person.) In remembering a past to mourn and celebrate it also constructs a present to fear and condemn. Organizing the 'division of grief' is among the nation-state's most vital tasks. Yet sometimes the very act of erasing what the state wants forgotten causes it to live on. So Suheyla *abla*'s father saw not a park but a graveyard, a graveyard inhabited by 'storming spirits' never finally mourned. When the grandson of Şeyh Said was re-arrested in 1996 the journalist and novelist Ahmet Altan wrote,

> Abdulmelik Fırat, Şeyh Said's grandson . . . First we hung the grandfather and now we are leaving the sick seventy-year-old grandson face to face with death in the darkness of a prison cell. May God preserve him, but should anything happen to this Kurdish aristocrat in prison, will the honour of our society be assured? Can a society that hangs his grandfather and kills the grandson be an honourable society? Murder does not bring honour to a community (*Yeni Yüzyil*, 2 February 1996, cited in Fırat 1996: 174 – my translation).

Another journalist commented:

> I am talking about Abdulmelik Fırat, who has lived like a political prisoner since he was two years old, who has rotted for 17 of his 72 years in a cell, and who now in the last days of his life has been suddenly handcuffed and arrested upon two sentences by an informer. Have the grudges of 1925 not died down yet? Have the years of bitter tears and spilt blood not yet salved their traces?

8. "Children picking up our bones/ Will never know that these were once/ As quick as foxes on the hill;/ And that in autumn, when the grapes / Made sharp air sharper by their smell/ These had a being, breathing frost;/ And least will guess that with our bones/ We left much more, left what still is/ The look of things, left what we felt/ At what we saw . . ./ We knew for long the mansion's look/ And what we said of it became a part of what it is . . . Children/ Still weaving budded aureoles,/ Will speak our speech and never know/ Will say of the mansion that it seems/ As if he that lived there left behind/ A spirit storming in blank walls . . ." (from 'A Postcard from the Volcano': Stevens 1990).

Islam, Kurds and the Turkish Nation-State

After seventy years has our great state not yet learnt to forget, to make peace, forgive, love and grieve with its enemies? (1996: 176 – my translation).

Perhaps Suheyla *abla*'s profane knowledge partly illumines Şeyhmus's claim that although many Kurds are now discovering their Kurdishness, his family has always been aware of their ethnic separateness and their rights.

However, even if this is true, Şeyhmus's grandfather was obviously Kurdish in a different way to both his son and his grandson. Faruk *ağabey*, like his father, is intimately familiar with the close relationship between Sunni Islamic practices and local culture, conforming to and manipulating its structuring of social life when appropriate in the village. But he himself is an atheist, and is particularly unsympathetic towards Islamist prescriptions for organizing the political sphere, arguing in rather romantic terms that the Kurds' conversion to Islam resulted in the extinguishing of local political traditions, including the public participation of women in decision-making. If Faruk *ağabey*'s father expressed his dissent from the regime of the day through some form of religious discourse (resulting in his occasional exile), Şeyh Faruk constructs his in more nationalist vein. Here in one generation we have a transition from an oppositional identity clustered around Islamist tropes (with a potential for de-politicizing ethnic differences between peripheralized Kurds and village or rural Turks by a common culture of resistance to a perceived anti-Islamic centre), to an identity constituted in more discrete ethnic categories, wherein alliances between Kurdish and Turkish subjects become problematic. Among other things, this corresponds with the reinvigoration of state-sponsored Turkish nationalism in the wake of the 1980 coup. This transition is also articulated with the urbanization of Turkish society, in which the centre itself is 'ruralized' and its production of a polemical Westernized distinction or civility is muted. In the difference between Faruk *ağabey* and his father we are confronting not the sudden invention of ethnic Kurdishness but the changing of its meaning over time.

Profane Knowledge and Kurdish Nationalism

Faruk *ağabey*'s children too are Kurdish in a way different to their grandfather, nationalists who if not totally ignorant of village life (Şeyhmus at least) are disinterested and only imperfectly acquainted with any form of Islamic living. Unlike that of many Kurds brought up in Istanbul, the Kurdish of the children is very good – so good in fact that the eldest daughter is in demand to translate foreign poets into Kurdish, and has completed several books. Her husband Remzi is one of the few publishers of texts in Kurdish in Turkey, though his potential market is not large – the Turkish

Republic's educational policies have ensured that the emergence of Kurdish as a literary language in Turkey (unlike what has happened in Iraq) has not occurred. Şeyhmus claims the result has been an artificial freezing of the Kurdish dialects in Turkey; having been unable to develop 'normally', they don't have any words for the constitutive elements of modernity.

This is not a problem unique to Kurdish. Asad argues that modern Arabic, for example, has since the nineteenth century undergone a thorough lexical, grammatical, and semantic transformation, becoming more like European languages than it was in the past. 'Such transformations signal inequalities in the power (i.e. in the capacities) of the respective languages, in relation to the dominant forms of discourse that have been and are still being translated' (Asad 1986: 158). Turkish, it is true, has had the dubious benefit of the state's Turkish Language Institute's periodically protesting the bastardization of the language. Kurdish in compensation has Kübra (Şeyhmus's sister) making up new Kurdish words while translating from English. Yet, if all languages are increasingly impregnated with the discursive categories of modern forms of knowledge (both technical and social), the banning of Kurdish in Turkey for seventy years has ironically prevented its participation (on whatever terms) in such a 'rejuvenation'. 'Purity' in this case leads not to the salvaging of Kurdish but to its obsolescence. Living languages incorporate new words with their associated range of contested meanings, which both allow the elucidation of new practices and choke off the unproblematic continuation of the old. The ban on Kurdish has locked the language out of this process, ambivalent as it may be.

How does Faruk *ağabey*, as a *bilincli* Kürd[9] think about the Kurdish problem? In what sense is it accurate to call him a Kurdish nationalist? And in which way is his identity different from his father's? For Faruk *ağabey* himself says that he does not want a Kurdish Parliament, but a Parliament of Kurdistan, a Parliament composed of representatives of all the minority ethnic and religious groups in 'Mesopotamia'. This is in keeping with Faruk *ağabey*'s claim that many of the members of the Turkish Parliament are not Anatolian at all, but from backgrounds in what is now Bulgaria, the former Yugoslavia, Greece, Georgia, etc. Indeed, he argues that the Republic is a *göçmen* (immigrant) regime in which the elite are cut off from their own roots and tradition, and have become

---

9. *Bilinçli* can be translated as conscious or aware. Şeyhmus used it to describe Kurds who know their own history. Compare this with *şuurlu* Muslims (also meaning conscious or sensible), the word used by some Islamists to distinguish themselves from other non-Islamist Muslims. Both categories seek to express the possibility, even necessity, of subjects' achieving a further awareness, knowledge or commitment, setting up the potential for a rivalry between them.

more Turkish than the Anatolians (Turks or otherwise). This *göçmen* elite are thus doubly displaced, both counterfeit Turks and traitors to their own ethnic identity. They are accused, too, of having founded a militaristic, oligarchic and *devşirme* state, a state that has attacked the traditions (and religion) of the local people on behalf of the English and French. *Devşirme* was the word used to describe the levy (recruitment) of Christian boys to be trained as Janissaries (soldiers and bureaucrats) in the Sultan's service. For Faruk *ağabey* the word refers to the process of losing one's culture, traditions and morals, as well as servitude to the authority of another, with its associated lack of honour. As evidence Faruk *ağabey* runs through the list of the presidents of the Turkish Republic, most of whom came from *göçmen* families. Faruk *ağabey*'s *devşirme* theory gives the nod to non-essentialist notions of identity, in acknowledging that people can become Turks or Kurds. Nevertheless, the verbs *türkleştirmek* (to make Turkish) or *türkleştirilmek* (to be made Turkish) are used in the context of an essentially true identity, the identity that is being given up. Disloyalty, then, is a ground for eviction from the palace of legitimate authority.

The illegitimate expropriation of power and positions by *devşirme* politicians from those to whom they rightfully belong is neatly symbolized for Faruk *ağabey* by someone like the head of the Izmir Chambers of Commerce, a migrant from Bulgaria who according to Şeyhmus's father arrived in Turkey with his family in the 1950s. Faruk *ağabey* described to me how closely he examines such a man when he appears on television, his body language, speech and ideas. This 'poetics of masculinity' is particularly important for *Şeyh* Faruk, brought up in a context in which to dominate others you have to dominate yourself, and where this authority has to be seen as arising from acknowledgment by others of your own self-domination. Faruk *ağabey*'s hypersensitivity to slights on his own status becomes on this reading as much a matter of class, gender and cultural history as a revelation of insecurity in his own character.[10] 'Just a *sıradan*

---

10. Şeyhmus has a constant battle (which has entered family folklore) with his father's profligacy, his conspicuous and unwise spending. According to the children, salespersons' eyes light up with glee at the mere entrance of their father into a department store, as Faruk *ağabey* always buys the most expensive product without either bargaining or shopping around for a better price – to do so would be an admission of a material concern he would not wish to display in front of a stranger. Şeyhmus seeks to do all the shopping, especially when money is short, as it is at the end of every winter. Indeed, his attempts to get immediately the once-a -year agricultural cheque out of his father's control creates a recurrent tension. 'You never buy me anything,' accused Faruk *ağabey* once, as Şeyhmus staged a desperate rearguard action against a shop assistant trying to sell his father an electronic diary. Şeyhmus told me he found it for half the price at Sirkeci the next day.

adam' (a man from the ranks), concludes Faruk *ağabey*, but a man who is also his own age, and a millionaire to boot. Here Faruk *ağabey* is comparing his own lack of wealth and status with those of this man, and then connecting it to the way the state, because of its *devşirme* ideology, has made him rich and ignored the claims of the legitimate Anatolians (who are almost synonymous with the Kurds). Faruk *ağabey*'s political critique is an analogue then of the story of his own unjust disempowering: his life is not external to the narrative he expounds. In contrast Remzi, the husband of his daughter Kübra, does not think that the proportion of *devşirme* politicians would be anywhere near as high as Faruk *ağabey* puts it at. But Remzi does not come from an *ağa* (landlord) or *Şeyh* family.

How does Faruk *ağabey* analyse the present Kurdish rebellion in Turkey? Is he convinced by the PKK's claim to be the legitimate representative of the Kurdish people? Şeyhmus told me a story to show how widespread he perceives support for its struggle is. There is a football team in Diyarbakır, he said. Its left back, Abdullah (Apo for short) is an acknowledged disaster, responsible for more goals against his own team than any other. But every week he is the first selected in the team. As the back of his own net billows once again and the ball is picked out of its corner by the disconsolate goalie, the crowd rises as one and chants, *En büyük Apo, Apo en büyük*! ('Apo is the greatest, the greatest is Apo!'). Truncheons slapping against thighs, the police shift uneasily and stare up into the stands. For Apo is also the name of Abdullah Ocalan, leader of the PKK (Kurdistan Workers' Party), public enemy number one in Turkey.

According to Faruk *ağabey* there have been some 38 local revolts since 1923, though none as big as the PKK movement. Faruk *ağabey* knows the names of the leaders of each of the major rebellions, and jokes that Apo is Allah's recompense to the Kurdish people for not giving them their own country. For Faruk *ağabey* the PKK's struggle is different to all the other revolts for four reasons – (i) it has a 'scientific' ideology; (ii) it has a proper organization; (iii) it has a committed and disciplined army; and (iv) it is not local, but involves all the people (that is, it is not kinship-based, nor tribal, nor denominationally-driven (Alevi or Sunni).

When I commented that many, including most of the Turkish communist groups, might see a logical contradiction between national liberation struggles and Marxist-Leninist ideology, Faruk *ağabey* argued that class struggle was not possible in Kurdistan, simply because it was too under-developed. 'What bourgeoisie? what proletariat? what comprador bourgeoisie? what industry? what factories?', he asked. Class struggle could only commence after the establishment of an independent nation: first 'we must take our national rights'. Again one hears an echo of Kemalist discourse:

at the 1923 Izmir Economic Congress for example, after the people had proved themselves ready to die for the nation in the war against the Greeks, they were solemnly entreated to work for it. Four non-antagonistic classes were identified (workers, industrialists, farmers and merchants) as an economic mobilization replaced the military one. A similar will to nationhood would unify the nascent classes in Faruk *ağabey*'s Kurdistan.

How ironic it is, then, that while the Izmir Economic Congress was in full swing the Lausanne negotiations between the victorious Turkish nationalists and the *Entente* Powers (England, France, Greece and Italy) had broken down. For Faruk *ağabey* tells the story that, while the talks were temporarily postponed, Atatürk engineered a Kurdish delegate to stand up in national costume in the parliament in Ankara and give a speech in Kurdish supporting the new regime. According to Faruk *ağabey*, Lord Curzon (the British Foreign Minister) was not fooled by the stunt, but sought to maintain the provisions of the 1920 Treaty of Sèvres (signed by the Sultan) that allowed for an autonomous Kurdistan. But other postwar problems of Empire loomed more important (including negotiations over Iraq), and Curzon did not pursue the matter. Whether such a speech actually occurred, and whether Faruk *ağabey*'s interpretation of it is valid, are perhaps less important than what his narrative affirms – the duplicity of Atatürk in betraying the Kurds who had also fought for the nation.[11] Kurdish has certainly never since been spoken from the podium of the National Assembly.[12]

11. In fact Robert Olson reveals that Atatürk himself suggested, while the Lausanne negotiations were at a stalemate, some kind of regional autonomy for Kurds in a meeting held with seven journalists near Istanbul the night of 16–17 January 1923. The minutes of the meeting were published in the journal *2000 Ikibin'e Doğru* (Towards 2000) in 1988, to the disapproval of the Turkish Government. The conversations had indeed been published earlier, but with Atatürk's discussion of the Kurdish question omitted. Robert Olson himself concludes, rather similarly to Faruk *ağabey*, that acknowledgments of possible Kurdish autonomy were made in times of crucial juncture 'to facilitate the goals and objectives that the Turkish nationalist government was pursuing at the time' (Olson 1991: 30).

12. Faruk *ağabey* also told me, unprompted, about the Kurdish regiments organized in the 1890s during the reign of Sultan Abdulhamid II, and then later by the Young Turks after 1909 – the regiments intimately involved in the Armenian massacres of the 1890s and 1915. According to Faruk *ağabey*, the same Kurdish tribes that were recruited by the Ottoman centre to consolidate and enforce its rule over the eastern periphery were also the tribes taking advantage of similar offers of privileges (tax exemptions, special educational provisions for children, wages) to act as village guards/irregulars for the state against the PKK.

'Med TV': Facilitating Kurdish Diaspora

Faruk *ağabey*'s assent to Kurdish nationalism's deconstruction of the founding myths of the Turkish Republic is perhaps summed up best by his decision to buy a satellite-sensitive antenna specifically to pick up the broadcast from England of the PKK's illegal television channel, Med TV.[13] Med TV itself is a reflection of the incredible explosion of electronic media in Turkey over the last five years or so. Since 1990, when the first pirate television channel began beaming experimentally into Turkish cities via satellite from Europe, Turkey has moved, as Ayse Öncü comments, 'from a scarcity of images directly controlled by the state, to an abundance of them, fueled by competition among increasing numbers of commercial channels' (Öncü 1995: 23). By 1996 no less than 1,058 local, 108 regional and 36 national radio stations, and 229 local, 15 regional and 15 national television stations (secular and Islamist) were broadcasting across the country.[14] In this sense Med TV, which started its transmission in 1995, is just one more facilitator of the babble of words, music, images, and propaganda encircling the globe. But its disputation of state television's official version of the eastern problem, as well as its contradiction of the coverage of the closely-censored (but occasionally revealing) commercial channels, has led the state to declare its viewing a crime. Enforcing such a decree is of course another matter.

Private television gains its revenge on the state's regulation of its political content (through the notorious Anti-Terror Law, Article 8 of the Constitution), not merely through its marginalization of the state channels by the stealing of their viewers, but by its unintentional commodification of the images on TRT (Turkish Radio Television). With the advent of Islamist stations packaging a contrary Islam, TRT's creation of a world-view and coverage of state and government affairs, once seen as uncontroversially educative, is now demystified, relativized as but one self-interested perspective among others. At the same time its content too has had in part to shift from presenting useful information for its ideal 'citizen-viewer' towards entertaining a heterogeneous and often ill-educated – even uncivilized – consumer.

If commercial television has transformed the way the audience watches state television – marginalizing, commodifying and relativizing it – it is

---

13. Med TV is currently broadcasting from Holland, as pressure from the Turkish Government has forced its closure and relocation several times.
14. *Yeni Yüzyil*, 9 October 1996.

striking how closely Med TV, with its limited resources, resembles TRT. Öncü's summary of the historic intent of TRT's radio and TV coverage: 'the creation of a sense of national unity, through homogenized official Turkish, national folkloric music, a shared sense of historic occasion, and loyalty to the nation' (1995: 25) – could also be a description of Med TV. It, too, addresses its viewers as prospective members of a national community, disseminating an assumed shared knowledge while constituting a political subjectivity. So one of the evening programmes is a fascinating game show, a contest reminiscent of the competition organized by Carnival Islamism in the tent at Ramazan, but one that awards no prizes save a nationalist glow. In it a youth panel of both sexes answers questions on Kurdish history, on Kurdish literature, on landmark geographical sites in Turkish Kurdistan, on Marxist-Leninism and on famous Russian writers like Gorky. Şeyhmus's family gathers around the television and answers the questions as well. Like TRT, Med TV too is concerned to nurture 'Kurdish' folk dance, national costumes and music. Like TRT, it propagates a standardized Kurdish, as it teaches literacy to children whose first language may be Turkish, German or Swedish. News is presented first in Kurdish (*Kurmancı*) and then repeated in Turkish for those Kurds who speak a different dialect (for example *Zazaki*).

However, unlike TRT, Med TV is not the handmaid of a nation-state. Rather it expresses resistance to a coercive Turkish identity used as one of the foundations for the official culture of the Republic. On the other hand the PKK's possession of a technology that was not so long ago the sole privilege of the state confounds the distinctions between 'nationalist critical longing and nostalgic or eschatological visions, [and] actual nation building – with the help of armies, schools, police and mass media . . . A certain prescriptive anti-nationalism . . . need not blind us to differences between dominant and subaltern claims' (Clifford 1994: 307). The establishment of a Kurdish Parliament-in-Exile signals the building up of a state *in absentia*, a state with no territory to manage (no liberated zones) except, with the aid of Med TV, the private sphere of the home.

Do its programmes, beamed to both Europe and Turkey, encourage a homogenization of modes of response to the Kurds' vastly different migration experience in cities like Berlin (for example), Copenhagen, or Istanbul? For Şeyhmus's *bilinçli* Kurdish family in Istanbul, life is lived as a kind of exile, as part of a diaspora of an imagined nation that is not yet. Kurdish nationalism results in the creation of a diaspora more willed than passively experienced. *Bilinçsiz* (unaware) Kurds, like my dentist in Kuzguncuk, are simply not part of it. In Faruk *ağabey*'s case the homeland as an imagined memory is only tangentially related to the cultural practices of Kurds living in Kurdistan. This notion of diaspora simultaneously serves to provide a cultural critique – the imagined homeland purged of customs unworthy of preservation, as well as those obstructing the exiles' return to their future. Faruk *ağabey*'s exile in Istanbul condemns him to a disconnectedness from everyday life in the general community, unlike the more communal experience of diaspora enjoyed by Ahmet *ağabey* and his friends in Kuzguncuk.[15] For not only is Faruk *ağabey* distinguished from his occasional village visitors by his status, knowledge and eloquence, but the making of new Kurdish political myths and community is a dangerous practice, liable to unwelcome gate-crashing by the security forces.

Finally, if Med TV facilitates a private diasporic Kurdistan in the belly of Istanbul, is it contributing at the same time to the winnowing of Turk from Kurd in the 'Turkish' diaspora in Europe? For part of its news each night is devoted to the protest activities of Kurds in the various states of Europe, as well as their clashes, physically or polemically, with more nationalist Turkish groups in tune with the Turkish consulates. Precisely because modern Kurdish nationalism is diasporic, it is also 'born global'. The coagulating of Kurds under the banner of the PKK in countries as distant from Turkey as Australia and Canada and their collecting of money to support the movement suggest the discourse of Kurdish nationalism is reorganizing the ethnic politics of immigrant communities in the metropolitan countries as well. In countries with large and well-organized Kurdish populations, Turks may not only be stigmatized as foreigners, aliens etc. in racist domestic discourses of state or civil society, but as oppressors of Kurds to boot, hardly worthy of much sympathy. Though Med TV itself cannot be watched in Australia, Kurdish nationalism as a transnational practice is politicizing Kurdish subjects (in the context of the national policy of multiculturalism) in Sydney as much as those living in Istanbul or Frankfurt. The first *Zazaki* (a Kurdish dialect) radio programme in the

---

15. Further, Faruk *ağabey*'s (and even more so Suheyla *abla*'s) isolation is not helped by their choice of housing, as they have rented since their arrival in Istanbul apartments in various city *sites*, those post-1980 clusters of uniform high-rise residential blocks sprouting up along the highways and byways of the metropolitan area. Advertised as places capable of screening out the undesirable cultural pollutants/of Istanbul living, *site* lifestyle is popular partly because of its homogeneity. Thus at Şeyhmus's *site*, where the *kapıcılar* (cleaners/caretakers) were at first housed in the basements of the apartment buildings, the complaints of other residents that *kapıcı* children were cluttering up the playground forced the manager to expel them from their cellars to trudge in from their rented flats in the sea of slums surrounding the *site* oasis to deliver the fresh bread at six o'clock in the morning. That most of them were Kurds was probably no coincidence.

world made its debut in Melbourne in 1997 on one of the multicultural/multilingual stations.

Conclusion

In short the double, ambivalent life of Şeyhmus's family in Istanbul is structured not so much by the exclusion of Kurds on the basis of their discursified difference (and inferiority) but, on the contrary, by the state's determination forcibly to include Kurds within an ethnic Turkish norm itself in crisis. Similarly, if recent Kurdish migrants to Istanbul now meet with some fear and loathing from native İstanbullis (themselves earlier migrants), this is probably due as much to the existence of the PKK movement itself as to any deep conviction of racial superiority. The double life of Şeyhmus's family arises not merely because the disdain they feel for the regime and its justifying myths, and the illegal activities they pursue to bring about its collapse, are kept hidden from their neighbours. It is double also because diasporic living is not only characterized by resistance to 'host' states, but also by inevitable numerous accommodations to the normalizing processes of the wider society itself. Diaspora is constructed by subjects constantly winning the battle while losing the war. For Şeyhmus's family diaspora is lived as a struggle against assimilation.

But what is envisaged by assimilation policies as the desired norm is of course peculiar to the particular historical context. The verb 'to assimilate' suggests a journey from one identity to another. It is also a journey to which a moral economy is affixed. To arrive is virtuous not only according to whether the traffic was voluntary or compulsory, but according to the social valuation of the old self abandoned or the new self embraced. The definition of the identity from which one departs and the identity which one attains is overtly laid down by the dominant power in its transforming project. Successful assimilation is demonstrated only by conformity to a few key symbolic markers – resistance to assimilation by non-conformism to those selfsame signifiers. The rest, as has been said, is silence.

The human targets, then, of nation-state homogenizing projects are defined (in their essential nature) by their divergence from the prescribed ideal; just as that ideal is constructed out of the targets' negative nature. If in the single-party period Kurds' successful transition to Turkishness was represented by their becoming modern, and symbolized by their adoption of neckties or abandonment of national dress, Kurdishness was marked by not knowing modern Turkish, or by an allegiance to 'fanatical' Islam. Perhaps Kurds' successful assimilation nowadays is signified less by becoming Republicans and more by conspicuously consuming the paraphernalia of commodity nationalism, especially the national flag.[16]

The tokens of 'having arrived', then, are not fixed but change over time, even if the state does not renounce its assimilatory project. Assimilation politics pursued by the state often result in an incessant politics of exclusion – paradoxically, given their *raison d'être* in the moral ideal of equality and social harmony. For once the desired identity is sketched out, and the corresponding deficiency of the 'assimilees' noted, the process is put in place for the exclusion of those who cannot or refuse to transform themselves. As long as assimilation is considered incomplete, i.e. as long as assimilation as a policy is pursued, those who have not yet commenced their journey or who have dallied somewhere along the way become the targets of state hostility and intervention, of reports, lies and damned statistics. Given the abstract nature of the desired qualities (i.e. civilized, courteous, Turkish, modern etc.) and the pinning down of their meaning only by recourse to the presumed clarity of their antonyms, the bar is capable of being forever raised, resulting in an official politics that is inherently (and ironically) exclusivist.

But when Şeyhmus's brother goes to watch Beşiktaş play football, is he assimilating? And is it only Muslims who are contaminated by parking in the underground car park of Istanbul's newest shopping malls and ascending in the elevator to buy Benetton? Identities, especially those projected as normative by the discourse of the nation, have, as has been noted, their own specific tests of loyalty, their own special hoops to jump through. Other facets of subjects' lives that do not explicitly oppose this primary identification are not directly subject to the state's censure on nationalist grounds. So Turkish nationalism may not have much to say now about the production of consumer identities by the incorporation of more and more goods and services into the cash economy, or the increasing commodification of social life. Despite the ceaseless efforts of nationalist discourse to construct 'pure' identifications, hybrid identities may in fact rule, but this 'does not necessarily mean that "hybrids" identify with [them]' (Diken 1997: 175).[17]

16. One indication of the legal pressure applied to people to display the national flag was the recent four-month gaol sentence given to members of a legal political party for not hanging the flag from the party headquarters on *Cumhuriyet Bayramı* (Republic Day) (*Yeni Şafak*, 26 February 1996).

17. See for example Tekellıoğlu (1996) on the furore surrounding the rise of arabesk music and its ambiguity *vis-à-vis* official music.

In sum the difficult life of Şeyhmus's family in Istanbul derives not from state practices that stress a racialized difference between Turks and Kurds, but from policies designed to render them identical. At the same time Faruk *ağabey*'s inability to extricate himself from an economic dependency on the village (and the village's ambiguous relationship with both the national economy and the national war)[18] leaves him vulnerable to local challenges directed at both his symbolic and economic dominance. Moving to Istanbul has heralded an attempt to both shore up and renew symbolic and economic capital. In Istanbul the family has sought anonymity in the relatively homogeneous social space of the middle class *site*. Here, in contrast to the oppositionary locality produced by Kurds in the informal neighbourhoods and squatter housing of the city, Şeyhmus's family lives in proud solitude, polite to neighbours but reluctant to borrow even a cup of sugar. Significantly, their decision to come to Istanbul was neither an example of chain migration nor did it involve the activating of kinship links. And, equally telling, Şeyhmus's family has not been the nodal point for a trickle of subsequent immigrants from the village to the city. Kurdish nationalism in this case is not a discourse hailing subjects from the rural poor but from the Kurdish aristocratic feudal class, subjects moreover intimately familiar as socially empowered authorities with the practices of Islam as pursued in Kurdistan.[19]

We will see however in Part III of the study that if most *bilincli* Kurds have had some close encounter with Kurdish Islam, not all are as violently secular as Faruk *ağabey*. The red, gold and green of Kemalist Kurdish nationalism, in brief, does not draw dry the well of Kurdish identity.

18. Gülay Günlük-Şenesen writes that in 1994 20 per cent of the total world arms trade was delivered to Turkey. In 1995 the general budget allocations to the Ministries of Defence, Education and Health were 11.5, 10.1, and 3.6 per cent respectively. But the budget allocation to the Defence Ministry is only one source of arms funding. There is also the Defence Industry Support Fund, which is financed, among other sources, by taxes on income, fuel consumption, alcohol, cigarettes and transfers from the national lottery. See Günlük-Şenesen: 1995.

19. In his work *The Struggle for Recognition* (1995) Axel Honneth argues that violation of the implicit rules of mutual recognition is as much the cause of social conflict as is struggle over material interests. True, the processes of change in the Kurdish areas of Turkey have resulted in the financial ruin of Faruk *ağabey*. But I would maintain that his feeling of indignation at the experience of disrespect is as vital to his commitment to the Kurdish nationalist movement as any thirst for financial restitution.

Part III

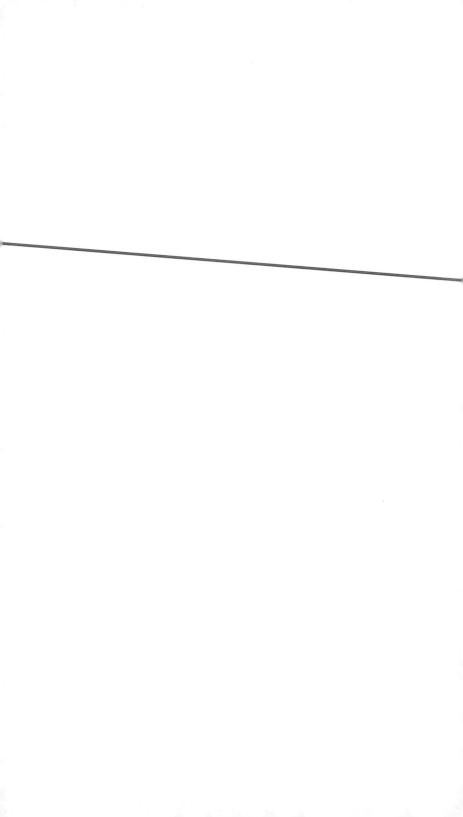

–9–

Islamist Politics and Ethnic Cleansing

Introduction

In Part I we looked at the heterogeneity of political Islam, and the pluralization of its energies into at least three competing tendencies: liberal, bourgeois and carnival Islamism. Yet in some ways this disunity is its strength – for in appealing to different constituencies Islamism extends the possibility that its discursive pearls of wisdom become the common currency in political discussion and debate. On the other hand we have seen also how in one particular local context (Kuzguncuk) the cajoling tones of liberal, bourgeois and carnival Islamism have fallen on ears deaf to their respective blandishments. If Islamist vocabulary is instrumental in giving Muslims voice, disputes over its demands lead to disharmony within the chorus of protest raised against the Republic's production of civility. In this process competing Islamisms selectively call forth affinities within Republicanism itself: in Fetih Paşa Korusu the malcontents of carnival Republicanism devour sliced bread side by side with the 'laic Islamists', while in the surrounding suburbs other Islamist groups refuse to employ a knife.

In Part II we examined the protest engendered by the Turkish Republic's production of nationality, with special reference to the emergence of a transformed Kurdish identity marked by resistance to its forced inclusion within modern (Westernized) Turkish identity. Here the state's assimilation project veers between a flat denial of Kurdish existence (in which case the basic condition for a politics of assimilation – the construction of an antithetical but bridgeable difference – is negated), and the necessity confronted by the state to think, speak and legislate about the Kurdish question. Thus we have the state refusing to recognize as real a language that it simultaneously outlaws through legislation.

Yet as we noted both in the case of Şeyhmus's family and with the Republic, demarcation of the role of Islam in the construction of Kurdish and Turkish nationalism respectively is vital to their making. In Part III we will attempt to bring these two dimensions together, to see to what extent the state's production of a Turkish national identity has worn off on the Islamist movement, despite its rejection of republicanism, and similarly, to analyse in this context the sometimes antagonistic, sometimes uneasily cooperative relationship between secular Kurdish nationalism and Kurdish Islamism, as well as the ethnic sensibility of Kurdish Muslims.

Islamist Democratization and the Return of the Repressed

Ali Bulaç reminds us that not so long ago someone asked the Refah Party's highest council whether mentioning the word 'Kurd' was permissible, and the religious experts decided that even if its use were legal, the present was not a propitious time to utter the dreaded 'K' word (1992: 96). Such a comment should sober up those who consider the Islamist critique of the Republic's deficient democracy (*vis-à-vis* Muslims) a sure indication of its commitment to plurality. For there is an emerging counter-orthodoxy among some commentators on Islamist politics in Turkey today that situates the movement and its deconstruction of the founding myths of the Republic as major participants in a more general assessment of the political role played by these myths. In this reading the Republican elites, whilst claiming for themselves the legitimizing trope of progress and civilization, have resembled the bourgeoisie in Marxist analysis: the class whose universal claims obscure their particularistic interests. Here in the name of the general will, the state felt free to guide society into the enlightenment designated for it. Within this analysis then, the Islamist unmasking of the Republic's dictatorial practices is interpreted as a contribution to the gradual emancipation of civil society from a repressive Jacobin republicanism.

Yet a problematic essentialism is sometimes stuffed into that conceptual ragbag 'civil society' at the same time. For often enough the newly heard voices of civil society (answering back to the governmental discipline of the Republican project) are interpreted as the return of the repressed, the 'real Turkey reasserting itself against official and state culture' (Robins 1996: 72). But is this real Turkey so unambiguously the remnant of the old Turkey neither effaced nor eradicated by the Republican order? Is it, as Feroz Ahmed describes, the arrival in the cities of an 'Ottoman-Islamic' culture, a villagers' culture 'that has hardly been touched by the secular culture of the Republic [*sic*] and [has] therefore continued to identify with the only cultural tradition they knew'? (cited approvingly in Robins 1996: 75). Have they, have Faruk *ağabey* and his family, really been living on the moon?

But perhaps contemporary social movements in Turkish civil society are often described in this way because both the intentions and the categories imbuing the discourse of Turkish-republicanism are so clearly identifiable in the various texts and practices of the new regime.[1] Here the ideal subjects of Turkish-republican discourse as well as their polemical interlocutors are inscribed as distinctive through the operation of a native orientalism. Constituting themselves as civilizing shepherds, the elite conceived the people as uncivilized sheep. Whether intellectuals or activists, proponents of the idea that civil society's recovery of 'lost worlds' is indeed the revenge of the real Turkey sometimes employ a similarly simplistic division of society. Yet the black and white villains and heroes imagined and disciplined by the discourse of Turkish-republicanism beg the anthropological question about the effectiveness of such discourse in constituting subjects, and the extent to which agents have accepted it as legitimate – or partially resisted, subverted, misconstrued or synthesized it.[2] Such a view forgets

1. Though the Kemalists may have stolen their ideological sandals from the clay feet of the Young Turks, and before that from the *Tanzimat* reformers of the long nineteenth century, it was only the Nationalists who were able to implement effectively a total programme. Some of the key – and not so key – moments in the biography of Turkish-Republican discourse include a report on religion in 1928 suggesting the introduction of organs and hymns into mosques; the compulsory examination in the history of religion (at the instigation of Atatürk) for all degrees in the Faculty of Letters in Istanbul Darülfünün between 1925 and 1930; the 1941 publication of an expanded version of the famous Leiden *Encyclopedia of Islam* in which the entry on 'Kurds', as I discovered to my surprise through a comparison of the English- and Turkish-language editions, had been doctored by the omission of the section on Kurdish nationalism; the founding of the Turkish History and Linguistic Societies; the engagement of Henri Prost (architect of colonial urban planning in Morocco) as chief town planner of Istanbul; the establishment of the Institute of Turkology at Istanbul University in 1924; the opening of a Sculpture School in Ankara soon after the founding of the Republic; the banning of *culs de sac*; the introduction in 1931 of the first beauty contest; the dissemination of childrearing manuals; the formalization of folklore studies; the archaeological digs seeking confirmation of Hittite society's Turkic precedents; the banning of certain types of music on TRT (Turkish Radio and Television); and the re-naming of geographical and urban landmarks, especially in the Kurdish-speaking areas.

2. Even in Said's *Orientalism* (1978) there is a question over the efficacy of orientalist ideas. On the one hand Said says that discursive orientalism needs to be separated from the 'brute reality' (p. 5) of eastern nations and cultures. That is, orientalism may constitute the idea of the Orient for the West, helping it to rule the East and constitute itself as the Orient's binary opposite; but this is not the whole story for the lives of orientals. On the other, the book's express purpose is to 'inventory the traces upon me' (p. 25). Here orientalism is not irrelevant, but partly productive of [Said's] subjectivity. The necessity of doing an inventory is Said's acknowledgement that orientalism, in constituting occidentals, also constitutes orientals. 'Western' subjects of course are constituted solely by orientalist discourse; but the internal politics of metropolitan countries means that subjects are never only 'Western' (as Said's interpretation of Jane Austen's novels admits). They are class subjects, gendered masculine or feminine, regionalized etc. By using the word 'traces', Said notes that he too is not solely constituted through orientalist discourse.

too the Republic's success in making 'real people', even people with fractured subjectivities. Perhaps more importantly, it obscures the similarities between the present-day recovery of lost identities and the historic project of Turkish nationalism, whose intellectuals were also concerned, particularly in the 1930s and 1940s, to revitalize a 'real' Turkishness groaning under the weight of an alien Arab Islam. Students of modernity might therefore be better advised to study the successive series of claims to cultural difference, repressed identity, and rediscovered alterity as constitutive of the political dimension of Turkish modernism itself, rather than accepting as self-explanatory the rhetorical terms (tradition, authenticity, backwardness, modern, etc.) in which such modernist struggles play themselves out.

With such concerns in mind we might also profitably mention the vital relationship between modernity, nationalism and democracy, in which rule in the name of the people, for the people, by the people is at once implicated in the problem of exactly who 'the people' are, necessitating their continuous representation in discourse. Democracy on this basis may be justified or reside not so much in the fact that the people (through their representatives) make the laws, but in its appeal to an essential (and often lost or betrayed) identity that the government embodies, protects and ensures. Islamism's claim to democracy derives not from the scope it gives to the people for the making of laws (*şeriat* is assumed, if not quite *in toto*) but from its appeal to a cultural homogeneity or essence in which Islamic law is merely the outcome of the people's desire (thus discursively represented). In this sense both Islamism and nationalism are claims for legitimate sovereignty, in that their authority is granted only through the consent of the represented. No government or opposition can refrain therefore from representing those whom they represent, or from constituting their constituents (which in a nutshell explains why all modern states have problems with the status of refugees and migrants).

Rather than presume that Turkish national identity signals the liberation of the native pre-Ottoman or pre-Islamic cultures, or that current social movements herald the re-emergence of the historically repressed or peripheral cultures of the pre-Republic, it is more fruitful to consider them beneficiaries of the possibilities opened up by the very richness of the process of modernity in Turkey itself. The jarring conflicts of Turkish modernity lie in its instituting a plurality of fields of social relations, whose imaginary significations and internal struggles bring them into unstable alliance or fragmented enmity one with the other. In this maelstrom, dualistic contrasts between official and real Turkey, which focus on their choosing as significant what the other has forsaken, ignore how they interpenetrate each other on other grounds, and what they in fact share. This is to ignore, as the different Islamisms of Kuzguncuk, Fetih Paşa Korusu and even Dilruba show, the way actors produce 'glocalities' that do not conform to visions of dichotomous caste status and the distinction between despised Muslims and the rest. And it ignores Turkish nationalism. What Carlo Levi wrote about East and West Berlin in the late 1950s could have been penned in respect of the reputed split between the ideal nation and the real people: 'They faced each other like champions of two different cultures, without any possible contact. But they were champions of the same mold. Whoever observed them without their arbitrary and make-believe fierceness, realized that in that very arbitrariness, in that fierceness, in that non-existence, in that desperation, they were identical' (Levi in Borneman 1992: 24). In a way, what makes them identical is their claiming of the category of 'the people' exclusively for themselves. For if the real people are the Anatolians, as Faruk *ağabey* posits, what about the *göçmenler* (migrants) from the Balkans, for example, who now call themselves Anatolians? Or if the real people are Muslims, as Islamism suggests, how do we understand those laicists who do *namaz* five times a day? And if the real people are Turks, as the basis of the state's legitimacy holds, where do we fit in Kurds who call themselves citizens of Turkey? Is there room for the varying practices of other people in the fantasy of a binary politics that pits the official nation against the real people?

Islamist claims to reconstruction of the nation's civility are not, as we have seen in liberal, bourgeois and carnival Islamism, unified reforming visions. Nor therefore are their democratic commitments. Yet in most Islamist versions of the official culture vs. the real people, the Republic is interpreted as having defrocked the one element that could keep various ethnic groups from each other's throats – Islam. Does their critique, however, of republicanism's insufficient democracy amount to anything more than the rhetoric of an ascending counter-elite determined to trans-late its emerging economic power into the political sphere so as to forcibly stamp its impress upon the cultural life of the society? The question should not only be asked theoretically but investigated practically: the hope that Islamist assertion is on balance an understandable and positive political response to the Jacobin civilizing will of the Republic needs to be examined empirically.

It is the suggestion of the following sections that the Islamist movement's response to the Kurdish problem, its intervention in the social imaginary signification of the modern nation-state, should be one of the litmus tests in determining an answer. (Its relationship to the socio-cultural field of gender politics could be another.)[3] In short, is Islamist interrogation of the Republic's historic modernizing agenda the prelude to its own democratization? Or does Islamism's privileging of 'Westernization as secularism' over 'modernization as nationalism' leave it vulnerable to the charge of propagating a green Kemalism?

Confessions of an Islamist

The Islamist movement, according to its own admission, has been remarkably quiescent *vis-à-vis* state policies towards the Kurds. So in a recent book detailing the massive war migration in the south-east of Turkey, Kemal Öztürk questions, 'Has an Islamist position been made clear on the Kurdish problem, which for the last ten years has assumed the highest place on the national agenda?' and goes on to ask, 'In the fifteen reports suggesting solutions to the Kurdish problem is there one representing Muslims?' He concludes by saying, 'Unfortunately the answer to both questions must be "no"' (Öztürk 1996: 104). Öztürk's comments are interesting for three reasons: first, his assumption that a distinct Islamist stance is possible regarding the Kurdish problem. Second, his deploring of the fact that such a position has not been enunciated. And third, the rather disingenuous claim that the lack of a clear response in the name of Islam is synonymous with no position being taken at all by the religious *camia* (community), as if the *de facto* positions of Muslims, i.e. their actual practice, could be dismissed as quite so unproblematic.

In these next sections, on the contrary, I hope to demonstrate that there are in fact several different responses to the Kurdish question within the

---

3. Though not wishing to investigate the problem here, it is certainly a puzzle why the Islamist movement caters for gender difference – indeed, encourages and justifies it both politically and theologically – yet does not consider it legitimate for Muslims to organize themselves on ethnic lines. In other words, why is the [possible] separatism of Kurdish Muslims perceived to be a threat to the Islamist *ümmet*, but not the manifest apartheid of the Islamist women's movement? Such an inconsistency is made even stranger by the Koran's insistence on the created nature of both gender and ethnic difference. Further, what is going on when Islamist women, utilizing a different and competing vision of the 'functional co-dependence' of men and women than Kemalism, refuse to acknowledge the vastly different subject positions of Turkish and Kurdish women. So the Islamist Istanbul Rainbow Women's Platform, which is made up of more than 40 women's associations, has no group representing the particular interests of Kurdish women, suggesting that the category of 'Islamist woman' (like 'Muslim') is also taking on hegemonic or ideological significance *vis-à-vis* Kurds.

Islamist Politics and Ethnic Cleansing

Islamist movement itself, and that these different responses reveal both the continuous politicization of ethnic identity in Turkey, and the nationalization of religious identity – despite the professed intention of the Islamist movement to 'ethnically cleanse' its politics. Secondly, I will argue that the Islamist movement, which not only bears the fingerprints of nationalistic discourse but has been 'raised on its slogans', (as one writer in the Islamist newspaper *Yeni Şafak* put it) is unable to find a position properly sensitive to Kurdish suffering as a direct consequence of its constituting rhetoric. That is to say, the Islamist movement's problem is not so much a lack of theological clarification but a function of its political mobilization and historical imagination.

To elaborate these points, I would like to begin from where Umit Sakallıoğlu left off in a recent paper examining the theoretical underpinnings of the TOBB report.[4] She notes firstly that Turkish nationalist discourse and the politics of the state are not concerned to emphasize the inferiority of the Kurd but to force Kurds to make themselves into Turks. This being the case, the question to what extent Islam counters (or supports) such a project becomes central, and Sakallıoğlu ends her critique by asking 'whether the high profile of Islam in the [south-east] region has come to resemble its past historical role of expressing a distinct [Kurdish] identity?' (Sakallıoğlu 1996: 17). (We have noted earlier how the same question could be addressed to state Islam and Turkish identity.) In the light of state policy, Sakallıoğlu's second query, whether the Islamist movement can unite both religious Turks and Kurds in a common discourse, must be answered very carefully.

To investigate these questions it would be useful to begin by briefly detailing the reasons Islamists themselves divine for the failure of Muslims to engage with the Kurdish issue. In other words, with the Islamist movement's self-diagnosis. For it is generally agreed that believers are bound to a world-view that provides a solution to every possible problem pertaining to human relations, as well as giving them the opportunity to achieve eternal life – peace on earth, peace in heaven. Any deficiencies in practice are traced to Muslims themselves, not to Islam. So Ramazan Değer (1996: 146) explains in a forum devoted to the Kurdish problem, '*Biz başkalarının Müslüman olmasını istiyorsak, ilk önce bizim Müslüman olmadığımızı anlatmamız lazım*' ('If we want others to become Muslims, we must first explain to them that we are not (true) Muslims ourselves'). Such an attitude

---

4. Union of the Turkish Chambers of Commerce and Commodity Exchanges, Report on *The Eastern Question: Diagnoses and Facts*, July, 1995, in Sakallıoğlu 1996.

is widely shared by Kurdish Muslims when discussing the shortcomings of the wider Islamist movement *vis-à-vis* the Kurdish problem. In this case 'true' Islam is not to be found in the actual practices of Muslims (which can be analysed sociologically like any other human activity) but in a discursive construct used to critique their behaviour. But what are the explanations offered by those who would explain why Muslims, constituted by such a singular discourse, paradoxically share the sins of the wider community in respect to the Kurdish problem?

Öztürk, after noting that Kurdish and Turkish Muslims are splitting in much the same way as did Kurdish and Turkish leftists in the 1980s, attributes the passivity of the Islamic community on the Kurdish question to the day and age in which the religious movement is living, in that it does not fully understand the transformed concepts (especially that of *milliyetcilik* – nationalism) with which it is confronted. Thus 'to produce politics on this sensitive [topic], when the Islamist movement has not been able to fully find itself, has not been possible' (Öztürk 1996: 106), and he goes on to say that the emergence of an important section of the Islamist community out of the Turkish nationalist movement has been a great hindrance.

Mehmet Pamak, whilst confessing that Muslims are the most backward political group in Turkey (*en geride kalanlar Müslüman olmustur*) in regard both to the general defence of human rights and their concern for the plight of the Kurds, argues that because Muslims have for years been grouped under rightist, nationalist, conservative or *mukaddesatçı* (followers of the holy) banners, and have in fact expropriated such terms to describe themselves, it is only natural that 'Islamist consciousness has conformed to such an understanding' (Pamak 1992: 344). This is not the circular argument it first appears to be, once we consider the importance of recognition by others in the making of self-identity.[5] Pamak ascribes the double standard of Muslims to an education system that is suffused through and through with Turkish nationalist propaganda:

5. Charles Taylor is perhaps the best-known writer theorizing the 'politics of [mis]recognition'. Because cultural particularity is dialogically constituted, Taylor takes it for granted that the non-recognition of cultural difference is a form of latent violence: since identity is dependent on exchanges with others, non-recognition actively extinguishes identity. (There is, though, a slight logical flaw here: if identity is relational, then 'mis-recognition' is analytically impossible.) On the other hand, 'mis-recognition' is simultaneously productive, as Mehmet Pamak maintains. See Houston 1998: 238ff.

Turkish Muslims have always given their support to the struggles of the oppressed Palestinians; we have organized meetings, conferences, panels and protests; we have striven to raise public awareness; even those of us who couldn't do anything have felt and shared their pain, wept and prayed. Everything we did was correct and in keeping with Islam, which commands us to be at the side of the oppressed. But when it comes to the plight of Kurds, in which the oppressors are not Israel but the administrators of the Turkish Republic, our position changed and we were unfortunately unable to show the same sensitivity (Pamak 1996: 18).

For Abdurrahman Dilipak, the insensitivity of the Muslims (Islamist intellectuals and writers included) is a result of their mental laziness, of their unwillingness to question established doctrines, particularly nationalism. 'Thinking in clichés and stereotypes we have been unable to break the nationalist mould' (Dilipak 1992: 86). In a variation on the same theme, Ilker Satana complains that the position of the Muslim community for the last twelve years has been a complete fiasco (*gerçekten tam bir fiyaskoyla sonuçlanmıştır*), and attributes this to the ethic of the existing system and its epistemological standards, which have affected the perceptions of Muslims, whether they want this or not. Satana sees the problem in an *asker-millet* (soldier-nation) collective consciousness that allows the ruling 'political class' to manipulate the sensibilities of the population (Satana 1996: 14). Müfid Yüksel takes the same tack, discerning a heavy dose of nationalism circulating within the Islamist movement, from which Muslims have not yet been able to free themselves (*bazı imajlardan hala kurtalamamışlar*) (1993a: 33).

Like many Islamists, Ali Bulaç too is more concerned to investigate why Muslims do not take an Islamic stance than to examine the (Islamic) stance they do actually adopt (which may be provisionally summed up as opposing ethnic particularity in the name of Muslim fraternity); but his analysis is more thoughtful than most. Firstly, Bulaç asserts that Muslims have been scarred by the terrible persecutions they were exposed to, particularly during the single-party period: *Bana dokunmayan yilan bin yil yaşasın* ('Let the snake that doesn't bite me live for a thousand years!') (Bulaç 1992: 93). This well represents the defeatist attitude of many religious people when confronted with state oppression. Secondly, Bulaç argues that the Turkish Islamist movement developed relatively late compared to those of other Muslim countries, but is also peculiarly tied in with Ottoman history and the disintegration of the Ottoman Empire. Historically, of course, the later Caliphate was in Istanbul, and from the beginning of this century to the late 1970s the Islamists and the Turkish nationalists have been arm in arm. Bulaç gives the example of Mehmet

Akif, who despite being among those 'least affected' by Turkish chauvinism, refers in his *Istiklal Marşı* (Independence March) to the *kahraman ırk* (heroic race). The advent of the Cold War and the 'threat' of communism is seen by Bulaç as another contributing factor to the long-lived alliance between right-wing Muslims and nationalists: *'Halen de bir bütün olarak Müslümanların sağcı ve milliyetci çevrelerle göbek bağlarını kestikleri söylenmez; özellikle "örgütlü din" adı verilen dini cemaat ve tarikatlar tam da sağcı ve milliyetcidirler'* ('Even today, it is difficult to say that Muslims as a whole have cut their umbilical chord with rightist and nationalist circles; in particular those religious groups and *cemaat* referred to as "organized religion" are thoroughly rightist and nationalist') (1992: 94). Behind these cohabitations Bulaç sees the long-term effects of the erosion of the Ottoman Empire's *ümmet* (community of believers) principle under the influence of the winds of nationalism blowing from Europe, and its replacement by a nation-state resting on the foundation of Turkish racism. Muslims, of course have not been immune from this state-building process, and on the Kurdish issue have actively participated in the denial of a separate Kurdish identity.

Conclusion

Examples could be multiplied, I think, without encountering too many varying views. Islamist writers, or the ones concerned enough to wonder at the general inability of even *şuurlu* (conscious) Muslims[6] to progress beyond mere platitudes about Islamist fraternity and face up to the responsibility for remedying the situation, or challenging the collective thinking of the Islamist movement, have put their finger on some of the more common-sense reasons for this indifference. Why can't believers take their required place at the side of the oppressed? Because they aren't pure enough Muslims (yet), and still allow extraneous influences (history, politics, ethnic sentiment) to defer their rendezvous with solidarity. That is, the continued insensitivity of Muslims to the infringement of the Kurdish people's natural rights, despite the clear condemnation of racism by Islam, is seen as testifying to the depth of Muslim alienation – even severance – from their roots. Thus, many presentations of the Kurdish problem by Islamists begin, naturally enough, by reference to the Koran, interpreting

---

6. In Ayşe Saktanber's (1994) article on the drawing of Islamist women into the struggle against secularism, the total absence of any concern for issues beyond the framework of this polarization is striking.

two verses from the *Rum* and *Hucurat suras* claimed to be key texts on ethnic difference: 'Among his signs . . . is the diversity of tongues and colours' (*Rum*: 23) and 'Men, We have created you from a male and a female and made you into nations and tribes, that you might come to know one another. The noblest of you in God's sight is he who is most righteous' (*Hucurat*: 13). The problem in short is constructed as purely an external one, a legacy of history from which the newly emerging Islamist movement has not yet fully freed itself. It should be clear, then, that the failure of Muslims to get a pass mark in the Kurdish examination is not attributed by Islamists to the making of an Islamic movement in itself.

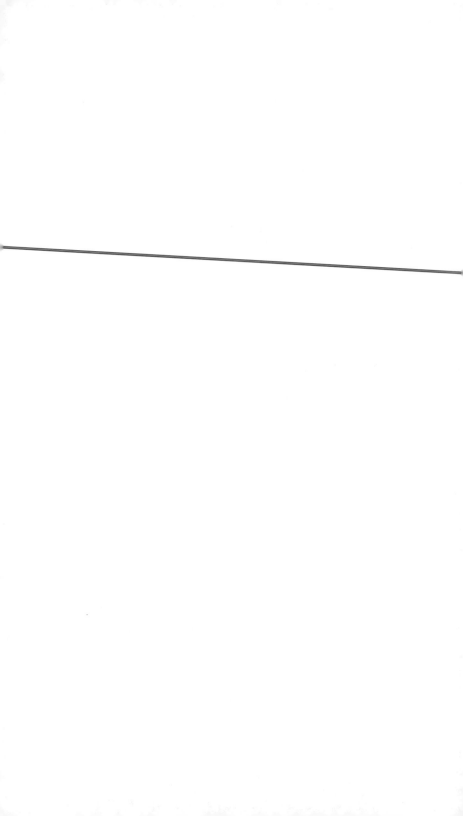

–10–

Islamist Responses to the Kurdish Problem: Statist Islamism

Introduction

Despite the attempts of various Islamist writers to posit reasons why the vast majority of Muslims do not take an Islamic interest in the Kurdish question, it is obvious that the Islamist movement, like the state, does have to talk about the Kurds if it wishes to talk about politics at all. Thus we should be able to examine the various positions taken by Islamist groups without necessarily entering into the debate over which position better reflects the truly Islamic vision. Rather than attempting to survey the explicit or implicit positions of the literally thousands of Islamist *tarikats*, educational and social foundations, organizations, businesses and community groups, however, I propose to bundle up their responses to the Kurdish question into three distinct and competing discursive packages. We might call these different discourses statist Islamist, Islamist, and Kurdish Islamist for the sake of simplicity, while acknowledging that they sometimes share the same recycled scraps of brown paper and bits of discarded string. These three constellations of truth-claims and values are not ethnically exclusive: many Kurds constitute themselves as political subjects through Islamist ideas, and some may even be partisans of the struggle against communism or leftist atheism embraced so enthusiastically by statist Islamism. On the other hand, not many Turkish Islamists imbibe until inebriated the draught of Kurdish Islamism.

We should note too that the same group or political party in different times and contexts may be informed by, or at least manipulate the categories of, the competing discourses – the history of the Refah Party's relations with the Kurdish elements within its own ranks is a prize illustration of this. The Refah Party's rhetoric on the Kurdish question veers between statist and Islamist discursive realms depending on whether they are in government or not, whom they are addressing or appeasing, and which way the winds of political fortune are drifting. Nevertheless, their constant care to prevent the Constitutional Court closing down the Party (as happened again in 1998) means that Refah is disinclined, whether by conviction or necessity, to dispute the boundaries laid down by the National Security Council. This disinclination is a constant thorn in the flesh of the Kurdish parliamentarians and their supporters in the Party, and leads to a high level of cynicism among the more *bilinçli* (self-aware) Kurdish members as well as some high-profile public departures. The fallout for example from Refah's 1991 electoral agreement with the racist *Milliyetci Çalışma Partisi* (Nationalist Action Party) crippled the Party in the south-east for some time. Necmettin Erbakan himself is cynically inconsistent: while on a Prime Ministerial visit to Libya he claimed that 'in Turkey there is no discrimination on the grounds of sex or race. There is one problem however. That is the terror problem. Because of this problem Turkey has given 10,000 martyrs in five years. Half of these are from our security forces . . . [That is, there is no Kurdish problem in Turkey but] only this terrorist problem. This movement will be finished soon' (*Yeni Şafak*, 7 October 1996). Yet Erbakan's repetition of the hard-line position of the state was partly transcended by a speech at the fourth Party Congress in 1993, when he made a distinction between terrorism and the Kurdish problem (see Çakır 1994). But at the fifth Congress in 1996, held when Refah was the senior party in a governing coalition, Kurdish parliamentarians were silenced when they sought to make the party accountable to the promises it had made three years earlier (see *Radikal*, 16 October 1996).

On a different note, the Refah Party's youth wing, the *Milli Gençlik Vakfı* (MGV – National Youth Foundation), announced a fortnight after the fifth Congress ended a special appeal for the families of soldiers killed in the war against the PKK (*Yeni Şafak*, 3 November 1996). It had preceded this a few weeks earlier with a *Mevlüt* read for the dead soldiers. Nevzat Laleli, president of the MGV, spoke at the ceremony, saying 'We are tied to our martyrs in our hearts and in our blood. We owe a great debt to our martyred soldiers who have fallen for the Motherland' (*Yeni Şafak*, 16 September 1996). Here we see no 'disinterested' Islamist mourning, no weeping for the families or souls of the Kurdish guerrillas killed in the fighting. Indeed Refah's often strident affirmation of a particular notion of Muslim brotherhood as the cure for social disharmony is sadly all too often a signifier of Turkish nationalism, as it wilfully ignores the correspondence between the public domain and the dominant or sovereign ethnicity.

Statist Islamism

I will not dwell overly-long, however, on the discourse of statist Islamism, as its stance towards the mere acknowledgment of Kurdish ethnicity is censorious. Secondly, its repetition and support of the state's slogans, policies and practices *vis-à-vis* Kurds, including the strategies pursued by the military to contain the situation in the south-east, are rather unconditional, as its main practitioners have long since been integrated into the economic and party-political systems.[1] In this sense, the main gripe of the statist Islamists with the order instituted by the Republicans is over the finer points of its application and not necessarily with its overall authoritarian structure.[2] On the other hand, this does leave some room for discontent, for the devil, as is often said, is in the detail.

Nevertheless, most of the Islamists cited above have state Islamism in mind when they criticize Turkish Muslims for their lack of interest in the Kurdish problem. As Altan Tan remarks, far from the solutions advocated by Muslims being rational or realistic, 'they deny that there is even a problem, being unable to mention the word' (1996: 27). Perhaps the best example of this, and the group I will take as a case study, is the public rhetoric of Fethullah Gülen (Fethullah Hoca) leader of the educational and media empire consolidated around the *Zaman* newspaper and the *Samanyolu* television station. Though once a disciple of the famous Kurdish religious figure Bediüzzaman Said Nursi (1873–1960), Fethullah Hoca (Gülen) has been following his own lights since his split from the *Nurcu* (light) movement in the early 1970s. Since then the organization has established hundreds of educational institutions extending from Turkey to the former Soviet Republics and all the way to Australia – Işık College in Broadmeadows, Victoria, which opened its doors for business

---

1. So the journal *Islam* for example, in a feature on the terror problem in the 'South-East', has an interview with both the Erzurum Security Director and the Erzurum Governor, who claim that the PKK is simply an Armenian front seeking to change Turkey's borders and establish a Greater Armenia. See *Islam*, Dec. 1993.

2. But what then makes statist Islamism Islamist? The political practice of Islamism exists in various degrees of critical distance from different aspects of society, for society itself is not unified but (more helpfully imagined as) a field of tensions (see for example the clash between labour and capital). Islamism as a magma of social imaginary significations (themselves internally contradictory) collides then with the social signification of Turkish-republicanism (also internally inconsistent), leading to as many alliances as enmities with the contending spheres of society. Islamism is not then solely 'over/against' society as an antagonistic alternative but also 'in/for' it, as both critic and stalwart. Statist Islamism is Islamist, then, in its moral condemnation of the values engendered by an anarchical liberal capitalism, and is active in constructing an anti-laic oppositional lifestyle, not only or even mainly against the culture of the professional Kemalist elites, but against the 'poor man's Kemalism' of working-class radical (communist) politics. Kemalism (modernity) on this reading is appropriated differently by different classes.

in 1997. The tenor of the schools may be judged by the comments of Mustafa Kalemli, the president of the Turkish Parliament, who, after visiting central Asia, claimed that arguments surrounding the introduction of eight years of compulsory education in Turkey could be resolved by taking as an example the schools of Fethullah Gülen in that region. 'Six thousand kilometres from my own country, under our flag, next to the bust of Atatürk, I listened to the Independence March' (*Zaman* (Australia), 7 April 1997).[3] That Fethullah Hoca has made the Turkic Asian Republics the chief target of his educational expansion is hardly surprising: some form of pan-Turkism is intrinsic to his mission, as the following extract from a sermon makes clear:

> Despite the passing of 1,400 years since its writing, the Koran is a book whose voice cannot be silenced. And the Turks, who have stood as its protector since the ninth century, have not yet exhausted its riches. But let me say this. They have understood it with such modesty, with such devotion to the truth it contains that since the age of the Prophet and his Companions no people has so acted as its defender, so become the standard-bearer of its message. To say this is not racism . . . The duty and function given to this people is a blessing. Two centuries before the Ottomans came into this world we have the prophecy of Muhyiddin Ibni Arabis'. There he wrote the names of the Ottoman Sultans. 'Sultan Selim will come to Damascus and will find his grave prepared', he said. He described the state that would emerge two centuries after his death. And he said something that fills my eyes with tears. Apart from the Companions of the Prophet himself, no other people will have such a message given to them as the great message entrusted to the Ottomans for the sake of humanity . . . But why? Because they became the castle for belief and for the Koran . . . Since the ninth century they have protected the Koran, saying 'This is my book.' . . . We cannot say that from time to time their hand did not slacken. It did, it did, but now this people is once again the source of hope for the world. It will extend its hand to those of the same race (*ırkdaş*), those of the same seed (*soydaş*), and to the world and while the dark clouds of distress are clearing this society will once again be one society . . .

3. Mardin (1989: 81) notes that Said Nursi too dreamt of establishing an educational institution that would bridge the gap between the Islamic education taught in the *medrese* and the scientific curriculum instituted by the secular reformers. Whether Said Nursi would have approved of the dream's realization in the educational empire of Fethullah Hoca is another question. Indeed Said Nursi's relationship to the Kurdish question is a topic of great dispute. Mardin's rather cautious concern to quarantine Bediüzzaman Said Nursi from secularist charges of Kurdish nationalism is contradicted by both Malmisanij (1991) and Rohat (1991).

The world is needy for your breath. While the world waits do not play the small games of the anarchists. You will breathe your breath in Uzbekistan, in Turkmenistan, in Mongolia, in the Crimea. They are waiting for you . . . You will explain Hazreti Muhammad. This great work is waiting for you. Don't let your hearts be burdened with the small work [of protest]. Let Allah be your, and our helper (from Çakir 1990: 112, 113 – my translation).

The sermon displays all the main theses of the Turkish-Islamic synthesis. There is the notion of a divine duty given to the Turks, a duty that not only constitutes the Turks as a race (*ırk*), but is carried out for the blessing of all humankind, as well as for the edification of the Muslim world. There is the claim to primacy among the Islamic peoples, a claim proved by the deeds and longevity of the Ottoman Empire, which is in the process Turk-ified, as it is not merely its Islamic genius but its Turkish identity that sets it apart. There is the criticism of any opposition to the state as anarchy – witness the slanderous claim earlier in the sermon that the Islamist women protesting in the street about the exclusion of covered girls from University on account of their headscarves were really men dressed up in long coats and veils. Last, there is the implication that Fethullah Hoca, as the leader of the community facilitating the Turkish people's once again fulfilling their destiny as the bearers of a world historic mission, is himself the hope of the world, as well as the one who will reunite the Turkic nations. In this case the comment made by one of my Islamist Kurdish friends, that Fethullah Hoca wants to be the new Caliph, and that if he becomes so he will massacre the Kurds, may not be as far-fetched nor paranoid as it initially sounds.

This heady mixture of nationalism, Islamism and authoritarianism ('to shout slogans in the street and cause disturbance is anarchy, whoever does it' (1990: 113), is better seen perhaps in an interview in *Zaman* (the newspaper of the '*Fethullahcılar*') with Professor Dr Oktay Sinanoğlu, a Nobel Prize nominee for Molecular Biochemistry. Here the vision splendid of a Greater Turkey, leaping out of the backdrop to reclaim its rightful place at the centre of world history, is painted in primary colours:

In the Turkish and Islamic worlds a great responsibility rests on us. The West knows very well that if any state can liberate the Islamic world it will be the Turks. For this reason the West's one mission has been to destroy Islam from within. In order to shake the Turkish leadership the English worked for 250 years to bring down the Ottoman Empire . . . But if this people can find itself we will be confronted with a new Turkey. This might seem a dream, but imagine this tableau. First let us reform our education system and like any honourable country liberate ourselves from a colonial mindset. Old Turkish will become well known again. All the sciences will be taught by high-quality teachers.

We will progress by taking strength from our historical heritage. Turkish will be the language of education in all schools. With the combined countries of the Turkic world we will establish a 'Turkish World History Institute'. Many scientists will be working assiduously inside the newly founded 'Turkish Language Foundation'. We will take what Ataturk did a step further. Everyone will write in the new revised Turkish put forward by the foundation. As a result a market of 250 million people will emerge for newspapers. A newspaper will be read by two million people. A book will sell two million copies. There will be shared television channels. The resources of the Turkic world will be pooled and used by the Turks. We will enter into joint ventures with others, and establish customs unions. There will be cooperative laboratories producing meticulous research. The whole world will stand in awe . . . We will say to people, 'We give you Turkish citizenship as a reward.' Everyone will plead for citizenship and queues will form outside the gates of Turkish Consulates around the world. To talk Turkish will become a fashion in America. When you walk around New York the signs above the shops will be in Turkish. Upon picking up the journals you'll see they'll be in Turkish . . . Turkish will become a world language. This will happen because first the Turks will be reunited, who will then awaken and help all Islamic countries. Even in the Western countries the unhappy, the wretched and the restless will become our cause, and we will open up schools to bring them some humanity. Every school we establish will give education in their own tongue, but they will teach Turkish and Turkish literature as well . . . They will come from around the world to plead for a customs union. 'If you reform your system and make progress in human rights and democracy perhaps then we will take you,' we will say. In the surrounding countries the candidates who gain our support will be elected and in gratitude make their first post-election visit to us . . . If we desire we will interfere in other countries' affairs, even cause a coup. But our character will not let us do such a thing, as we will help other peoples in pursuit of the good (*Zaman* (Australia), 2 June 1997 – my translation).

The programme is remarkably Kemalist. Science is conscripted once again to turn the blowtorch of its merciless truth upon the past and prepare the way for the new virgin order. Knowledge is harnessed to ensure that the new generation manifest themselves as the boon to the peoples of the world that they in fact are. *Hayatta en hakiki mürşit ilimdir* ('Knowledge is the truest guide in life' – Ataturk) proclaims the facade of the Faculty of Letters, History and Geography in Ankara. *Pozitif bilimler aklın ziyası ise ulum-u diniye de kalbin nuru oluyor* ('If the positive sciences are the light of your mind, theology is the halo of your heart') says Fethullah Hoca (*Yeni Şafak*, 7 August 1996). The new nation-(super)state will be constructed, like the Republic it supersedes, through its school system. Not merely science but Islam too will be instrumental in establishing a rational yet pious cadre to manage the system. Obviously the community led by Fethullah Gülen rides in the vanguard to ensure such a dream of rational mastery comes to fruition.

Not all Muslims, as may be imagined, are happy with this particular expropriation of Islam, especially its unstinting support for the ruling authorities of the Republican order. So for example Fethullah Hoca is attacked in an article entitled *Ihaneti Anlamak* ('To Understand Betrayal') in the Islamist journal *Ak-Doğuş*, in which the writer, after commenting upon Fethullah's constant self-deprecation in his sermons, asks him why in that case 'you have not yet left your work, and your claim to be a guide to the people? . . . What right do you have to invite them to obey the state in the name of Islam? . . . From where do you get the gall to make Muslims the passive object of every kind of political pressure and oppression under the mask of non-politicalness?' (Çakır 1990: 106). Reference is made here to Fethullah Hoca's well-known propensity to weep over his own unworth- iness while preaching, especially while supplicating God. Esra Özyürek argues that Fethullah Hoca's 'unmanly' weeping while petitioning God strengthens rather than subverts a hierarchical relation between men and women, as an analogy is constructed between the believer's passivity and powerlessness before God, and women's obedience to men. One wonders whether the same correspondence is not being evoked between the indi- viduals that 'bear' the (chosen) race and the state (similarly constituted) that represents it/them. Can an 'anarchist' be anything other than a traitor (*hain*)? Communicating with God, says Fethullah Hoca in a recent sermon, is inherently dangerous, 'as it always contains the threat of challenging God's authority' (Özyürek 1997: 49), of encroaching upon His domain. The believer's humble position before God mirrors the woman's position before men, which mirrors the loyal Turk's position before the state.

The condemnation of Fethullah Gülen by less statist Islamists (see the next chapter) is compensated by his commendation by secularists. Şahin Alpay in *Milliyet* newspaper for instance proffered a selection of Fethullah Hoca's opinions in an article on liberal democracy and Muslims, declaring that Gülen's interpretation of Islam was apposite in Turkey's struggle to democratize and modernize.[4] Among the quotes, taken from an interview with Fethullah Gülen and published in book form by the staunchly secularist *Milliyet*, is the claim that 'Customs Union, and inte- gration with the West, is inevitable in the age we are living in. We cannot lose from this.' Indeed an 'unreasonable hostility to the West will leave

---

4. Fethullah Gülen as icon of reformist Islam has been praised by non-Turkish scholars too: Dale Eickelman in a recent article commends him as a religious moderate (2000: 126).

us stranded outside the times'. Traditional Islamic education is criticized as 'excluding science and philosophy, despite the commands of the Koran'. As a result, 'the development of an artistic sensibility was obstructed'. In like vein, 'We are fighting a war with dogmatism and fanaticism'. The 'we' here presumably are Turks, for 'the Turks have evolved a tolerant, non-fanatical Islamic perspective', and 'represent Islam's universalism very well. The world has a need for such a representative and such an interpretation.' Fethullah Hoca divines this perspective as deriving from the cultural roots of contemporary Turkish identity: 'First there is Islam, secondly our Turkish ethnic origins in Central Asia, and thirdly Sufism, the soul of Islam' (*Yeni Şafak*, 7 August 1996).

What place then for the Kurds (indeed any non-Turkic Muslims, as well as Christian Turkish citizens) in Fethullah Gülen's burning discourse on Turkish supremacism? Political activity in the name of a Kurdish identity, which must of necessity protest at state practices, contravenes Fethullah Hoca's dictates in at least two ways: firstly it is anarchical, and secondly contemptuous of the special duty bestowed by God on the Turkish people. Condemning the PKK as simply terrorists is hence a logical response. But Fethullah Gülen's Kurdish politics do not cease with his criticism of the PKK. When the Iraqi Kurdish leader Mesut Barzani was received in Ankara in 1992 by President Demirel, who also made a statement about recognizing 'the Kurdish reality' in Turkey, Fethullah Hoca wrote in an article in *Zaman* that such an admission was a threat to the 'unity of the state'. He went on to argue that 'there should be no concessions made to [solve] the Kurdish problem, and the problem of *Kürtlük* (Kurdishness) should be disposed of by Islamic education' (Bulut 1992: 15). What Fethullah Hoca intends by 'Islamic education' is perfectly clear, as his schools in Central Asia show. Since the Kurdish problem is the problem of *Kürtlük* (Kurdishness) – i.e. the very feeling of being Kurdish – 'encouraging' Kurds to change their self-perception will eliminate the problem. The new Islamic education heralds an old assimilationism that Kurdish Islamism will not take kindly to.

In fact, the historically dominant education system in Kurdistan even during the single-party period was the Kurdish *medreseler* (theology schools), in which the principal language of instruction after Arabic was Kurdish, written not in the Latin alphabet but the Arabic. According to Müfid Yüksel, it was the secularist *Nakşibendi* mullah M. Emin Bozarslan who first printed Kurdish books in the Latin alphabet. Though greatly reduced in number and strength, some of the Kurdish *medreseler* are still operating (Yüksel 1993a.). Fethullah Hoca's schools, therefore, will not be the only institutions offering an 'Islamic education' in Kurdistan.

In short, statist Islamist discourse, as exemplified in the enterprise headed by Fethullah Gülen, conceives the Kurdish problem as residing in the Kurdishness of the Kurds. Transform this identification, and there will be no Kurdish question left to ponder.

–11–

A Plague on Both Your Houses!
The Kurdish Problem According to
Islamist Discourse

Introduction

The second discursive parcel passed around Muslim circles is one we
have provisionally named Islamist. Unlike statist Islamism, which is both
Turkish-supremacist and submissive to ruling authority, Islamist discourse
on the Kurdish problem gives its assent to the existence and equality of
Kurds as a *kavim* (people/nation) and to Kurdish as a language, but calls
for the subordination of such an identity to an Islamic one. At the same
time Islamist discourse is also resolutely anti-Turkish nationalist. It bears
its adjective-free status proudly – not Turkish nor statist Islamism, but
plain unadorned Islamism. This correction stands pointedly in judgement
over Kurdish Islamism as well. Islamist discourse stakes a claim to be an
ethnically neutral political actor: in the new social contract posited by
Islamism, ethnic irons are withdrawn from the fire in the name of a more
universalistic identity. In the context, however, of the hegemony of the
Turkish sovereign in the public sphere, is the Islamist plague on both houses
quite the even-handed third way it purports to be? Is even-handedness
what is called for here? Before considering these questions, however, we
should examine the main features of Islamist discourse, to discover which
elements of Islamic vocabulary have captured its historical imagination.

Muslim Identity and Its Critique of the Nation-State

Some of the major discursive planks of Islamism are usefully but polemically
nailed together in an article by Abdurrahman Aslan in the book *Kurt Sorunu
Nasıl Çözülur?* (How Can the Kurdish Problem be Solved?), the published
proceedings of a conference organized by the Kurdish Islamist journal
Nü Bihar. Aslan began his speech by proclaiming that he would define
himself simply as a Muslim, because he did not wish to describe his

identity using modern dimensions or concepts: 'A modern identity is useful only for today . . . whereas a Muslim identity is valid for the other world too' (Aslan 1996: 88). What is a modern identity? Aslan goes on to argue that those individuals or societies who constitute themselves by grasping at the modern term *ırk* (race)[1] are dining at the exotic table of a new historiography, a history tracing its origins to the glories of pre-Islamic civilizations: 'The Turks have discovered Central Asia, the Iraqis the Babylonians, the Kurds Mesopotamia, the Egyptians Pharaoh and the Algerians Carthage' (1996: 87–8). He omits to add that the Islamists themselves have long been feasting on the period of the *Asrı Saadet* as their own defining cuisine.

Noting that most of the Muslim speakers proffering solutions to the Kurdish problem were approaching the subject with demands based on ideologies other than Islam, Aslan wondered what would happen if Muslims had never heard of the concept of 'culture'. For this concept was invented only after 1800:

> If this word didn't exist, with what would we have expressed our desires? . . . If we didn't know this term, as Muslims we would have met our needs in Islam . . . But once this word was invented, you were able to discuss the culture of the Kurds, the Arabs, the Persians, the Turks. If you had been living 200 years ago you would never have used the secular concepts of race and nation (1996: 89 – my translation).

Aslan's comments are directed to both Turkish and Kurdish notions of cultural specificity, but his diagnosis of the current conjuncture in world history makes it clear that his critique is aimed particularly at extant Kurdish petitions for political rights on the basis of their ethnic identity. Gleefully embracing apocalyptic predictions of the imminent collapse

---

1. *Irk* is translated in the dictionary as 'race' (and *ırkcılık* as 'racism') but the concept perhaps better corresponds to the English word 'ethnicity' (with all the problems this entails). Obviously the Turks or Kurds or Persians do not constitute what has been traditionally understood in racist social science and in everyday speech as separate genetic or biological entities (races). Occasionally however the metaphor of *kan* (blood) is placed in close proximity to nationalist fantasies of *ırk*; so the Nobel Prize candidate in Molecular Biochemistry, Professor Dr Oktay Sinanoğlu, can hypothesize in the article cited above that 'Hitler said there was a pure-blood (*safkan*) German race (*ırk*). I am reading the Roman historians and the developments that occurred after them. In one excavation in Europe, and even in Germany, sometimes you can see people with slanting/almond eyes. From the Alps to the bottom of Italy the Huns came and settled but because they forgot their language they melted away and disappeared. If you stirred up European blood (*kan*) half of it would turn out to be Turkish' (*Zaman* (Australia), 2 June 1997).

of the nation-state, especially in its post-colonial form, Aslan argues that if yesterday statelessness for a nation or community was a disadvantage, to be a possessor of a nation-state today carries an equivalent negative meaning. Indeed, 'to incite people to define their identity according to their ethnic origin *at this critical point in history* [my stress] is an insult to them'. For 'Not only do we Muslims reject the nation-state theoretical model, we also reject in the expectation of developing the *ümmet* [commonwealth of believers] the organizational modes that accompany it' (1996: 91). Though Fethullah Hoca's Turkish nationalism (and statist Islamism) is in principle included in such a condemnation, the decisive nation-founding struggle 'at this critical point in history' is of course Kurdish nationalist. In an ironic echo of the Kemalist accusation that Islam imperils the very direction of universal history ('Let us not deceive one another, the civilized world is miles ahead of us. We have to catch up with it and enter the circle of civilization. Gentlemen, uncivilized people are trodden under the feet of civilized people' (Atatürk, in Mango 1996: 6)), Aslan implies that those who still think in the imagery of the nation-state or even with the concept of culture are outdated, protesting feebly against the turning of the historical tide.

Aslan is no lone voice in Islamist circles linking both the subject-instituting discourse of nationalism and ethnic identity to the West (post-French Revolution), nor in claiming that in contrast his own identity derives from Islam. Ahmet Taşgetiren, a columnist for the *Yeni Şafak* newspaper, begins his speech at the conference in the same way: 'I am a Turk by race. But as for identity, I define myself as a Muslim' (Taşgetiren 1996: 93). Taşgetiren's intervention clarifies Aslan's passing claim that 'cutting' Muslims was what Kemalist ideology knew best, that this constituted its defining characteristic. For Taşgetiren too, the Kurdish problem is an accessory after the fact: if it is possible to talk of an assimilation project intended for the Kurds, it is equally valid to speak about a forced cultural transformation aimed at all Muslims in Turkey, the republican state having abolished their alphabet and changed their history, their religion and their law. Consequently 'There isn't much difference between the Turkish problem and the Kurdish one . . . in fact both Turks and Kurds are drowning in the same problems' (Taşgetiren 1996: 94).

If Islam was and remains the chief target of the regime, and the Kurdish problem a side-effect of this enmity, the solution to the Kurdish problem lies not in some sort of special social recognition for Kurds or local autonomy for the Kurdish regions (however worked out), but in reconstituting the system along Islamic lines. Taşgetiren ends his speech by calling for just such an order.

Indeed, if the problem originates in the forced alienation of Muslims from the Koran, perhaps logically there is no Kurdish problem at all? And lo and behold! *Iktibas* journal, in its answer to a survey conducted by another Islamist journal *Hak Söz*, concludes exactly that. 'As Muslims we are not convinced that there is a Kurdish problem. We are of the opinion that the problems confronting Muslims in Turkey and the whole world reside entirely in their distancing from Islam' (in *Hak Söz*, April 1992, p. 7).

If there is no Kurdish problem, perhaps there are no Kurds either? Or maybe the Muslim's ethnic identity is of such little consequence that, as an article in *Yeni Şafak* proclaimed, 'I am a Kurd but I could be Chinese' (*Yeni Şafak*, 17 November 1996). Indeed Islamist discourse can easily slip from a grudging admission of the created reality of ethnic difference into bravado slogans exalting the suppression, even erasure *tout court* of all ethnic traces from the new Muslim subject. So in the same article Nihat Nasır breathlessly announces that, 'I do not consider anything important beside being a Muslim, and I condemn those who, despite their Islamic identity, see any value in their Turkishness, Kurdishness, Arabness, etc., even if I stand alone' (ibid.). Here we are confronted with a wilful individual self-creation, celebrating the sloughing-off of the historical and social determinants of identity in the name of a radical Islamic express-ivist autonomy. As there is no Kurdishness worth speaking about, Nasır concludes that Kurds cannot have been exposed to oppression on the grounds of their ethnicity but because of their religiousness. Logically, then, 'the regime prefers a Kurd who compromises with it than a Turk who for the sake of Islam gives no concessions' (ibid.). But how do Kurds cooperate with the regime? By downplaying their Kurdishness and assim-ilating, of course, in which case naturally they have no problem.

The Islamist critique of nationalism as non-Islamic makes no distinction, then, between state-sponsored nationalisms constructing an emergent national identity, and reactive nationalisms explicable only in terms of their negative inscription, or even denial, within the discursive practices of the new nation. Ihsan Işık, for example, at a different forum also devoted to the Kurdish problem, can declare himself to be 'as much against Turkish nationalism as I am against Kurdish nationalism' (Işık 1993: 375). Similarly Ramazan Keskin rebukes Kurdish delegates for talking too much about Kurdish history and language. 'Presumably we did not come to this sym-posium to contemplate whether there are or are not any Kurds in Turkey . . . We came to speak about the oppression the peoples of Turkey are subjected to. True, because of a double standard we haven't explained sufficiently the sufferings of the east and south-east. But this doesn't mean the Muslims who live in Turkey's other regions haven't suffered too' (Keskin 1993: 251–2). Keskin's heavy-handed insensitivity to the historical experience of Kurds and their obsessive need to assert again and again their own existence, his impatient dismissal of their special misery, points to a wound that Islamists seem unable to staunch.

Yet interestingly, medical metaphors are often employed by Islamists in their attempts to grasp the parameters of the Kurdish problem. So writers frequently opine that unless a proper *diagnosis* of the *condition* is carried out, the correct *remedy* will not be *prescribed*. Nationalism is asserted as *festering* in Western imperialism's drive to expose and thus subjugate the Muslim *ümmet* accustomed to sheltering under the umbrella of the Ottoman Empire. This is regularly summarized as the *recrudescence* of the Crusader mentality (*haçlı zihniyet*). If the Turkish Republic itself is sometimes *classified* as the West's greatest tactical triumph, Kurdish nationalism too is *treated* as Western-inspired, sometimes through the claim of the West's direct *injection* of funds, but more often as *symptomatic* of an ideological *infection*. Thus the *body* politic (the Islamic *ümmet*) is labelled as *sick*, being *under attack from foreign-bodies* that *contaminate* its holistic entity. The *cure* then is to *purge* it, by ridding the body politic of that which penetrates it, and restore it to *health and strength*.

Such a contention between on the one hand the life-threatening process put in train by the laic regime (and behind it, by imperialism), and the political order instituted by Islam on the other also means that Islamist discourse does not look kindly upon the call for alliances, strategic or otherwise, with secular groups that may also be struggling against the state. In Ali Bulaç's pithy words, 'The Turks, Arabs and Persians did not occupy Kurdish geography . . . The French Revolution occupied us with foreign and enemy ideals' (Bulaç 1996: 107). Any democratic front composed of the very groups taken in by such concepts is skating on thin ice. Of course this includes the PKK, projected not as representing – whether one likes it or not – a section of Kurdish public opinion, but as herding the *zavallı Müslüman Kürt Halk* ('the unfortunate Muslim Kurdish People') between the rock of PKK terror and the hard place of state violence. In contrast Kurdish Islamism, as we shall see, cannot afford to be so cavalier in disavowing Kurdish nationalism nor its peak representatives.

Islamist Slants on the Narrating of History

In like vein the unhappy *Müslüman Kürtler* are sometimes addressed as *Selahaddin-i Eyyubinin torunları* (Saladin's grandchildren) or even *Şeyh Saidin torunları* (Şeyh Said's grandchildren), titles that emphasize or even seek to constitute the exemplary religiousness of both the dead Saladin and his living fictive descendants. Nomenclature here is the fuel powering the political intervention. So Abdulvahhab Elgursi uses both metaphorical devices to delineate the dimensions of the Kurdish problem, polemically querying whether 'the solution lies in offering *Selahaddin-i Eyyubinin torunları* to the Marxist-Leninist movements'. 'Of course not,' he concludes, 'rather than solving the problem these will only make the illness chronic' (Elgursi 1993: 269). If historical figures as remote from modern times as Selahaddin Eyyubi are pressed into service, how much more is Şeyh Said's 1925 uprising hermeneutically up for auction, occupying as it does what Hobsbawm has called the 'twilight zone' where 'the memory of our grandparents overlaps with the history textbooks' (in Deringil 1996: 13).

And not just the memory of our grandparents. For the grandson of Şeyh Said is still living, and his interpretation of the event that resulted in his grandfather's execution abuts at a strange angle to both the official historiography of the state and the take of Islamist discourse. For if the Republic damns the rebellion as the work of a regressive Islamic nostalgia for an abolished and backward social order, Islamism reveres it for the same reasons. M. Emin Akın for example identifies Şeyh Said as the man who led 'the most serious and virtuous Islamic revolt in the Republican period' (Akın 1993, 357), while Nurettin Şirin calls for Muslims to emulate the man who 'carried out an honourable Islamic uprising against the despotic laic regime' (Şirin 1993: 349). His grandson, Abdulmelik Fırat, is rather less one-dimensional in his appraisal. Indeed, he told me the story of a recent walk he had taken in the park in Diyarbakır where his grandfather's body was thrown 'like rubbish'. While scattering rose petals and saying a prayer for the seventieth anniversary of Şeyh Said's hanging he heard the clear voice of his grandfather saying, 'Don't be sad, I'm not here, I'm in the mountains with my friends.' 'Interpret that as you will,' Abdulmelik Fırat said to me with a smile.

Fascinatingly, Abdulmelik Fırat recounts the same story in more detail in his book *Fırat Mahzun Akar*. Here he writes that his grandfather said,

> My son, don't search for me in this unconsecrated ground. Didn't I write to you in my own hand from the shadow of the gallows, 'In the name of God, the merciful and compassionate. Our existence comes from God, and we will again return to him. Don't say that those slaughtered for the way of God have died, for they are living. But you seem unable to grasp this. I have no anxiety about hanging from that worthless bough. Without a doubt, my struggle is for God, for religion and *for my people.*' Didn't you read that letter? I am now in the plains, the streams, the springs, the rivers, and on the mountaintops of

Kurdistan. I am in the midst of those children who listen to my voice . . . Don't be angry with those collaborators who work for the enemy; they are still stricken with fear of the wolf that has leapt upon them. The voice of my children in the mountains will open their ears (Fırat 1996: 122).

In fact, Abdulmelik Fırat's own changing assessment of his grandfather's revolt is a translucent image of Kurdish Islamism's disillusionment with the charms of Islamist discourse. In an earlier interview he gave in 1989 Abdulmelik Fırat noted that 'despite 64 years having passed since Şeyh Said's rebellion . . . his relatives have not yet been able to read prayers for his soul at his graveside' (in Yılmaz 1992: 97). In that same interview he again quoted the final testament of his grandfather, but this time Şeyh Said's last sentence was reported as being, 'Without a doubt, my struggle is for God and the Islamic religion' (1992: 92). That is, here there was no mention of his sacrifice being '*for my people*' (see above). In six short years, then (1989–1995), years in which an already grim situation in the east and south-east had deteriorated appallingly, Şeyh Said's grandson had also refocused his position, now perceiving a common communion between his grandfather's uprising and the present rebellion of the PKK guerrillas on the plains, streams and mountaintops of Kurdistan. The account of his grandfather's new insight into his own rebellion casts some light on Abdulmelik Fırat's public support of HADEP (the Kurdish party), not Refah, at the 1996 general election.

The meaning of the Şeyh Said revolt, like the signifier *Selahaddin-i Eyyubi*, varies therefore according to the discourse within which it is affixed. As Abdulmelik Fırat's broadened imputation of his grandfather's aims illustrates, the mere pinning like a medal of the epithet 'martyr' to the person of Şeyh Said is insufficient. A martyr for what? For whom?

Radical Disobedience and Vulgar Utopianism

One major difference between statist Islamist and Islamist discourse on the Kurdish question resides in their differing valuations of the state's legitimacy. Statist Islamism counsels patience and obedience for 'Muslims suffering in the south-east' (as they are nominated; not for 'Kurds suffering in Kurdistan'), while representing the present conflict as originating in the attempts of outside forces to destabilize the nation, as well as in the ambitions of internal enemies (irreligious communists and anarchists) to destroy the present order. In this case, faithful Muslims are entreated to stand by their state, not just because it is the last Turkish 'castle', but because those threatening it will bring atheism in its place. Statist Islamism is not of course the privilege only of religious organizations close to the state (like the *Fethullahcılar*): one's ears, to use a Turkish expression, can be guests to variations on its themes everywhere.

In the course of my residence in Kuzguncuk, for example, even my local barber, Ramazan, had become conscientized. In the second year of my fieldwork he grew an Islamist beard, and permanently tuned the radio in working hours to the station owned by the *Türkiye* newspaper, broadcasting vital advice – as one was coming up for air, head dripping wet – on religious quandaries, for example 'Does one need to start *namaz* from the beginning if someone knocks on the door before one finishes?' 'Please don't cut my hair un-lawfully,' I used to joke with him. But riots by leftists on May Day 1996 in Kadikoy, not far from Kuzguncuk, left him and his friends in ill humour. Ramazan showed me a picture from the newspaper of the protesters holding up a picture of Lenin, and asked, 'Is he a Turk? No. Then what's he doing there?' For Ramazan, people who did such things were *vatandaş hainler* (traitors to the nation), were all PKK and communists who wanted to 'split Turkey'. I left that day rubbing my clean-shaven chin and wondering whether barber Ramazan and co. were not all [grey] wolves in sheep's clothing, nationalists in religious drag.

By contrast, Islamist discourse on the Kurdish question finds the republican regime illegitimate and accordingly pleads for the active withdrawal of Muslim consent from the existing system. Rhetorically at least, vulgar Islamism accuses the state of being as atheist as its erstwhile leftist opponents. If the laic and nationalist Turkish state is irredeemably compromised by its defining principles, only a social order conforming to Islamic law can be sufficient. Not just reform, then, but a contrary utopia. So Elgursi claims that 'the solution of the [Kurdish] problem is found in rejecting all human answers and systems. In fact the real problem has emerged from these human (*beşeri sistemler*) systems. For in the period when Islam was the authority, there was no Kurdish problem, nor any other problems . . . For thinking and intelligent people is there any better solution than God's system?' (Elgursi 1993: 269, 270). Yet the claim that permanent solutions to the problem can only be assured by a revolutionary new system dismays many Kurdish Muslims who do not want to wait for the dawning of an Islamic (or socialist) order for a remedy to assimilative racism. In its resolute anti-nationalism, Islamist discourse concurs with the 'red' Kemalism of Turkish communism, which calls not for the unity of Kurdish and Turkish Muslims, but for the unity of Turkish and Kurdish workers to cooperate in throwing out American imperialism before sitting down together to discuss problems of ethnic discrimination. For in their political imaginations the Muslim *ümmet* and the Marxist working class are both exemplary multicultural, even international or universal communities.[2]

Yet even the revolutionary installation of 'God's system' in the shape of the Islamic Republic of Iran has not managed to solve the Kurdish problem, if the publication of a book entitled *Kürdistan Hainleri* (Kurdistan Traitors) is anything to judge by. Translated from the Persian into Turkish in 1996, the book mimics the worst polemic of statist Islamism, but here in the name of the Iranian Islamic regime, whose founding became the inspiration of a number of Islamist groups and journals in Turkey in the late 1980s and early 1990s. So the book opens by praising the revolutionary subject:

> A people made a revolution, and broke open the fetters that had bound their hands and feet for 2,500 years . . . A great leader, unequalled in history, guided this historic revolution . . . This revolution drained the roots of despotism and imperialism, brought social justice, did away with poverty, ignorance, oppression and corruption, and destroyed the injustice and cruelty of those who had domi-nated this country . . . But the imperialists, for whom this country was the hen that laid the golden eggs, were of no mind to leave . . . [And so the plotting began,] the leftist parties, taking advantage of the Kurdish people's poverty and disadvantage, worked to incite them. They started to scheme against the Iranian Islamic revolution for the profits of imperialism (Çamran 1996: 5–7 – my translation).

Why were the imperialists able to destabilize the Kurdish provinces? Because in the period before the revolution 'Zionist orientalists' in America and Europe had 'propagated the idea that the Kurds were a separate people with their own culture and language'. But in fact 'the Kurds are Iran's true people. And their languages, cultures and nation have originated in Iran' (1996: 17).

2. In practice, however, ethnic subjectivity becomes problematic for political class-consciousness, as it does for conscious Muslims. In turn, Islamists accuse Marxist theories of class conflict of fermenting social divisiveness, just as they do the production of ethnic solidarity in a multicultural context. Islamism, in contrast, is projected as a commitment to a voluntary polyethnic religious community submitted to the rule of the knowledgeable and virtuous, even if women are ineligible to become judges or members of the *ulema* (legal fraternity). This gendered division of social life is defended as functionally providential, as is the division of labour. Yet given that class and ethnic structuration is endemic to industrial economies organized on capitalist lines and modern systems of democratic sovereignty respectively, Islamist movements can only seek to manage their activating impulses, not abolish their sources. Rational management of the social realm is itself an intrinsically modernist ambition, possession of which undercuts the claims of both Islamist movements and their opponents that Islamism is somehow an alternative to modernity, not an alternative modernity.

Suspicion, however, that the Islamic state in Iran has been reconstructing itself less on the grounds of polyethnic pan-Islamism than on Shiite and Iranian (but not necessarily Persian) nationalism since the death in 1989 of Imam Khomeini is disillusioning many of its former Islamist supporters in Turkey. For in its numerous dealings with neighbouring countries and their various internal political struggles Iran is seen as acting not so much in accordance with principles of Islamic solidarity as in its own interests as a regional power (and often in support of foreign Shiite minorities). This places Islamists in Turkey in a difficult position, and chafes at their own raw nationalistic nerves. But not everybody is prepared to jettison the inspiration that the Iranian revolution offers.

Nevertheless, even some of those most impressed by the Iranian Islamist Republic confess to occasional doubts. For example in an interesting article in *Akit*, written in response to the Iranian military's excursion into northern Iraq in pursuit of Kurdish rebels in 1996, Yılmaz Yalçıner admits to being puzzled over the apparently similar justifications used by Iran and Turkey in their defence of such border crossings. For unlike Turkey the Islamic Republic of Iran does not have a centralist structure but a federal one, and 'every ethnic element is a partner in the state. There is even a province named Kurdistan.' Why then is the rhetoric familiar? And what is it that the Kurds desire? After chanting the obligatory Islamist mantra that Kurdish nationalism wants a laic national Kurdish state, Yalçıner also canvasses the deficiencies of the Islamic Republic:

> The Iranian Islamic Republic, despite the plural Islam or shared state imagined by the Imam, has unfortunately not always been totally successful . . . According to the late Dr Fehmi Sinnavi, the Kurds find Iran guilty of insufficient love by its refusal to teach the Kurdish language and by its sending of non-Kurdish administrators into the region. Iran in its turn conceives the Kurds as potential separatists who will embolden other minority peoples, and hence accuses the Kurds of threatening the unity of the state (*Akit*, 1 August 1996 – my translation).

Yalçıner concludes by advising the Islamic Republic to remain wedded to the spirit of Imam Khomeini.

Islamism and Autonomy

In general, however, enthusiasm for the Iranian model has died down, and Islamist proposals for solving the Kurdish problem do not often toast the Islamic Republic of Iran as worthy of emulation. Unhappily, Iran too has been contaminated by a nationalist logic. But this disappointment has not dented Islamism's self-confidence in its own internal resources as sufficient to solve any problem, and in particular to cut the knot of the Kurdish question. In this regard Islamism as utopia is engaged in a search for purity, as any degree of hybridity necessitates a counter-movement toward disentanglement. This drive towards purity is simultaneously a plea for autonomy, as the sought-after and divinely-ordained order legislates only according to its own significations and principles, and not those of the West. And the project of autonomy, as Castoriadis argues, can be seen as one pole of the 'dual institution' of modernity itself, a cultural orientation permanently at war with the divergent logic of capitalism or expanding rational mastery (Castoriadis 1997a; Arnason 1989). In the name of a more inclusive social contract Islamism may reject notions of national identity as the basis for state sovereignty, but it can hardly give up on the ideal or imaginary signification of autonomy and sovereignty *per se*. And ironically, then, neither can it ever attain its own purity, at least not while the modern signification of autonomy itself remains an esteemed goal. Indeed, in desiring to be free from Western law and hence to become a law unto itself, Islamism's rootedness in modernity is revealed. Autonomy here is activated in the form of a collective subject, the ruled making the rules that will rule them, as the agitating spirit of autonomy urges. For as the people become voluntarist, not traditional Muslims, the Islamic law instituted by their struggle is simply their self-legislation.

At the same time the field of meanings mined by the terms the 'West' and the 'modern' to aid in the purification of Islamist discourse is rather extensive. Is the West merely a signifier for imperialism? In this case Islamist discourse is pulled (with the conspiratorial left) towards a nationalistic grammar of external threats and rampant foreign agencies, whose main aim in life is to destabilize the Middle East and Islam. Or is it modernity and its significations (like nationalism) that need to be opposed, and not only the Western powers? Or can Muslims by contrast be Islamist and modern at the same time, but not Western? And if they can, according to what criteria are the various contending cultural orientations within modernity to be adopted or annulled? Why, for example, is a practising knowledge of one's Kurdish identity vilified as separatist and Western-inspired, but not the practical organization of Islamist businesses according to capitalist management techniques?

This elasticity, even confusion, over the relationship between the West and the modern is not of course peculiar to Islamist discourse – they are as often presented as synonymous in self-congratulatory Western versions of acultural modernization theory too. But the tendency of Islamist polemic to lump them together often precludes a more creative engagement with, and reinterpretation of modernity in the name of a premature 'No'.

Saying 'no', however, does not sidestep the necessity of bestowing new meanings on what is inherited or adapted from modernity, on what is at hand. There can never be total discontinuity. However, saying 'no' does repress an open discussion of the principles employed in Islamism's selective appropriation of the modern. So on the Kurdish problem it fails to consider how its own category of an essential or *öz* (true) Muslim identity, when used to subordinate Kurdish claims, may at the same time construct a hierarchically-ordered modernist subject, a subject culturally plural (Muslim plus Kurdish/Turkish/Arab, etc.) but politically singular (Islamist). As Judith Butler notes, modern identity is as much a normative ideal as a descriptive feature of experience (Butler 1990: 16).

Conclusion

Dr Sinnavi's analysis and critique of the present situation in Iranian Kurdistan stands as a succinct illustration of the north/south magnetic poles that tug at Islamist discourse on the Kurdish problem. On the one hand Islamism, unlike statist Islamist discourse, is sympathetic to the realization of the cultural rights of Kurdish people, to the teaching and speaking of Kurdish in schools, to the broadcasting of Kurdish by the mass media, etc. Abdullah Ünalan, for example, is not atypical when he proposes among other things that 'the education system, its curriculum and textbooks should be re-organized, cleansed of provocative statements that diminish Kurds. As much place should be given to famous Kurds as to Englishmen, Germans and Frenchmen in the textbooks' (Ünalan 1993: 230). On the other hand Islamism is antagonistic to any Kurdish political subjectivity that may undermine Muslim identity, an identity cast in the furnace of its struggle with Republicanism and behind that, with secularism's perceived schoolmaster and mentor, the West. Yet in Islamist discourse the exact relationship between Kurdish cultural and political rights is often unclear, and the question whether Kurds can actually win their own cultural rights without an accompanying political subjectivity is glossed over. Islam may bestow cultural rights on Kurds, but can Islamists?

If for statist Islamism, then, the Kurdish problem resides in the Kurdish-ness of the Kurds, for Islamist discourse it lies in the ethnicity of ethnics, full stop. Or more exactly, it derives from the *şuurlu* (conscious) subjectivity of ethnic actors: Kurdish, Turkish, Laz or whoever. For Turkish Muslims, this subjectivity is explained as a consequence of state patronage; for Kurdish Muslims of being deceived by Kurdish Kemalist look-alikes; and for both of them a consequence of the West's deliberate release of the feral beast of nationalism, which has run wild and destroyed the ordered gardens of Islam more effectively than any marauding invader. For the feral beast has adapted well to its new environment, and the marks of its footprints are difficult to distinguish from those of the native animals to be found grazing in the pages of the Koran: the *aşiret* (tribe), *kabile* (tribe/clan), *kavim* (people/nation), *halk* (people/community) and *ümmet* (community of believers).[3] Yet Islamism's romantic concern to return the social ecology to its indigenous state would paradoxically require an artificial and highly organized intervention in cultural life, specifically to prevent the Islamist subject from becoming an endangered species. Ethnic actors are perceived in this sense to be feral Muslims, competing for the same eco-system. In ultimately attributing all such feralism to the West, Islamist discourse refuses to consider the plurality of sources of ethnic assertiveness. Its 'plague on both houses' suggests a statist concern to curtail ethnic differences in the name of a unifying and overriding notion of Islamic identity.

But I will explore this problem further after unwrapping and opening up the Islamist movement's third discursive offering *vis-à-vis* the Kurdish question, namely the parcel of ideas and analyses termed Kurdish Islamist.

3. Part of the problem of associational taxonomy lies in the translation of the Arabic words and the range of meanings each possesses. The Islamist movement in Turkey is valiant in its efforts to ensure that Muslims learn to read Koranic or classical Arabic, precisely in order to assuage the fear of the revealed Word of God's being drowned out by paraphrased vernacular versions of the Koran, or interpreted by ill-considered exegesis reading contemporary political prejudices into the text. But to debate the possible extension (or otherwise) of Koranic terms to such constitutive significations of modernity as nationalism – in other words to attain such a level of proficiency in Arabic and the Koran – becomes a lifetime labour (of love?), and is therefore a rare skill, given the demands of a commodity-dominated economy and a technocratic education system. At the same time we see an interesting spiritual division of labour between men and women, in the not insignificant numbers of girls able to read the Koran out aloud in Arabic, while not fully aware of the meaning of the words being recited. For young women, especially from poorer families, an ability to read the Koran may become a desirable asset for the marriage market, as well as a source of income.

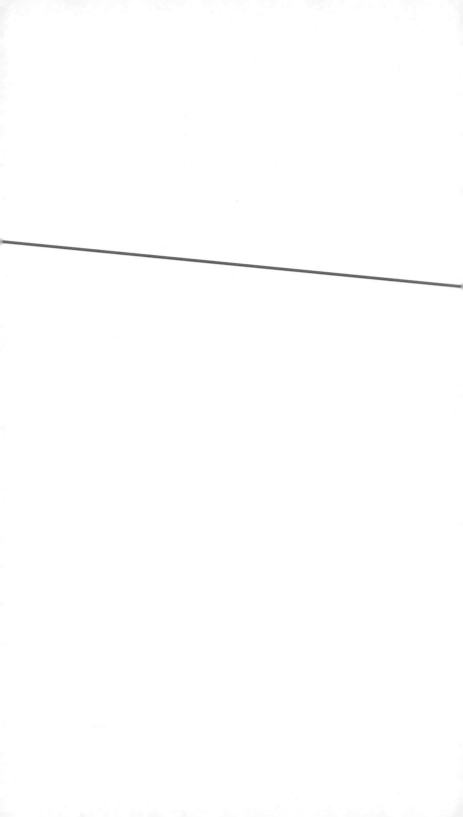

–12–

Allah Delights in Diversity: Kurdish Islamism on the Kurdish Question

Introduction

Perhaps the best way of sketching out the distinctive features of the three competing discourses is to return briefly to the 1996 *Selahaddin-i Eyyubi* (Saladin) Symposium (see page 32), organized by the Refah-controlled Greater Diyarbakır City Council to mark the 900th anniversary of the First Crusade. The spectre of the Kurdish problem haunted the conference, as *Selahaddin-i Eyyubi*, like a blank cheque, was inscribed with the values informing the positions of various players in the current political struggle, and then cashed in for their respective benefit. For example, a Kurdish speaker in the summing-up session argued that *Eyyubi's* greatness lay in his establishing a state that did not seek to buttress its power by allowing any one ethnic group to dominate. He was immediately rebuked by the Chair, who went on to claim in good Islamist fashion that it makes no difference if we arabize, turkify (*türklestirilsek*), or kurdify – the Muslim's true essence remains unchanged. In this context, the simple fact of acknowledging that *Selahaddin-i Eyyubi* was Kurdish was censured as a form of *Kürtcülük* (Kurdism), while the deliberate avoidance of all references to his ethnic origin in the name of his status as a Muslim was never admitted to be the political act it so clearly was. On the other hand, the Islamist censure should also be understood in the light of the conference's opening address, when the representative of the state, the Governor of Diyarbakir, initiated proceedings by telling the audience that they were to be introduced to a 'great Turkish warrior'. This claim stood uncorrected by the Chair. Thus in the Islamist response – the repudiation of all and any politics based on ethnic difference – to statist Islamism's Turkish chauvinism, the high wire that Kurdish Islamism must walk is spotlighted.

In brief, Kurdish Islamist discourse seeks to defend both the particularity of Kurdish Muslims against their belittling by Islamism's Muslim universalism, and also the universality of Islam against the prejudice of statist Islamism's Turkish particularism.

Islam and Ethnic Difference

If Kurdish Islamist discourse aligns itself with Islamist discourse over the reasons for Turkish Muslims' and the wider Islamic movement's indifference towards the Kurdish problem, there is less in common in their analyses of the cause of the problem itself. At its simplest, the Islamist re-narrativization of Turkey's history with de-islamification as its main drama means that the oppression of Kurds is traced ultimately to the Republicanism of the state (i.e. to its denial of the Islamic tolerance of the Ottoman polity in the pursuit of a French-style secularism) and only secondarily to its Turkish nationalism. That is, Turkish nationalism is seen as a result of modernization, not as one of its constituting elements. Kurdish Islamism, on the other hand, though only too aware of Kurds' suppression as Muslims by the Republic, does not wish – or is unable – to reduce such experience to Kurds' Muslim selves. Rather it is forced, by dint of the Republic's refusal to recognize Kurdish ethnic difference, to conduct a political struggle on the grounds of cultural identity as well. In other words Kurdish Islamism is concerned to mount a defence of the notion of Muslim cultural plurality, against Islamist discourse's strong critique of it.

So in reply to Abdurrahman Aslan's claim (see page 158) that the demand for cultural recognition is a concept invented only 200 years ago, the next speaker at the conference bar one retorted that 'our friend spoke as if culture was an influence in social life that only appeared because of the French Revolution. But the Koran itself says "If an invader enters the land, he destroys both lives and culture"' (Varlı 1996: 99). The rest of Varlı's speech is devoted to tracing references to the Kurds as a separate entity in various texts, including the Old Testament. Similarly, Atasoy Muftuoğlu in his address at the *Mazlumder* conference on the Kurdish problem explicitly denies that the present-day demands of Kurds are any different to the demands they have made throughout the long history of their relationship with others, especially difficult latecomers to Anatolia such as the Turkish tribes: 'In the past the Kurds have demanded that Kurdistan's conditions be reformed; today they want the same thing' (Muftuoğlu 1993: 206).

In like vein Osman Tunç, countering the enthusiastic conviction of both Aslan and Ali Bulaç that the life-cycle of the nation has entered its dotage (and hence, in good Hegelian fashion, that the Kurdish problem has already been solved), attempts to deflect the 'either/or' of Islamism by suspending judgement on a Kurdish state. Tunç argues that the problem should be divided into two categories: its political, economic and administrative

dimensions, and its social and cultural ones. In order to solve the political
dimension of the problem, before anything else Kurdish identity must be
recognized:

> As long as this political dimension is not realized, there can never be any serious
> progress towards a solution. But while I want to stress the importance of recog-
> nizing Kurdish identity, I am not concerned to promote a nation-state identity
> or to denigrate the possibility of all the different ethnic groups (*uluslar*) living
> together affectionately. But on a practical level I want a society under the rule
> of law in which the Kurds' own identity, like the identities of all the groups
> living in the region, is accepted and expressible in the public sphere. I am not
> using this idea to revive once again a nation-state consciousness (Tunç 1996:
> 144 – my translation).

Tunç here is not fussed about arguing which guiding political principles
are better able to deliver such an outcome, but neither is he willing to risk
miring the Kurdish question in the quicksands of a thoroughgoing Islamic
reform programme. Instead, he chooses to stay closer to the issue, to seek
ways the Kurdish problem can be solved without necessitating a prior
and radical draining of the whole swamp. For as he said to me in an interview, 'A root-and-crop reform will be a long time in coming, if ever.' In
that same interview he made it clear that in his opinion Islamist discourse's
critique of ethnic identity is unnecessarily straitjacketing, as well as bad
Islam. For even when Turkey's Muslims do manage to free themselves
from the thrall of the state,

> they get ambushed by a second obstacle: that of the *ümmet*. This is the same
> mistake the left in Turkey used to make ... Now Muslims repeat this same
> utopian idea in the form of the *ümmet*. 'Let the whole Muslim world be freed,
> then there will be a single state, and after that we can give you the freedom to
> speak your own language if you want to, you can dress how you want to, you
> can live your own culture', they say. To think like this is just a daydream,
> there is no traffic in this direction ... It is as if Muslims think that Kurds are
> tearing the Islamic *ümmet* apart, as if Kurds, by requesting their legitimate right
> to speak their own language or live their own culture are splitting the Islamic
> world. But there is no such intention. To be scared that it is the Kurds who pose
> such a threat is an injustice. And for Muslims to propagate this in the name of
> religion is an incorrect understanding of Islam.

The Politics of *Ümmetcilik*

Tunç himself, after working as a journalist in Turkey, lived for seven years
in Saudi Arabia, where he studied theology in Mecca after fleeing the

1980 military coup. Well educated in Islam, he is not interested in criticizing the felicity of the idea of the *ümmet*. Rather he dislikes how the concept is applied by Turkish Islamist discourse to stifle discussion of the specific repression of Kurds by adducing an equivalent (or even greater) Muslim suffering, or how it is used to conflate the particular experience of Kurds with the general dismantling of a retrospectively harmonious Islamic order. In this scenario, then, the attempts of Kurdish Islamist discourse to witness to the continuing denial of Kurdish language and identity, etc. are perversely interpreted as further evidence of the insidiousness of the problem. That is, the existence of the Kurdish problem is both the prime exhibit in the crime of the West and yet, if handled by Kurds, condemns them to complicity with the act. For though it might be admitted that Kurds as Kurds suffer as a result of Islam's disestablishment, should they protest as Kurds they are accused of reinforcing that very process. In this case the particular tragedy of the Kurds becomes merely symbolic, an emblem of the 'abolition' of Islam.

Osman Tunç is not the only advocate of Kurdish Islamism to focus on the various meanings that the signifier *ümmet* possesses, nor to interrogate how the word is used. Ibrahim Kaya, for example, notices that, 'Whenever Kurdish identity is put on the agenda, Kurds especially are reminded of the unity of the Islamic polity (*ümmetcilik*).' This despite Turkish Muslims' being those 'whose memories need to be jogged over the indivisibility of the *ümmet*, for the separatism is done in their name . . . As a result their most important obligation is to purify the politics pursued on their behalf, combat the insecurities it causes, and cease their splitting of the *ümmet*' (Kaya 1993: 148). Muhammed Çağrı for his part decries the interpretation of some *Islamcilar* (Islamists) that 'the Kurdish people's struggle for their most natural rights is contrary (*aykiri*) to the politics of the *ümmet*. This interpretation is not based on knowledge of the *ümmet* but on the denial of the Kurds' (Çağrı 1993: 81).

Süleyman Kursun brings a more sober note to his exposition on the *ümmet*. He begins by apologizing to the Symposium for the 'weakness of my Turkish, as I have not been able to leave my home for a year. [Secondly] I know that what I say today will be recorded and passed on to internal security. But I don't feel any unease of conscience. Because this state is not a legal state.' Kursun, like many Kurdish Islamists, is quickened to sketch out the proper relationship between the imagined communities of the *ümmet* and the *kavim* (ethnic group/tribe/nation), between the politics of *ümmetcilik* and *kavmiyetcilik*. This to deflect Islamism's tendency to set them at loggerheads. 'Just as almighty God,' he argues, 'created the earth and life, he has created the variety of colours (*renk*) and languages.

Allah Delights in Diversity: Kurdish Islamism on the Kurds

To reject this variety is as stupid as denying the earth and its life . . . In fact *ümmetcilik* is an idea, a theory. It has to be bedded down on a foundation. That foundation is the different ethnic groups (*kavimler*). Almighty God created each people with their own true authenticity. It is not possible for one people to melt another away' (Kursun 1993: 215).

What then would this truer *ümmetcilik* consist of, and how can the internal relations between the different *kavim* (peoples) that constitute it be envisioned? According to Haşim Haşimi, real *ümmetcilik* exists if you 'respect the rights of all, raise your voice against injustice, protest against the abuse of human rights and struggle for others to take up those rights' (Haşimi 1993: 234). In other words, it exists when you want for others what you want for yourself. That many Kurds feel Islamist discourse falls manifestly short of such a practice is clear in some of the angry responses made to the indiscriminate Islamist attack on any form of ethnic identity. Mehmet Metiner, for example, rejects the charge that *Türkcülük* and *Kürtcülük* are the same thing. 'When did Kurds ever write on the mountains "What happiness to those who can say 'I am a Kurd'"', or "One Kurd is worth the whole world"?' (interview). Or again, 'is it Kurdish racism to claim that the problem can only be solved within the boundaries of democracy?[1] To want a recognition of Kurdish identity, to want the cultural rights of Kurds recognized, is this Kurdish racism? Dear friends, we need to analyze the problem properly' (Metiner 1993: 148). Ramazan Değer notes sadly that for Muslims, 'If you put the Kurdish problem on the agenda, you are a Kurdish nationalist (*Kürtçüsünüz*)' (Değer 1996: 148).

In contrast *ümmet şuurlu* Islamists, especially those who in the name of a recently liberated Islamic identity consider themselves progressive in their rejection of the Turkish–Islamic synthesis, are theoretically disposed to generalize the rule and deny the possibility of any ethnic political activity at all. In this case, Turkish and Kurdish nationalisms are read as equal, and equally denounced. 'If we can't be [aggressively] Turkish', they seem to say, 'you can't be [defensively] Kurdish.'[2] This is especially true for those who have split from the extreme Turkish nationalist party, the MHP (National Movement Party). So in two recent publications chronicling the writers' journeys from fascist Turkist to Islamist, both writers cite

1. Another fault line dividing Kurdish Islamist and Islamist discourse is conflict over the legitimacy of the concept of democracy, which for some is included within that constellation of ideas originating in the West, and hence needs to be submitted to criticism or Islamification. I merely mention the issue here, and will discuss it briefly later (p. 182 ff.)

2. Hamit Bozarslan argues that the pan-*Turanism* (Turkism) of the MHP (National Movement Party) distinguishes itself from Kemalism on at least one key point: it interprets Turkish nationalism as a doctrine of civil war (1996).

the famous press release prepared in Çanakkale prison by ex-*ülkücü* (the name claimed by the cadres of the anti-communist MHP) and sent to the Islamic newspapers in 1990, rejecting nationalism and announcing that, 'We have abandoned the *ülkücü* movement because we have discovered that its leadership, its ideology and its organization are anti-Islamic' (Sümbül 1996: 84–5; Yusufoğlu 1993: 126). In discovering 'real' Islam the ex-*ülkücüler* have also discovered that the violence of the movement's leader, Alparslan Türkeş – despite its justification in stirring slogans like 'Let our blood flow for the victory of Islam' – does not represent a *cihat* for an Islamic order (*Allahın nizamı*) but a human one, one that explicitly rejects the aim of a *şeriat* state. Yet if Kurdish identity is no longer perceived to be a threat to the unity of a reified Turkish nation, it is now seen as a menace to what Yusufoğlu calls *tevhid şuuru* (monotheistic consciousness), a danger to the *ümmet*. Similarly ex-MHP member and convicted murderer Sümbül concludes his book by calling on Muslims to change the Kemalist regime that oppresses Kurds:

> we should put in its place an order founded on God's commands, not one based on those of famous Turks or Kurds. Then rather than killing each other for the nonsense of not obeying 'my rules', we will have the right to force each other to conform to justice, saying 'Why don't you obey the rules of Him who created both you and me?' (Sümbül 1996: 111, 112).

This privileging of an *ümmet* identity is not of course limited to Turkey. In many Muslim countries (and in Western countries with a large Muslim diaspora) Islamist notions of the priority of the 'community of believers' over the nation enjoin Muslims to disengage from secularist or state-Islamic regimes. To some extent this reflects a globalization of a particular interpretation of Islam (amongst commentators too).[3] So a friend of mine in Istanbul has cast his crust of bread upon the tumultuous waters of Islamist activities, by translating into Turkish a book published in London by the Islamic Foundation entitled *Ummah or Nation? Identity Crisis in Contemporary Muslim Society*. The book's themes are familiar enough to Turkish readers, especially its proposal to counter Muslims' lack of unity and averred identity crisis with an overriding 'ideology of supreme loyalty' (Al-Ahsan 1992: 146).

---

3. For example in his new book *The Power of Identity* (1997) Manuel Castells entitles his brief section on Islamist movements '*Umma* versus *Jahiliya*: Islamic fundamentalism'. But Kurdish Islamism is also a part of the wider Islamic social movement. How and why, then, does Islamist discourse become for global scholarship on Islam the essential proto-type of political Islam?

Yet this unfortunate phrase is not, as we have seen, the only definition of *ümmetcilik* in Turkey. Kurdish Islamist discourse is concerned to show that on the contrary Islam does not cancel ethnic subjectivity, and that such subjectivity is not a Western innovation. Rather, the Muslim *ümmet* should be understood as catering for created ethnic difference, indeed to be predicated on it. This may or may not entail argument for or against an independent Kurdistan, but it does recognize as a minimum the equal rights of different ethnic groups to the same services (education and media in their own language, for example). If the democratization of the political structure in Turkey proves incapable of granting such rights, Kurdish Islamist discourse finds no objection in Islam, or in Islamic law, to their realization through a federation, or by autonomy, or in an independent state for Kurds. For assimilation of any kind hinders the ability of such created ethnicities to fulfil what the Koran sees as their proper duty: that of allowing the different ethnic groups to get to know each other (*Hucurat* 13). The inference here (though not always clearly drawn) is plain: ethnic difference could not have been created merely to alleviate the very problem (cross-cultural communication) engendered by its creation. At a more basic level, Allah delights in diversity, otherwise humanity would have all been created the same.

The Law of Freedom

If the political connotations of the word *ümmet* are disputed between Islamist and Kurdish Islamist discourse, so is the range of meanings dredged up by two other key terms, *şeriat* (shariah) and Islamic *kardeşlik* (fraternity). Though *şeriat* may also be commended as the long-term solution to the Kurdish problem by many Kurdish Islamists, this is not to say that the same vision is evoked in the uttering of the word. *Şeriat* for Kurdish Islamists should be seen, beside its technical meaning, as having the same meaning that 'secularism' does for Alevi Muslims: as being a refuge, and providing a legal space that gives one permission to be Kurdish. *Şeriat* as freedom then becomes the topic of discussion, Islamic law being understood as consenting to Kurdish identity. Here we see the gulf of meaning opening up between Kurdish Islamist and Islamist positions. For Islamists *şeriat* as a solution to the Kurdish problem carries with it connotations of assimilation, in which everyone throws in their ethnic hand and picks up a new non-cultural Islamic identity. For Kurdish Islamists *şeriat* acknowledges the created difference of human beings, and urges a political structure that caters for just such a difference. '*Islamiyet Kürtlere ne veriyorsa ona raziyiz*' ('Kurds will be satisfied with whatever Islam gives')

(Münis 1996: 22), says the Chair of the Mersin Immigrant Foundation: and what Islam gives is not merely the negative possibility of not being Turkish, but the positive possibility of being Kurdish too.

Likewise Islamic *kardeşlik* is a contested term. In Islamist discourse it implies the cessation of separatist claims in the name of Islamic unity (i.e. against the enemies of Islam). For Kurdish Islamism it demands the necessary (if as yet unforthcoming) support of Turkish Muslims in Kurds' struggle for God-given natural rights. *'Ne Türk, ne Kürt, biz Müslüman kardeşiz'* ('We are neither Turks nor Kurds, we are Muslim brothers'), say religious Turks. *'Biz üvey kardesler olmak istemiyoruz'* ('We do not wish to be foster brothers')[4] reply religious Kurds. That is, for Kurdish Islamism Islamic fraternity involves not merely the acceptance of, but active support for, the protection of ethnic difference, not its cancellation in some meta-Islamic identity. Presuming, then, the currency of such a principle, Altan Tan requests that his Muslim Turkish brothers and sisters take responsibility for solving the Kurdish problem. 'If you want a state for yourselves, want that for us. If you want autonomy for yourselves, want that for us. If you want law for yourselves, want that for us. If you want unity, solidarity, fraternity, if you want a unified legal state for yourselves, want that for us' (Tan 1996a: 78). *'Bu yapıldığı anda gerçek kardeşlik tahakkuk edecektir'* ('When this happens, true Islamic *kardeşlik* will be realized').

This should not be taken to mean, however, that all religious Kurds are unhappy with a politics that minimizes ethnic distinction in the name of Islamic unity and *şeriat*. Kurds too may give their assent to the position chiselled out by Islamist discourse. For many Kurds, any practice that calls *Türkcülük* (Turkism) to heel has some attractions, which is perhaps why the Refah Party traditionally polls heavily in the Kurdish areas. Yet even here a different motive may be discerned in the endeavour of those Kurds seeking to de-politicize their own Kurdishness and re-constitute themselves solely as Muslim political subjects. Islam in this case is experienced as a relief (from exposure to power) rather than, as in the elaborations of many Islamists, a remedy (for Kurdish resistance to power). With such

---

4. One of the proofs of Islamic *kardeşlik* cited by Kurdish Islamists and Islamists alike is a claim about the giving and taking of girls (*kızlar*) in intermarriage. The proof demonstrates at the same time that the problem is between the state and Kurds, not Kurds and Turks. Yet note the casual patriarchal assumption at work: Islamic brotherliness between males (as the main political actors in the public sphere) is ensured through the exchange of sisters. But who would give their sister to a foster brother?

different agendas amongst those promoting the *ümmet*, Islamic fraternity between Turkish and Kurdish Muslims is well primed to issue in disappointment.

Universalism vs the Solidarity of Muslims

This inability of Islamists to countenance, let alone desire, the possibility of autonomy for Kurds lays them open in turn to the charge of rejecting not just politics in the name of ethnicity, but ethnic diversity itself. Kurdish Islamists often cite the saying of the Prophet as a rebuke to their perceived refusal to stand in solidarity with their fellow-Muslims in reclaiming usurped rights: '*Zülme karşı susan dilsiz şeytandır*' ('He who is silent in the face of oppression is a dumb devil'). Because ethnic identity is part of the 'created order', its exposure to forced assimilation or to non-recognition should trigger the protest and resistance of Muslims, regardless of their own particular ethnicity. This would extend so far as taking the side, if justice so required, of the non-Muslim against Muslim oppression. 'Turk-Kurd, Greek-Armenian, all have been created by Allah . . . Whenever an ethnic group is persecuted, those who say "I am a Muslim" must come out against [the persecutors]' (Kavuncu 1992: 9). Kurdish Islamist discourse here stands in contrast with the more Manichaean vision of Islamism, with its focus on innocent international Muslim suffering at the hands of the West and its constant pains to define itself over against the (deficient) Western other. That is, its citing – in the name of justice for all – of Turkish Muslims for hypocrisy discourages Kurdish Islamism, at least rhetorically, from displaying the same selective moral outrage.

So the Kurdish scholar Müfid Yüksel, for example, is concerned enough to note that Kurdish has not been the only language marginalized by the dominance of the official national language: 'Syriac and Pontic Greek in particular have suffered the same fate' (1993a: 390). In fact Müfid himself, who comes from a long line of notable Kurdish religious leaders, was one of the least prejudiced people I met in Istanbul, as well as being an avid collector of the wisps of arcane knowledge that wafted like puffs of wind around the streets of historic Istanbul. He took two Muslims and myself on a walking tour of Fatih, where he translated the Ottoman inscriptions of every fountain, doorpost, mosque and tomb we passed. He preferred to call the city Constantinople in deference to its Byzantine heritage, and claimed that the Ottomans, when putting minarets on some of the churches made into mosques, merely 'circumcised the city'. He hoped for the day when Armenian [i.e. Christian] architects would once again design the *medreses* and mosques of Istanbul. Our sightseeing tour of Fatih took for ever, because the three believers egged each other on to even greater heights of religious piety in every historic mosque we visited. The shade in the dusty courtyards was pleasant enough as I waited for their mosque crawl to finish. The Refah-run Istanbul municipality employed Müfid as an adviser on relations with the city's Alevi groups, though not himself Alevi.

'What happiness to those who can say I am a Kurd'

Müfid was not the only Kurdish Islamist I met who was extremely proficient in the building-blocks – Arabic, Persian and the sacred texts – of Islamic law. A certain Mustafa Bey, whom I met at the Islamist journal *Nü Bihar* (the only journal printed solely in Kurdish in Istanbul), was also an expert in languages. I was at his home for dinner one night[5] when Mustafa Bey mentioned in passing that when he was growing up in Kurdistan he was personally acquainted with old people who had half-tongues, their punishment for speaking Kurdish. The story illuminates another cardinal difference between Kurdish Islamist and Islamist discourse: Kurdish Islamists' disinclination to obliterate the distinction between their suffering as Kurds and their suffering as Muslims, as well as that between Kurdish and Turkish Muslims. He also told me a story about the Independence Tribunal's work in Diyarbakır in the wake of the 1925 Şeyh Said rebellion. On the appearance of a young Kurd before the court the presiding judge sentenced him to death saying, 'There is no need for an examination, nothing good comes from a man who doesn't know Turkish.'

Apocryphal or otherwise, the stories well up from a reservoir of anecdotes that water the memories of many Kurds and erode Islamist attempts to gain a dominant place on the slopes of Kurdish suffering. 'If Muslim Turks get cuffed once,' says Ramazan Değer, 'Kurdish Muslims cop two' (1996: 149). Değer too tells a tale, about his time in Diyarbakır prison:

> There were six of us, lined up in a row. A soldier came and shouted 'What are you?' at my friend. Out of fear he said, *Müslümanım* ('I'm a Muslim'). Upon hearing this the poor soldier was nonplussed, as he was expecting him to say 'I'm a Kurd', so he could prove that he wasn't. The fact is, Muslims don't go to

5. That same night the local *Hoca*, employed by the *Diyanet İşleri Başkanlığı* (Directorate of Religious Affairs), popped in to ask Mustafa Bey to translate a document. It turned out to be a 250-year-old Ottoman letter obtained from somewhere, which the *Hoca* was illegally planning to sell. *Hocaların söylediğini dinle, gittiği yoldan gitme* ('Listen to what the *Hoca* says, don't do what he does') goes the Turkish saying.

jail so much. Anyway, when he shouted 'What are you?' at the next man he too said, 'I'm a Muslim.' A third friend, confronted with the same question said, 'I'm a Muslim too.' The fourth one of us noticed that the soldier's face was getting redder and angrier, and he thought to himself, 'I'll have to say something else.' *Elhamdulillah Müslümanım* ('Praise God, I'm a Muslim'), he said in panic. The soldier latched on to the clue: 'What should you others have said? You should have said, "Praise God, I'm a Muslim!"', and he started to hit us. If we'd said 'I'm a Kurd', he would have said 'You're a Kurd, are you?', and bashed us there and then (Değer 1996: 149 – my translation).

Stories of suffering, even comic ones, don't only make Kurdish listeners aware of their peculiar solidarity. They also appeal to the charity of non-Kurdish listeners, who may be open to hearing something surprising in their words, or who may attack the sufferers for making them feel uncomfortable by confronting them with their hurt. Yet to ask for tolerance from the person wronged without proper contrition on the part of the wrongdoers (whether wittingly compliant in oppressive acts or not), is to listen indifferently to their stories. Tolerance, Islamic *kardeşlik* (and in this case its practical embodiment, the *ümmet*) can only first be offered by the oppressed, not by the advantaged. Otherwise it becomes another word for forgetting. The voice of Kurdish Islamism, like a tongue revisiting the nerve of an exposed tooth, speaks out of the pain of exclusion to ensure that Muslims remember. Its stories and anecdotes reclaim the right of victims to interpret their plight in their own vernacular.

So Mehmet Pamak, for example, like many other Kurdish Muslims, reminds one-eared Islamist listeners of the double dose of oppression that Kurds have experienced at the hands of the Turkish Republic's rulers. True, he says, all Muslims in Turkey have been wronged. But Kurds have been discriminated against for being both Muslim and Kurdish. He goes on to illustrate the difference in a parable, in the expectation that fiction cuts as deep as analysis.

If there were a Kurdish Republic,
If the regime ruling the country named it Kurdey,
If Turkish were forbidden and if Turks were made to read, write and talk Kurdish (if education in Kurdish were compulsory),
If all the mountains in the Turkish regions were decorated with the slogan 'What happiness to those who say I am a Kurd',
If every morning in every school Turkish children were forced to shout, 'I am a true Kurd . . . Let me exist as a gift to Kurdish existence',
If Turks who wanted their legitimate rights were made to eat filth and were subjected to every kind of torture,

If there were no modesty, honour, security of life or property in the Turkish
areas,

If Turkish clubs and social organizations were banned, but Kurdish fraternities
were encouraged to flourish and become centres for producing administrators
and ideologues for the state,

If 'Kurdish nationalism' were guaranteed by the Constitution and idolized as
an unchangeable, unchallengeable principle of social life,

If everyone were forced to be a Kurd and the Kurdish President went on TV
and announced to the whole nation, while looking into the eyes of Turks,
that Kurdey was only for those who say 'I am a Kurd',

And worse – if Kurdish Muslims didn't perceive the level of trauma experienced
by Turks but said, 'What difference does it make? We've all been oppressed,
you haven't suffered anything special.'

I wonder what Turks, especially Muslim Turks, would feel? (Pamak 1996:
17–18 – my translation).

Steps Towards a Democratic Front

Pamak's insinuation that when Kurds insist on their legitimate rights it often
ends in their arrest and torture suggests a more sympathetic understanding
of the practice of Kurdish nationalism than that expressed by Islamist
discourse. Kurdish nationalism (and in particular its most notorious representative, the PKK) is typically reviled by Islamism as a secularizing and
atheistic movement, a movement tarred with the brush of imperialism to
split the *ümmet* and ensure the West's pride of place in the New World
Order. Kurdish Islamist discourse is of necessity more variegated on the
issue of non-Islamic resistance to the policies of the state. In this case we
come to a last distinguishing trait of Kurdish Islamism, its tendency to
advocate provisionally a 'democratic' or pluralistic solution to the Kurdish
problem over against the explicit Islamist remedy of a utopian order. The
difference is encapsulated in the impressive eclecticism of the books on
sale in the waiting-room at the Kurdish Islamist journal *Nû Bihar*: scholarly
histories of Kurdistan jostle alongside novels and collections of short stories
and poems by new Kurdish writers, while Islamic devotional materials
elbow for space amongst the writings of prominent Kurdish dissidents,
religious or otherwise. This is not comparable to the liberal Islamism
discussed in Chapter 5, whose proponents, though willing to appear on
the same panel as their laic rivals, participate in a dialogue to find grounds
for living together, re-negotiating in the process their own particular
identities. By contrast Kurdish Islamism is goaded by the common pre-
dicament of Kurds to look favourably upon a coalition of differing political
persuasions.

Altan Tan, for instance, suggests that because neither Kurds nor Muslims alone can force a new, more equal Constitution, 'whoever has a problem with the state, whether Kurds, Muslims, Alevi, conservatives or leftists, should establish a democratic front. First let us eliminate tyranny and usurpation, and then let everyone go on their way with God's blessings. Let those who want to live together, live together; let those who don't want to, not do so; let those who want to establish a religious state do that; and those who don't do something else' (1996b: 76 – my translation).

Yet under what administrative and political structure will those who choose to live together do so? 'In a system of provinces (*eyalet*), organized not on ethnic or religious foundations but on local and geographic grounds. Each province will have its own assembly that oversees it. That Parliament will represent whoever lives in that province – Christians, Copts, Gypsies, Azeri, Arabs, Turks – whoever lives there will have equal cultural rights and a government that respects the laws. I don't see as practical a federation or autonomy whose borders can only be secured by an ethnic or religious cleansing' (1996b: 74). Tan envisions a rejuvenated Ottoman Empire model based on urban centres, but without an imperial capital appointing governors to administer and tax what would accordingly be perceived as political peripheries. Here we have a suggestion for a confederation of localities, as well as a plea for an end to a politics of forced modernization. Indeed Tan appeals to Kurdish intellectuals not to repeat the seventy years of Kemalist transformation and prejudice the decision of the Kurdish people *vis-à-vis* Islam. Yet it is not clear if his critique of the project of 'repressive developmentalist regimes' (Nandy 1994: 11), whether Kemalist or Kurdish nationalist, applies to Islamic developmentalism too. Could a decentralization of sovereignty advocated in the name of Islam resist the temptation to rationalize its ideals in other spheres of civil society also?

The editorial comment on a special feature about the Kurdish problem published in the final edition of the [Kurdish] Islamist journal *Yeni Zemin* (New Foundation) is just as interesting. After casting aspersions on the *Adil bir Düzen* ('A just order') slogan of the Refah Party, the anonymous writer goes on to say:

> At the Refah Party's fourth congress Erbakan called for the giving of cultural rights (radio, TV, education) to Kurds. Less than a month later at a rally in Nevşehir, he defined the conditions under which such freedoms should be bestowed. 'If Kurds are going to teach atheism and communism through such liberties then it is not possible to say "yes". But if they are going to explain Islam then "yes" is possible', he pronounced . . . In conclusion we are compelled to say this: 'yes' must always be said to the exercise of Kurds' basic human rights. For this reason in place of *religious* [my emphasis] or ideological

perspectives the problem will be better solved in the context of fundamental human rights (*Yeni Zemin* 1994: 18 – my translation).

In explicitly rejecting a religious nostrum for the Kurdish problem, the writer voices the suspicion held by many Kurdish Islamists that an Islamist solution would reduce the crime against Kurds to a mere element in a prior conviction, as well as delaying full redress until after the final denouement and victory of Islam.

If Altan Tan wishes to address the problem through a non-ethnic federalism, and *Yeni Zemin* with a discourse of human rights, Mehmet Metiner too is an advocate for a democratic solution, arguing that there is no contradiction between Islam and democracy.[6] Indeed, even *şeriat* is a plurality:

> In *şeriat* there is no single legal system. That is, *şeriat* is the name of the partnership of many legal systems. For example, the *Alevi* law is distinct, the understanding of *Hanefi* law is distinct, as is that of *Şafii* law. The name of this totality of understandings of law is *şeriat*. *Şeriat* is itself a plurality of legal systems. Every Islamic jurist puts forward what he understands of Islam . . . There are laws dealing with action and laws dealing with principle. Sometimes these laws contradict each other, sometimes they even reject each other.
>
> [*Interviewer – Chris Houston*:] "This requires tolerance?"
>
> Of course. In fact, the Prophet says, 'It is meritorious to make an interpretation, even if wrong. But for those who perceive rightly there is even more merit.' This is a great tolerance. This keeps the gate of interpretation open (*içtihat kapısı*) . . . Secondly, democracy in my opinion (and not many people in Turkey understand this) is a means, not an end. Democracy is a political procedure, and in my opinion it is non-ideological . . . That is, it is the people's own self-management . . . In the West democracy was ushered in as an ideology with enlightenment philosophy and modernity. Democracy is intrinsically a human creation: three or five people sit in the Parliament, institute laws that contradict the revealed laws of religion, and make everyone conform to such laws. The reason why *şeriat* circles see democracy as an expression of unbelief is that democracy, along with enlightenment philosophy, was imposed like a straitjacket. Democracy was propagated as an ideology. Can anyone defend the thesis that the French Jacobins were democrats? . . . They established

---

6. Mehmet Metiner has a long history of concern to mediate some of the disputes between the different Muslim groups. General Manager for the influential but now defunct Islamist journal *Girişim* (1985–1990), Metiner has been an influential participant in the slow democratizing of the Islamist movement.

institutions to represent their own truth. And because they established such institutions they were able to attempt to shape the whole community, to modernize it. In fact whatever the church priests used to do, the new intellectuals and republicans now did in the political sphere . . . One brought an oppression in the name of revelation, the other an oppression from the side of human creation. This is not democracy . . .

The shape of democracy may be different in different places, but its principles are always the same. (1) You will submit yourself to the judgment of the ballot box . . . (2) You will agree to the individual's right to self-determination. That is, the state should not impose an ideology, a religion, denomination, or legal system. The individual chooses these. (3) Democracy is the rule of the majority. But it is also pluralistic. In fact the majority should not swallow up the minority. Democracy is the regime in which the minorities' rights and liberties are guaranteed by the Constitution . . . If these three principles are put into practice, then democracy in its different varieties exists. For this reason I see no contradiction between Islam and democracy, and I count myself a democrat (Interview – my translation).

Despite this intimate binding of Islamic *şeriat* and pluralism, Metiner still concludes that only a democratic solution (not a religious one) can resolve Turkey's ethnic problem. (Compare this with Refah Party parliamentarian Hasan Mezarcı, who argues that democracy is a concept invented by infidels, and is useless for Muslims (1993: 142)). For Metiner the steps towards a resolution are clear: first, Kurdish identity needs to be recognized; second, Kurdish identity and cultural rights need to be guaranteed by the Constitution; and thirdly, the state needs to be democratized.

Kurdish Islamism and the PKK

But does Kurdish Islamism's preference for a coalition and a democratic solution to the Kurdish problem extend even to the PKK, the largest and most active Kurdish nationalist movement? It would be wrong to assume that Kurdish Islamists are necessarily anti-PKK because of its avowed anti-religiosity (though as the organization's 1991 pamphlet on religion shows, there seems to have been a strategic change in the rhetoric of the PKK leadership towards Islam). But on the other hand some Kurdish Islamists are, naturally enough, perturbed by the secular nature of the PKK's political programme. Positions among Kurdish Islamists range from cooperation (all those with a problem with the state should open a common front, and after realizing the common aims should pursue their own political preferences) through pragmatism (if the state finishes off the PKK something else will arise in its place, because the problem is created by the state), to downright hostility (the PKK and the Kurdish secular elite want to sever the Kurdish people from Islam and set up an atheistic state). Though this last position may be thought favourable for the military's campaign against the PKK (and there have been many rumours that in the Kurdish areas of Turkey *Hizbullah* was initially supported by the state), anti-PKK Kurdish Muslims are no less backward in defending their ethnic specificity. The dispute here with secular Kurds is over the characteristics of Kurdishness, not its existence.

Perhaps the highest Kurdish Islamist praise of the PKK that I encountered was by the writer Faysal Mahmutoğlu (even though at the end of the article he hopes that his envisioned democratic society would be established by Muslims).[7] Mahmutoğlu divides the problems faced by Kurds into two broad categories: first there are those produced by the Turkish state, the most serious being its determination to assimilate the Kurds. Second are those that originate within the internal organizational structures of the Kurds themselves, most importantly the 'feudal relations left over from the Middle Ages' (1993: 416). The popularity of the PKK with Kurds arises from its active anti-landlordism. 'I can give a hundred examples,' says Mahmutoğlu 'to show that the PKK is the only representative of the Kurds. Someone abandons their village and migrates to Istanbul and the western provinces because of landlord or mullah exploitation, and their children join the ranks of the PKK . . . Someone is killed in a fit of jealousy by a landlord because he gave a feast for his neighbours, and his children join the PKK . . . Or someone is driven from his village by the landlord's men for not voting the way the landlord had wanted, and the children of the people that stay behind join the PKK' (1993: 416–17).

Mahmutoğlu appreciates the PKK for both its struggle against Turkish state oppression and [corrupt] landlords or [manipulative] religious mullahs, the traditional elites of Kurdistan. Self-criticism here is made with the intention of reinstating a true Islam, of reforming the corrupt practices of those using religion for their own ends. But such self-criticism can also be interpreted as a moment in a modernizing nationalist narrative, as rational self-examination and social reform cleanse Kurdish life of those backward or repressive cultural characteristics perceived as obstructing the realization of nationhood. Kurdish tribalism, for instance, is often portrayed as impeding Kurdish unity; anti-tribalism therefore becomes a defining

7. Though one of the leading figures of the Kurdish Islamist journal *Cudi*, published in Germany, told me privately that they sometimes cooperated with the PKK's political wing in Europe.

article in the modernizing agenda of the PKK. In practice, of course, the manipulation of the fictive (imagined) kinships constructed by tribal power may be useful in the nitty-gritty of political struggle.[8]

Most other Kurdish Islamist writers prefer to focus on the state's role in denying Kurdish identity and are less concerned to critique the dominant social relations of Kurdish society. Indeed, many would be downright hostile to the claims of secular Kurds that Islam itself is responsible for Kurdistan's backwardness. Despite concerns, however, that the PKK propagates such attitudes, a significant number of Kurdish Islamists analyse the organization as representing an understandable reaction to the policies of the Turkish Republic. The solution is not found in defeating the PKK militarily but in drawing out the poison that inflames it. Compare this with the claim by the Islamist and Turkish *Nurcu,* Hekimoğlu Ismail, that 'the PKK is the work of international states . . . there is no Kurdish problem, just the problem of the PKK . . . because our people are one. They are fellow believers and brothers' (1993: 137).

Muhammed Çağrı recounts a story told him by a young Muslim from a village. 'The soldiers tied a young Kurdish guerrilla to the back of a jeep and dragged him through the village square. On the same day five or six youths from that village went to the mountains' (1993: 80). Atasoy Muftuoğlu thinks that the spite and enmity engendered by repression naturally manifests itself in violence. 'Kurds in Turkey now have an opportunity to act. The main reason for the birth of the Kurdish resistance is Turkish chauvinism' (1993: 207). Ibrahim Kaya too admits the PKK has the support of many Kurds: 'Because the PKK has given in equal measure an answer to the oppression and tyranny directed at Kurdish identity, the people have in one way appropriated this movement and have on an individual level become less Muslim. Indeed whether we like it or not, if not consciously then perhaps unconsciously they are becoming secular' (1993: 148).

These are not isolated remarks, but reveal a constitutive ambivalence within Kurdish Islamist discourse. The grudging admittance that the PKK, unlike Muslims in Turkey or the rest of the Islamic world, have at least defended the rights of Kurds makes it difficult for many Kurdish Islamists to condemn the organization out of hand. Walking around the south-eastern

---

8. Whether such patron–client relations can survive the urbanization of Kurds, and how they are remade or renegotiated in the context of city living is a complicated question in itself. Some might see the struggle to influence the Kurdish nationalist movement as a contest between feudal and bourgeois authority, between a religious and tribal elite employing a discourse of traditional rights and one using more modernist terms.

city of Antep once with the brother of an Istanbul friend, I was surprised to hear him speak Kurdish to a passer-by. His *ağabey*, a state-employed *Hoca* in Üsküdar, had never mentioned he was Kurdish. 'Oh yes,' said the younger brother, himself very religious, 'our *Hoca* brother has become Turkish.' When I asked him about the PKK he said, 'The PKK had a job to do and they did it. Now no one can deny the existence and the cultural rights of Kurds. But it is time for them to change or bow out, and let other solutions come to the fore.'

Even those Kurdish Islamists who dislike intensely both the PKK's Marxist flavour and its attack on their social and economic power are particular in the logic of their criticism. So in an interview I had with a notable but blind Kurdish mullah who had been forced to migrate from Kurdistan to Istanbul only that year (where he had established a *mescid/ medrese* in the basement of the apartment in which the interview occurred), the PKK was judged not for stressing *Kürtçülük* (as in Islamist discourse) but for being anti-Islamic: 'No one can call the Kurds racist, because the Kurds are not in power and are not able to oppress another ethnic group . . . Thus even those who defend the dispossessed have some right on their side . . . But the PKK will deliver the people from one tyranny and bestow on them another.'

Indeed, it is on the issue of the PKK that the discursive package of Kurdish Islamism most clearly shows the fraying string, the peeling sticky-tape that papers over the differences within. If state aggravation of Kurds eases sufficiently to allow Kurdish representation *qua* Kurdish in the political system, one wonders whether fragmentation of Kurdish nationalism on other lines (Alevism, liberalism, Islamism) wouldn't also occur. But as the military seem disinclined to permit a genuine democratization in the near future at least, the internal tensions between Kurdish Islamist groups are held in equilibrium as they defend Kurdish identity (or are at least prevented from spilling over into the formation of close partnerships with non-Kurdish associations of like mind) by the greater force of outside pressures, discouraging such a development.

Conclusion

The mix of interpretations and ideals bundled up in the discourse of Kurdish Islamism is distinguishable from both statist Islamist and Islamist discursive practices on the following grounds. Firstly, Kurdish Islamist discourse waters down Islamism's strong critique of nationalism *per se* by both defending the created nature of ethnic groups, and by making a distinction (in the context of Turkish modernity) between dominant and subaltern claims. Secondly, Kurdish Islamism questions the way the imagined community of believers (the *ümmet*) becomes in Islamist discourse a practising of *ümmetcilik* that seeks not the cooperation and mutual care of its various ethnic parts but their subordination to a 'higher identity' (*üst kimlik*). Likewise *Islam kardeşlik* (Islamic brotherliness) is interpreted by Kurdish Islamists as involving the sacrificial aid of Muslims (of whatever *kavim*) to reclaim the usurped rights of (in this case) Kurds. Yet if non-Muslim minorities are excluded by the production of the nation, Kurdish Islamism calls for solidarity with them as well. In the same way *şeriat* too is a contested term: is it a law of freedom or a legal suppression of cultural particularity? Thirdly, Kurdish Islamists refuse to reduce their oppression as Kurds merely to the level of being despised as Muslims, and hence are sceptical of a general (and utopian) religious solution to their peculiar injury. Thus the history of Kurdish suffering is not felt to be reducible simply to Muslim disestablishment by the state's civilizing drive. Fourthly, in keeping with such an analysis Kurdish Islamists are willing to consider the benefits of a democratic coalition in order to force a resolution of the Kurdish problem. Further, the local autonomy desired by Kurdish Islamists does not in principle rule out the establishment of a Kurdish state that would ensure the right of Kurds to speak their own language, educate their children in Kurdish and direct their own affairs, even if a confederation of local parliaments is posited as the preferred Islamic political structure. Fifthly and finally, this willingness to engage in a democratic front leads Kurdish Islamists to consider less polemically than Islamists the role of the secular Kurdish nationalist movement and its vanguard the PKK, though it opens up cracks between those more or less sympathetic to its struggle.

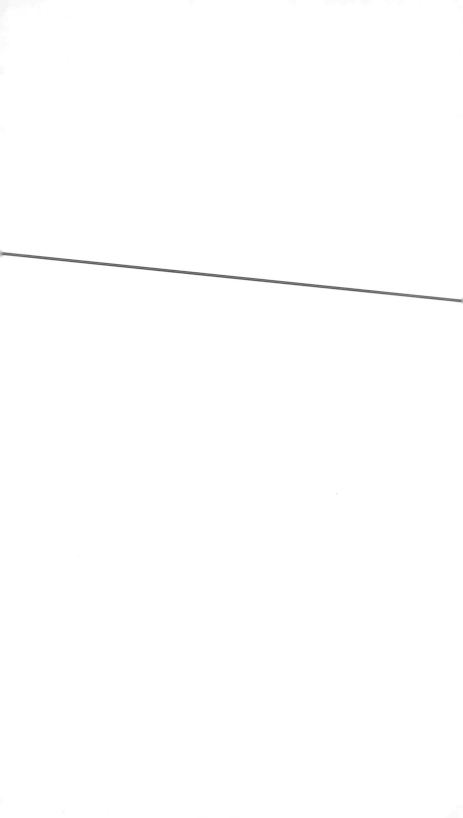

−13−

Conclusion: Islamist Politics and the Superseding of Ethnicity

I want to bring Part III to a close by briefly considering the political import of the plurality of Islamist responses to the Kurdish question. As we may remember, the positions of the myriad Islamist groups and associations can be usefully if provisionally grouped into three competing discursive packages, namely statist Islamist, Islamist, and Kurdish Islamist. Statist Islamism, to jog our memory, is exemplified by the organization headed by Fethullah Gülen, and inspired by the parsimonious realization that if there were no Kurds there would be no Kurdish problem. Accordingly the solution to the problem in the south-east lies in encouraging Kurds to change their self-perception. This is because *şuurlu* (self-aware) Kurds, religious or secular, threaten not only the momentum of Fethullah Hodja's Islamic politics but contradict by their very presence those claims privileging the special genius and duty of Turkish Muslims.

Islamist discourse, on the other hand, accepts the created status of ethnic difference but is concerned to rein in the political ramifications of such acknowledgement by subordinating Kurdish identity to an Islamic one. In Islamist calculations ethnic political subjectivity derives from a nationalistic self-love alien to the sources of esteem in an Islamic polity. The suffering of Kurdish Muslims at the hands of the Turkish state is evidence, then, of extraneous influences on the Muslim *ümmet*, while being barred from constituting the ground for any political resistance. Only an Islamic order can provide a permanent cure to the problem.

By contrast, in the historical context of the state's continual drive to produce a Turkish citizenry worthy of its beneficence, Kurdish Islamism defends the religious legitimacy of political struggle on the basis of Kurdish particularity. Islam is interpreted as licensing the collective right to linguistic self-expression of every *kavim*, Muslim or otherwise. Indeed, such rights are presented as existing prior to any particular religious commitment and the political demands stemming from such commitment. One can choose to be a Muslim, but not to be a Kurd. Consequently the Kurdish subject and the Muslim subject are not perceived by Kurdish Islamists to be in perpetual secret competition, unlike the rivalry between secular Kurdish identity and the broader Islamist movement.

What does this Islamist clash of interpretations reveal? Firstly, the dispute seems to inhere in the Islamist movement's situating itself as primarily in opposition to the enforced civilizing project of the Republic. Here Islamist political consciousness is spurred to action by the modernization of the heart of the Ottoman Empire undertaken in the name of the universality of Western civilization. Accordingly, in the cultural struggle between secular and Islamist forces, the mobilizing of the Islamist movement is threatened by the revival of other political identities similarly repressed by the modernizing ideology of the Republic's reformist elites. This includes in particular Kurdish subjectivity, long a target of assimilation in the name of the universality of the Turkish nation.

In this case the 'plague on both houses' pronounced by Islamist discourse upon the nationalism of both statist Islamism and Kurdish Islamism amounts to a remarkably indiscriminate imprecation. It refuses to differentiate between the modern nation-state's construction of a uniform national Turkish identity, and the response of Kurds to the resultant denial of their existence. In so doing it disregards the Turkish state's winning of sovereignty through its construction of ethnic Turks as national subjects. Instead, it pursues its challenge to the Republic's legitimacy by seeking to break the link claimed between Western civility and modernity.

Resistant, then, to the pristine secularism of the public domain established by the Republic and its own consequent exclusion from it, Islamist discourse turns a blind eye to the similar exclusion of non-sovereign ethnicities from the public sphere. This because the regime's constitution of ethnic identity is only of secondary interest to the Islamist critique. Indeed, in pointed contrast to Kurdish Islamism, Islamist discourse is proud to be adjective-free and ethnically unmarked. Yet ironically Turkish subscribers to Islamism's hostility against all and any ethnic political subjectivity have been pampered by the privileging of Turkish ethnicity in the public sphere. When, for example, has Islamism ever been known to call for a simultaneous dismantling of ethnic Turkish advantage (i.e. education in Turkish) as prerequisite to a new Islamist social contract? Hence Kurdish Muslims' standing suspicion that, in its indifference, the Islamist movement is also stained with the conceit of Turkish nationalism.

In short, Muslims have a diseased intellect – at least according to Islamists writing about the movement's response to the Kurdish problem. For Islamist discourse, the compromised stance of Muslims reflects the continuing influence of non-Islamic political philosophies on the religious

Conclusion: Islamist Politics and the Superseding of Ethnicity

community. The solution in brief is to be more Islamic, to revert whole-heartedly to a purity once corrupted but ultimately retrievable, despite infection from outside.

Yet reflection on Kurdish objections to Islamist neutrality would suggest that the cause of such indifference is quite the opposite: the movement is too Islamist, doomed by its prejudicial even-handedness to disunity. Perhaps the problem resides in the very making of an Islamist movement. At the same time this strong recommendation of Kurdish Islamists – be less Islamist when approaching the Kurdish problem – should not be seen as applying to Turks and Kurds equally. This because the political and historical context in which Turkish and Kurdish Islamisms are rooted (and thus Turkish and Kurdish nationalisms) is not the same. Ironically then, given its marginalization by the 'universalist racism' of the Republic's 'triumphant modernity' (Wieviorka 1993: 53), Islamism is tempted to pursue a reductionist destruction of Kurdish specificity in the name of its universality (to adapt a phrase from Göle 1985). Protagonists need to be wary of a prescriptive anti-nationalism (and laicists of a similar prescriptive anti-Islamism) that fails to distinguish between dominant and subaltern claims. This may mean that in the present context a Kurdish–Islamic synthesis (as a civil movement) should be separated conceptually from the Turkish–Islamic synthesis (with its etatist tendencies).

With this recommendation in mind, we may at last hazard an answer to the two questions raised by Sakallıoğlu (page 141). She concludes her discussion on the TOBB report by wondering whether Islam 'provides a unity between Kurdish and Turkish people that supersedes ethnicity and other particularisms?' Or alternatively, does it 'sharpen nationalist consciousness by putting its weight behind the formation of a Kurdish identity?' (1996: 18).

To take the second question first, I think it incontrovertible that Kurdish Islamism is a discourse on Kurdish identity.[1] In the context of state assimilationist policies towards Kurds, Islam is interpreted as a protector of ethnic

1. Kurdish identity should be seen as subject to many different constraints in the contrasting contexts of rural and urban environments. Yet in the village, too, a politics of ethnic identity is articulated. While doing her fieldwork in the Kurdish province of Hakkari, Yalçın-Heckmann recounts a story told her by villagers:

All the nations of the world were present at the Prophet Muhammad's court, and he was hearing the requests of each group. The Arabs approached him in the most respectful terms, saying 'ya Rasulullah, ya Rahmetullah, what can we do to be in your service'? and the prophet presented them with the Holy Land and all the oil. The Turks were next to approach the Prophet, and they too addressed him with reverence and due respect, 'ya Muhammad, ya Peyghamber, what can we do for your service?' and they were given their own country, Anatolia. The Kurds addressed the Prophet in their typical familiar

difference, not its terminator. Consequently Kurdish Islamists do not see a conflict between Islam as a universalizing principle on the one hand, and Kurdish identity as a particularistic one on the other. However, some oppose Islam to the PKK. Their disagreement with secular Kurdish nationalism is not over the existence of Kurdishness *per se* but over the place of Islam in defining it. Similarly, Şeyh Faruk *agabey*'s dispute with Kurdish Islamism (see Part II) is not over any vacillation on its part in advocating Kurdish identity, but originates from his differing strategies for attaining Kurdish rights.

Does Kurdish Islamism's defence of Kurdish identity translate into support for a *Kurdistan*, into partisanship for a Kurdish nation-state, Islamist or otherwise? Not generally, I would think, though in the programme of the Kurdish Islamist group gathered around the journal *Cudi* an independent Islamic Kurdistan is called for. (Interestingly, even the PKK is not explicitly seeking a Kurdish state, but is talking federation or local autonomy.) In the main, a Kurdish state is only instrumentally valued: if recognition of Kurdish ethnic difference can be assured within some other political structure Kurdish Muslims carry no torch for a formal state. On the other hand, many would see no contradiction between Islam and an institutionalization of cultural and political autonomy for Kurds, which may entail in all but name some functional equivalent of an independent legislature.

In sum, Kurdish Islamism is a discourse on Kurdish identity protesting against both the aggressive Turkish nationalism of the state and the unbrotherly lack of interest of the secularist elites' *bête noire*, the Islamist movement. But it is not primarily a culturalist discourse stressing the unique characteristics of Kurdish Islam. Indeed, besides insisting on the existence of the Kurds, Kurdish Muslims' aims are relatively modest: to win permission not to be Turkish, or Turkish-Muslim. True, the desire of

---

way, and said, '*halo Muhammad, ci dikey, cowani?*' which means 'hallo, Uncle Muhammad, how are you these days?' The Prophet was angry at their impudence and threw the Kurds out of his court saying, 'I don't care where you go, you don't have any country!' (1991: 114).

The story itself may attribute Kurdish misfortune to their own political *naïveté*, but it takes for granted both the separate existence and different religious/cultural practices of the various nations within the Islamic *ümmet*. If the joke at their own expense reveals, as Yalçın-Heckmann comments, the security of the villagers in their own ethnic identity, it also reveals their confidence in their Muslim identity. And it marks out an intimate bond between them: Muslim Kurds are constituted by their religious laxity.

Kurds to be recognized as non-Turks necessitates some explication of their ethnic difference. But beyond a moral demand for such a recognition (and the accompanying pledge about the right to foster their linguistic heritage, including education and media in Kurdish), Kurdish Islamism is generally uninterested in spelling out any positive cultural content to Kurdish identity. With secular Kurdish nationalism, its rival and partner in crime, it shares a common obsession: a driving need not so much to define itself (apart from being Muslim) but to say who it is not. This is, as Vali says, a politics characteristic of the targets of ethnic assimilation (1996: 50).

To return explicitly to Sakallıoğlu's question, it is clear that Kurdish Islamism does 'sharpen nationalist consciousness'. But whether this leads to a desire for an independent Kurdish nation-state is another matter. Indeed, the ambivalence of Kurdish Islamists towards the process of secular nation-building may even act to check separatist impulses. Since the act of state formation is only one expression of ethnic subjectivity, Kurdish Islamism's reticence here is no clinching sign that it is any less committed to a defence of Kurdish rights.

With these thoughts in mind, let us now turn to Sakallıoğlu's first query, about whether Islam can unite both religious Turks and Kurds in a common discourse that 'supersedes ethnicity and other particularisms'. As we have seen, Kurdish Islamists do not look favourably upon statist Islamists adumbrating their theory of Turkish Muslims as the chosen people, nor upon Islamist homogenization of the history of Turkish and Kurdish Muslims in reply. Consequently, a unification of Turks and Kurds under the green banner of Islam depends fundamentally upon the pluralization of the *raison d'être* for the Islamist movement's struggle. Such concord is possible only if the movement organizing in the name of Islam can widen its horizons to practise some form of compensatory discrimination for Kurds as a just retort to the unjust effacement of Kurdish identity. Put glibly the Islamist movement, like a green-caped, fez-donning Islamic super-hero, needs to fight to redress injustice first, not the wrongs of Muslims. (But as justice might be labelled a 'hypergood' for Islamic social theory anyway,[2] this re-ordering does not need to be seen as a concession to non-Islamic values.)

2. The term is Charles Taylor's. Hypergoods are 'goods which are innumerably more important than others, but provide the standpoint from which these must be weighed, judged, decided about' (1989: 63).

What is it then that prevents this opening up of a second front, this pluralizing of the Islamist movement's struggle? The answer lies, one suspects, in Islamism's attempt to create a *purified* political subject, a *new creation* cut free from both the superstitious 'folk beliefs' of traditional Islam, and the compromising encumbrances of any particular ethnic background. Here Islamist autonomy is won through a self-extinguishing creative act, a callousness towards one's old identity, and a wilful embracing of a new identity that brooks no rival loyalties. But it does not take much perspicuity to detect a whiff of the modern in this liberating of the Islamist self. Indeed the archetypal expression of such a creative but self-destroying act is of course the suicide bomber, who like Nietzsche's ideal philosopher becomes in himself 'a terrible explosive, endangering everything' (Nietzsche 1989: 281). To be sure, Turkey's Islamist movement has not yet produced such a self-squandering prodigy. Yet there is something of this willed 'self-execution' in the claim of Nihat Nasır that

> apart from my Islamic identity I do not in the slightest degree find as a pretext for praise or pride any value in being a Turk or a Kurd, a Laz, an Arab, a Circassian, Cossack or indeed any ethnicity, and I openly deride and condemn anyone who does. Even if I have to stand alone, I announce that I give no importance to anything except being a Muslim (*Yeni Şafak*, 17 November 1996).

The writer's rejection of his embeddedness in his own particular context, the fantasy of his self-projection as a singular subject detached from history or culture is palpable here. True, his autonomy as a singular subject easily slides over into a collective one, the autonomy of the Islamist movement purging itself from ethnic contaminants. But the effect is the same: creative self-extinguishment issues in the autonomy of a new communal-particular subject, which cannot abide any plurality in its professed unity.

This new Islamic identity, relieved of any retarding social baggage, is freed to create itself according to its own imagined history and tradition. But to do so, it needs to specify who and what it is not. Accordingly Islamist identity (1) defines itself in a reverse occidentalism against a Western 'other', and then on the presumption of its own homogeneity; (2) struggles to ensure that its possible stress points – other ethnic identities, gender struggles, class fractures – are not allowed space to assert their own separate demands; and in turn (3) denies corporate groups within the *ümmet* the right to participate in 'ethnic' politics; while (4) itself engaging in, and even being constituted by, the pursuit of such politics.

Can Islam then, to reiterate Sakallıoğlu's question, unite both religious Turks and Kurds in a common discourse that 'supersedes ethnicity'? To the extent that Kurdish Muslims accede to such a position, obviously it can. But the dissenting voice of Kurdish Islamism proves that many Kurds are not enamoured with the terms of an Islamic-brokered peace deal. For finally, Islamism in Turkey, as an identity discourse in its own right, cannot supersede but can only offer as a competing practice its own Islamic ethnicity. *Biz Kürt milliyetci, Türk milliyetci değiliz, biz Islam milliyetciyiz* ('We are not Kurdish or Turkish nationalists, we are Islamic nationalists'), declares Islamism.

As long as that is the best that Islamism can offer, many Kurdish Muslims will remain on a war footing.

Epilogue

Despairing of cajoling Ahmet *ağabey* into forsaking Kuzguncuk to do the five-minute walk to Fetih Paşa Korusu, I give up and conduct an interview in the quiet of the *Sek Süt* (Milk Industry Association) shop. We sit behind the packaged cheeses and creamy yogurts. My tape recorder refuses to turn, so I grab the pencil used to add up purchases, and scribble down his answers on a newsprint bag, folded origami-style for carrying eggs. I ask Ahmet *ağabey* about the Kurdish question. 'Only a Muslim,' he says, 'can write an objective history of the Kurdish problem. Because only a Muslim can be a non-ethnic partisan.'

The interview finishes and we blink out into the sunlight. Vassili comes around the corner trailing his deaf and doleful mother. Kissing and shaking hands, we pull up stools and drink tea at the taxi rank. Ahmet *ağabey* and Vassili get out their respective sacred texts and begin comparing verses. Vassili is searching for a reason for the existence of suffering.

I lose the thread of it and gaze across the road at the red Turkish flag pinned up in a bank window. How benign it looks, sitting there quiet each day, its once white crescent now greying like a favourite uncle's moustache. I think of the pastries on sale at Fetih Paşa Korusu and marvel at its openness, its willingness to champion the practices of both Muslims and laicists at the same time. I wonder too at the Islamist movement's reluctance to extend the same liberty to Kurdish Muslims, at its imperious demands that they be either ethnic or Islamist. I speculate idly whether Kurdish Muslims themselves offer a way beyond the project of rival Turkish and Kurdish nation-state building, whether their reluctant nationalism might indeed incorporate both local autonomy and trans-local solidarity.

A teaspoon tinkles. I am recalled from my reverie. Vassili's mother stares blankly down the street, at the gap between two buildings where the glitter of the Bosphorus sparks up at the eye. Vassili's and Ahmet *ağabey*'s fingers jab down on proof-texts upholding their claims. Neither one disposed to give ground. Perhaps they might arrive at some provisional relief to the great questions troubling Vassili's soul?

The waiting taxis roll forward along the kerb upon the departure of the front cab. Yakob *amca* walks slowly out of the synagogue beside the taxi rank sign. He murmurs the Torah faithfully every morning, himself his own congregation. The mosque next to the church next to the synagogue.

I ponder whether political Islam might likewise be able to come to terms with its own internal plurality.

References

Abu-Lughod, J. (1980) *Rabat: Urban Apartheid in Morocco*. Princeton, NJ, Princeton University Press.

Açar, F. (1991) 'Women in the Ideology of Islamic Revivalism in Turkey: Three Islamic Women's Journals', in R. Tapper (ed.) *Islam in Modern Turkey*. London, I. B. Tauris.

Akin, M. (1993) in *Kürt Sorunu Forumu*. Ankara, Sor Yayincilik.

Akşit, B., Mutlu, K., Nalbantoğlu, H., Akçay, A., and Şen, M. (1996) 'Population Movements in Southeastern Turkey: Some Findings of an Empirical Research in 1993', *New Perspectives On Turkey* 14, Spring.

Aksoy, A. and Robins, K. (1994) 'Istanbul Between Civilization and Discontent', *New Perspectives On Turkey* 10, Spring.

Al-Ahsan, A. (1992) *Ummah or Nation; Identity Crises in Contemporary Muslim Society*. Leicester, The Islam Foundation.

Al-Azmeh, A. (1993) *Islams and Modernities*. London, Verso.

Amnesty International (1996) *Turkey: No Security Without Human Rights*. London, Amnesty International Publications.

Appadurai, A. (1993) 'Patriotism and its Futures', *Public Culture* 5, 3, Spring.

Appadurai, A. (1995) 'The Production of Locality', in R. Fardon (ed.) *Counterworks: Managing the Diversity of Knowledge*. London, Routledge.

Arnason, J. (1989) 'The Imaginary Constitution of Modernity', *Revue Européenne des Sciences Sociales*, Genevas, Droz, Autumn.

Asad, T. (1986) 'The Concept of Cultural Translation', in J. Clifford and G. Marcus (eds) *Writing Culture*. Berkeley, CA, University of California Press.

Aslan, A. (1996) in *Kürt Sorunu Nasil Çözülür?* Istanbul, Nübihar.

Atatürk, M. (1989) *Atatürk'ün Söylev ve Demeçleri 11*. Ankara, Atatürk Araştirma Merkezi.

Ayata, S. (1996) 'Patronage, Party, and State: The Politicization of Islam in Turkey', *Middle East Journal* 50, 1, Winter.

Barkey, C. (1990) *The State and the Industrialization Crises in Turkey*. Boulder, CO, Westview Press.

Bauman, Z. (1985) 'On the Origins of Civilization: A Historical Note', *Theory, Culture, and Society* 2, 3.

References

Baykan, A. (1993) 'Islam as an Identity Discourse', *Arena Journal* 1.

Beilharz, P. (1996) 'Citizens of Cities', *Thesis Eleven* 46, August.

Bektaş, C. (1996a) *Hösgörünün Öteki Adi: Kuzguncuk*. Istanbul, Tasarim Yayin Grubu.

Bektaş, C. (1996b) *Ev Alma, Komşu Al*. Istanbul, Tasarim Yayin Grubu.

Bora, T. (1995) 'Turkish National Identity, Turkish Nationalism and the Balkan Problem', in G. Özdoğan and K. Saybaşli (eds) *Balkans: A Mirror of the New International Order*. Istanbul, Eren Yayincilik.

Boratav, T., Türel, O., and Yeldan, E. (1994) 'Distributional Dynamics in Turkey under "Structural Adjustment" of the 1980s', *New Perspectives On Turkey* 11, Fall.

Borneman, J. (1992) *Belonging in the Two Berlins*. Cambridge, Cambridge University Press.

Bourdieu, P. (1990) *The Logic of Practice*. Cambridge, Polity Press.

Bozarslan, H. (1996) 'Political Crisis and the Kurdish Issue in Turkey', in R. Olson (ed.) *The Kurdish Nationalist Movement in the 90's*. Kentucky, University of Kentucky.

Bozdoğan, S. (1994) 'Architecture, Modernism and Nation-Building in Kemalist Turkey', *New Perspectives On Turkey* 10, Spring.

Bulaç, A. (1992) in *Kürd Soruşturmasi*. Ankara, Sor Yayincilik.

Bulaç, A. (1996) in *Kürt Sorunu Nasil Çözülür?* Istanbul, Nübihar.

Bulut, F. (1992) *Türk Basininda Kürtler*. Istanbul, Melsa Yayinlar.

Butler, J. (1990) *Gender Trouble, Feminism and the Subversion of Identity*. London, Routledge.

Çagri, M. (1993) in *Kürt Sorunu Forumu*. Ankara, Sor Yayincilik.

Çakir, R. (1990) *Ayet ve Slogan. Türkiye'de Islami Oluşumlar*. Istanbul, Metis.

Çakir, R. (1994) *Ne Seriat, Ne Demokrasi, Refah Partisini Anlamak*. Istanbul, Metis.

Calvino, I. (1974) *Invisible Cities*. Orlando, FL, Harcourt Brace and Company.

Çamran, M. (1996) *Kürdistan Hainleri*. Istanbul, Evrensel Yayincilik.

Canclini, N. (1995) *Hybrid Cultures: Strategies for Entering and Leaving Modernity*. Minneapolis, University of Minnesota Press.

Castells, M. (1997) *The Power of Identity*. Oxford, Blackwell.

Castoriadis, C. (1997a) *World in Fragments*. Stanford, CA, Stanford University Press.

Castoriadis, C. (1997b) 'Anthropology, Philosophy, Politics', *Thesis Eleven* 49, May.

Çayir, K. (1997) 'Islamci bir Sosyoloğun Hal-I Pürmelali', *Yeni Şafak* 15, Eylül.

Çelik, Z. (1986) *The Re-making of Istanbul: Portrait of an Ottoman City in the Nineteenth Century*. Seattle, WA, University of Washington Press.

References

Çelik, Z. (1991) 'Le Corbusier, Orientalism, Colonialism', *Assemblage* 17.

Chatterjee, P. (1986) *Nationalist Thought and the Colonial World: A Derivative Discourse?* London, Zed Books.

Çinar, A. (1997) 'Refah Party and the City Administration of Istanbul: Liberal Islam, Localism and Hybridity', *New Perspectives On Turkey* 16, Spring.

Clifford, J. (1994) 'Diasporas', *Cultural Anthropology* 9, 3.

Copeaux, E. (1996) 'Hizmet: A Keyword in the Turkish Historical Narrative', *New Perspectives On Turkey* 14, Spring.

Deger, R. (1996) in *Kürt Sorunu Nasil Çözülür?* Istanbul, Nübihar.

Deringil, S. (1996) 'The Ottoman Twilight Zone of the Middle East', in H. Barkey (ed.) *Reluctant Neighbor: Turkey's Role in the Middle East.* Washington DC, US Institute of Peace.

Diken, B. (1997) *Strangers, Ambivalence and Social Theory.* Copenhagen, Danish Social Science Research Council.

Dilipak, A. (1992) in *Kürd Soruşturmasi.* Ankara, Sor Yayincilik.

Duben, A. and Bahar, C. (1991) *Istanbul Households: Marriage, Family and Fertility, 1880–1940*, Cambridge, Cambridge University Press.

Düzdağ, M. (1995) *Müslüman Aile.* Istanbul, Iz Yayincilik.

Eickelman, D. (2000) 'Islam and the Languages of Modernity', *Daedalus* 129, Winter.

Ekim (1995) *Siyasal ve Örgütsel Değerlendirmeler.* Istanbul, Eksen Yayincilik.

Elgursi, A. (1993) in *Kürt Sorunu Forumu.* Ankara, Sor Yayincilik.

Firat, A. (1996) *Firat Mahzun Akar.* Istanbul, Avesta Yayinlari.

Göle, N. (1985) 'Women of the Mediterranean; A Shared Destiny', *Unesco Courier* 4, April.

Göle, N. (1994) 'Islami Dokunulmazlar, Laikler ve Radikal Demokratlar', *Türkiye Günlüğü* 27, Mart-Nisan.

Göle, N. (1996) 'Authoritarian Secularism and Islamist Politics: The Case of Turkey', in A. Norton (ed.) *Civil Society in the Middle East.* Leiden, E. J. Brill.

Günlük-Şenesen, G. (1995) 'Some Economic Aspects of Turkish Armaments Spending', *New Perspectives On Turkey* 13, Fall.

Gürbey, G. (1996) 'The Development of the Kurdish Nationalist Movement in Turkey Since the 1980s', in R. Olson (ed.) *The Kurdish Nationalist Movement in the 1990's.* Kentucky, University Press of Kentucky.

Hakimcioglu, I. (1992) *Bir Müslüman Nedir?* Istanbul, Yeni Asya.

Hann, C. (1990) *Tea and the Domestication of the Turkish State.* Huntington, WV, Eothen Press.

Haşimi, H. (1993) in *Kürt Sorunu Forumu.* Ankara, Sor Yayincilik.

References

Holston, J. (1989) *The Modernist City: an Anthropological Critique of Brasilia*. Chicago, University of Chicago Press.

Honneth, A. (1995) *The Struggle for Recognition*. Cambridge, Polity Press.

Houston, C. (1994) *The Very Beautiful Democratic Novel*. (Unpublished Manuscript).

Houston, C. (1997) 'Islamic Solutions to the Kurdish Problem: Late Rendezvous or Illegitimate Shortcut', *New Perspectives on Turkey* 16, Spring.

Houston, C. (1998) 'Alternative Modernities: Islamism and Secularism on Charles Taylor', *Critique of Anthropology* 18, 2, June.

Human Rights Watch Project (1995) *Savaş and Insan: Türkiye'ye Silah Transferleri ve Savaş Yasalari Ihlalleri*. Istanbul, Belge Yayinlari.

Iktibas (1992) 'Kürt Sorunu ve Türkiye Islami Hareketi', *Hak Söz* 13, Nisan.

Inciroglu, E. (1994) 'Negotiating Ethnographic Reality: Team Fieldwork in Turkey', in C. Hann (ed.) *When History Accelerates: Essays on Rapid Social Change, Complexity and Creativity*. London, Athlone Press.

Ireland, R. (1994) 'Brazil and a Sociology for Hope', *Thesis Eleven* 38.

Işçi Partisi (1992) *Dine Devrimci Yaklasim Mi Kürt-Islam Sentezi Mi?* Istanbul, Varyos Yayinlari.

Işik, I. (1993) in *Kürt Sorunu Forumu*. Ankara, Sor Yayincilik.

Ismail, H. (1993) in *Kürt Sorunu Forumu*. Ankara, Sor Yayincilik.

Kadioğlu, A. (1994) 'Women's Subordination in Turkey: Is Islam Really the Villain?', *Middle East Journal*, 48, 4, Autumn.

Kadioğlu, A. (1996) 'The Paradox of Turkish Nationalism and the Construction of Official Identity', *Middle Eastern Studies*, 32, 2, April.

Kahn, J. (1995) *Culture, Multiculture, Postculture*. London, Sage Publications.

Kahn, J. (1997) 'Revitalization of Discourses of Race in Australian Politics', Unpublished Paper at La Trobe University.

Kandiyoti, D. (1997) 'Gendering the Modern' in S. Bozdoğan and R. Kasaba (eds) *Rethinking Modernity and National Identity in Turkey*. Seattle, WA, University of Washington Press.

Kavuncu, B. (1992) *Zehra Vakfi Bülteni*, Temmuz.

Kaya, I. (1993) in *Kürt Sorunu Forumu*. Ankara, Sor Yayincilik.

Keskin, R. (1993) in *Kürt Sorunu Forumu*. Ankara, Sor Yayincilik.

Keyder, Ç. (1987) *State and Class in Turkey*. London, Verso.

Keyder, Ç. and Öncü, A. (1994) 'Globalization of a Third-World Metropolis: Istanbul in the 1980's', *Review*, XVII, 3, Summer.

Kinross, Lord (1964) *Atatürk, The Rebirth of a Nation*. London, Weidenfeld and Nicolson.

Kirişci, K. and Winrow, G. (1997) *The Kurdish Question and Turkey*. London, Frank Cass and Co.

References

Kurşun, S. (1993) in *Kürt Sorunu Forumu*. Ankara, Sor Yayincilik.

Mahmutoğlu, F. (1993) in *Kürt Sorunu Forumu*. Ankara, Sor Yayincilik.

Malmisanij (1991) *Said-I Nursi ve Kürt Sorunu*. Istanbul, Doz Basim ve Yayincilik

Marcus, G. (1986) 'Contemporary Problems of Ethnography in the Modern World System', in J. Clifford and G. Marcus (eds) *Writing Culture*. Berkeley, University of California Press.

Mango, A. (1996) 'The Kemalist Project: The Struggle Between New Knowledge (*bilim*) and Old Knowledge (*ilim*) in Turkey', Unpublished paper.

Mardin, Ş. (1989) *Religion and Social Change in Turkey*. Albany, NY, State University of New York.

Mardin, Ş. (1993) 'Religion and Secularism in Turkey', in A. Hourani, P. Khoury and M. Wilson (eds) *The Modern Middle East*. Berkeley, CA, University of California Press.

Mardin, Ş. (1997) 'Projects as Methodology: Some Thoughts on Modern Turkish Social Science', in S. Bozdoğan and R. Kasaba (eds) *Rethinking Modernity and National Identity in Turkey*, Seattle, WA, University of Washington Press.

Mazlumder (1995) 'Dogu ve Güneydoğu'da Iç Göç Neden ve Sonuçlari', *Göç Raporu*, Kasim, Istanbul.

McDowall, D. (1997) 'Diary', *London Review of Books*, 20 February.

Meeker, M. (1997) 'Once There Was, Once There Wasn't: National Monuments and Interpersonal Exchange', in S. Bozdogan and R. Kasaba (eds) *Rethinking Modernity and National Identity in Turkey*, Seattle, WA, University of Washington Press.

Metiner, M. (1993) in *Kürt Sorunu Forumu*. Ankara, Sor Yayincilik.

Mezarci, H. (1993) in *Kürt Sorunu Forumu*. Ankara, Sor Yayincilik.

Muftuoğlu, A. (1993) in *Kürt Sorunu Forumu*. Ankara, Sor Yayincilik.

Muniş, Y. (1996) 'RP'den Ümitli Degilim' *Yeni Dünya* 3, Eylül.

Nandy, M. (1994) 'Culture, Voice and Development: A Primer for the Unsuspecting', *Thesis Eleven* 39.

Nietzsche, F. (1989) *Ecce Homo*. New York, Vintage Books.

Olson, R. (1991) 'Kurds and Turks: Two Documents Concerning Kurdish Autonomy in 1922 and 1923', *Journal of South Asian and Middle Eastern Studies* XV, 2, Winter.

Olson, R. (1996) *The Kurdish Nationalist Movement in the 1990's*. Kentucky, University of Kentucky Press.

Öncü, A. (1995) 'Packaging Islam: Cultural Politics on the Landscape of Commercial Television', *Balkan Media*, IV, 2.

References

Öncü, A. (1997) 'The Myth of the "Ideal Home" Travels Across Cultural Borders to Istanbul', in A. Öncü and P. Weyland (eds) *Space, Culture and Power*. London, Zed Books.

Öniş, Z. (1991) 'Political Economy of Turkey in the 1980's. Anatomy of Unorthodox Liberalism', in M. Heper (ed.) *Strong State and Economic Interest Groups*. Berlin, Walter de Gruyter.

Öztürk, K. (1996) *Insanliğin Göçü*. Istanbul, Birleşik Yayincilik.

Özyürek, E. (1997) '"Feeling tells better than language": Emotional Expression and Gender Hierarchy in the Sermons of Fethullah Gülen Hocaefendi', *New Perspectives On Turkey* 16, Spring.

Pamak, M. (1992) in *Kürd Soruşturmasi*. Ankara, Sor Yayincilik.

Pamak, M. (1996) *Kürt Sorunu ve Müslümanlar*. Istanbul, Selam Yayinlari.

Rabinow, P. (1989) *French Modern: Norm and Form in the Social Environment*. Cambridge, MA, MIT Press.

Robertson, R. (1990) 'After Nostalgia? Wilful Nostalgia and the Phases of Globalization', in B. Turner (ed.) *Theories of Modernity and Postmodernity*, London, Sage.

Robertson, R. (1995) 'Glocalization: Time–Space and Homogeneity–Heterogeneity', in M. Featherstone, S. Lash and R. Robertson (eds) *Global Modernities*. London, Sage.

Robins, K. (1996) 'Interrupting Identities: Turkey/Europe', in S. Hall and P. du Gay (eds) *Questions of Cultural Identity*. London, Sage Publications.

Rohat (1991) *Unutulmuslugun Bir Öyküsü: Said-I Kürdi*. Istanbul, Firat Yayinlari.

Roy, O. (1994) *The Failure of Political Islam*. Cambridge, MA, Harvard University Press.

Said, E. (1978) *Orientalism*. London, Penguin Books.

Sakallioğlu, U. (1996) 'Historicizing the Present and Problematizing the Future of the Kurdish Problem: A Critique of the TOBB Report on the Eastern Question', *New Perspectives On Turkey* 14, Spring.

Saktanber, A. (1994) 'Becoming the Other as a Muslim in Turkey: Turkish Women vs. Islamist Women', *New Perspectives On Turkey* 11, Fall.

Saktanber, A. (1997) 'Formation of a Middle-Class Ethos and its Quotidian: Revitalizing Islam in Modern Turkey', in A. Öncü and P. Weyland (eds) *Space, Culture and Power*. London, Zed Books.

Sassen, S. (1994) 'The Urban Complex in a World Economy', *International Social Science Journal*, 139, February.

Satana, I. (1996) 'Kürt Sorununda Islamci Siyaset Eksikliği', *Yeni Dünya* 3, Eylül.

Sayyid, B. (1997) *A Fundamental Fear: Eurocentrism and the Emergence of Islamism*. London, Zed Books.

References

Scott, J. (1990) *Domination and the Arts of Resistance*. New Haven, CT, Yale University Press.

Seal, J. (1996) *A Fez of the Heart*. London, Picador.

Seufert, G. (1997) 'Between Religion and Ethnicity: a Kurdish-Alevi Tribe in Globalizing Istanbul', in A. Öncü and P. Weyland (eds) *Space, Culture and Power*. London, Zed Books.

Şirin, N. (1993) in *Kürt Sorunu Forumu*. Ankara, Sor Yayincilik.

Sirman, N. (1995) 'Review of Martin Stokes: The Arabesk Debate, Music and Musicians in Modern Turkey', in *New Perspectives on Turkey*, Spring, 1995.

Starr, J. (1992) *Law as Metaphor*. New York, State University of New York Press.

Stevens, W. (1990) *Collected Poems*. New York, Vintage Books.

Stokes, M. (1989) 'Music, Fate and State: Turkey's Arabesk Debate', *Middle East Report*, September–October.

Stokes, M. (1994a) *Ethnicity, Identity and Music: The Musical Construction of Place*. Oxford and Providence, RI, Berg.

Stokes, M. (1994b) 'Turkish Arabesk and the City: Urban Popular Culture as Spatial Practice', in a Ahmed and H. Donnan (eds) *Islam, Globalization and Postmodernity*. London, Routledge.

Sümbül, M (1996) *Milliyetcimiyiz Müslümanmiyiz?* Bursa, Ümmet Yayinlari.

Tan, A. (1996a) 'Müslümanlarin Çözüm Projesi Yok', *Yeni Dünya* 3, Eylül.

Tan, A. (1996b) in *Kürt Sorunu Nasil Çözülür?* Istanbul, Nübihar.

Tapper, R. and Tapper, N. (1991) 'Religion, Education and Continuity in a Provincial Town', in R. Tapper (ed.) *Islam in Modern Turkey*. London, I. B. Tauris and Co.

Taşgetiren, A. (1996) in *Kürt Sorunu Nasil Çözülür?* Istanbul, Nübihar.

Taşkin, F. and Yeldan, A. (1996) 'Export Expansion, Capital Accumulation and Distribution in Turkish Manafacturing', in S. Togan and V. Balasubramanyan (eds) *The Economy of Turkey Since Liberalization*. New York, St Martins.

Taylor, C. (1989) *Sources of the Self: The Making of the Modern Identity*. Cambridge, Cambridge University Press.

Tekellioglu, O. (1996) 'The Rise of a Spontaneous Synthesis: The Historical Background of Turkish Popular Music', *Middle Eastern Studies*, 32, 2.

Thompson, J. (1990) *Ideology and Modern Culture*. Cambridge, Polity Press.

Touraine, A. (1994a) 'Democracy', *Thesis Eleven* 38.

Touraine, A. (1994b) 'Mutations of Latin America', *Thesis Eleven* 38.

Tunc, O. (1996) in *Kürt Sorunu Nasil Çözülür?* Istanbul, Nübihar.

Türkdoğan, O. (1997) *Etnik Sosyoloji*. Istanbul, Timaş Yayinlari.

References

Ünalan, A. (1993) in *Kürt Sorunu Forumu*. Ankara, Sor Yayincilik.

Vale, L. (1992) *Architecture, Power and National Identity*. New Haven, CT, Yale University Press.

Vali, A. (1996) 'Nationalism and Kurdish History Writing', *New Perspectives on Turkey* 14, Spring.

Van Loon, J. (1997) 'Racism, Culture and Modernity', *Theory, Culture and Society* 14, 3, August.

Varli, A. (1996) in *Kürt Sorunu Nasil Çözülür?* Istanbul, Nübihar.

Wieviorka, M. (1993) 'Racism and Modernity in Present-Day Europe', *Thesis Eleven* 35.

Yalçin-Heckmann, L. (1991) 'Ethnic Islam and Nationalism Among the Kurds in Turkey', in R. Tapper (ed.) *Islam in Modern Turkey*. London, I. B. Tauris and Co.

Yeğen, M. (1992) 'The Turkish State Discourse and the Exclusion of Turkish Identity', *Middle East Studies*, 32, 2, April.

Yeni Zemin (1994) Unsigned editorial: 'Gönüllü Beraberlik', *Yeni Zemin* 17–18, Mayis-Haziran.

Yilmaz, H. (1992) *Dogu Gerçegi ve Müslüman Kürtler*. Istanbul, Timaş Yayinlari.

Yüksel, M. (1993a) *Kürdistan'da Degisim Süreci*. Ankara, Sor Yayincilik.

Yüksel, M. (1993b) in *Kürt Sorunu Forumu*. Ankara, Sor Yayincilik.

Yüksel, M. (1997) 'Cezayir – Türkiye Ekseninde Berberiler ve Aleviler', *Ülke*, 29, Eylül.

Yusufoğlu, S. (1993) *Sentezli Düsüncenin Yogurduklari ve Doğurduklari*. Istanbul, Değisim Yayinlari.

Zürcher, E. (1995) *Modernleşen Türkiye'nin Tarihi*. Istanbul, Iletişim Yayinlari.

Newspapers cited in the text

Akit
Cumhuriyet
Demokrasi
Radikal
Sabah
Turkish Daily News
Yeni Şafak
Yeni Yüzyil
Zaman
Zaman (Australia)

Index

Index

passivity on Kurdish question, 140–3,
140n3, 142, 171
radical Islamism, 87–8
reasons for Islamist movements, 57n9
responses to Kurdish question, 147–89
passim
schooling, 54, 54n5, 57, 154
statist (bureaucratized) Islamism, 76–8,
77n10, 148–55 *passim*, 149n1,
149n2
Turkish supremacism, 153–4
utopia, search for, 43, 58, 164–7, 182,
189
and ethnicity, 62, 168–9, 179–181,
183, 188–9
and sport, 42n4, 68–9, 69n3
and *tarikats*, 53–4
and women, 1, 22, 43n6, 44–5, 56n8,
59–60, 66, 66n1, 140n3, 144n6
Istanbul, ix, 14, 16
City of Greater Istanbul Council, 36–9,
46–7, 49, 180
cosmopolitanism, 68n2
early town planning, 35–6, 35n1, 68,
68n2
exodus to suburbs, 20–2
influx from provinces, 19–21
Ottoman heritage, 179–80
'the Islamic city', 68, 68n2
touristifying of, 11, 20
world's largest Kurdish city, 105
and communal clashes, 7–8, 7n1
and globalization, 9–11, 16, 20, 25–6
and human rights, 96
see also architecture, global cities,
heritage conservation, housing,
Kuzguncuk, Üsküdar

jihad (*cihat*), 45, 176

*kardeşlik (*fraternity), 177–8, 178n4, 180,
188, 189
Kaya, I., 174, 187
Kemal, Mustafa, 13, 69
Kemalism, 3, 57, 70, 85, 89–90, 149,
149n2
as de-islamification, 91–2, 172
delegitimising Islamic identity, 92
historical antecedents, 137n1

Keyder C. and Öncü A., 11, 36, 37n3
Koran, 2, 26, 27, 29, 78n11, 87, 153, 160
courses for girls, 54, 54n5, 57
difficulty in exegesis, 169n3, 184
linguistic difficulty, 169n3
on ethnic difference, 144–5, 172, 177
reading competitions, 66, 73
'return to the K.' tendency, 93n6
Turks the guardians of, 150–1
Kurdish problem,
aspirations of Kurdish movement, 109,
123, 128, 167, 175–7, 175n1, 183–6
breakdown of civil society in SE, 96–7,
97n2
communal clashes in Istanbul, 7–8,
7n1, 96
denial of Kurdish identity, 88, 95,
95n1, 99–103 *passim*, 130, 135,
143–4, 174, 191
destruction of villages &dispersal of
population, 77n10, 88, 96, 105–6,
105n4, 128
geopolitical implications, 95
goal of a Kurdistan, 110, 177, 186,
193n1, 194–5
historical background to, 99, 120,
125–6, 126n11, 126n12
Islamic discourse, 110, 157–69 *passim*,
171
Kurdish language ban, 99–100, 99n3,
110, 123, 177, 180
Kurdish nationalism, 108–11, 157–8
Med TV, 127–9, 127n13
military action, 96–7, 114n2, 115n3,
148
nature of, 95–8
'problem of Kurds' or Kurds' problem?
97–8
problematics of coalition, 182, 185,
188, 189, 196
and human rights, 96–7, 97n2
see also PKK
Kurds, 2–3, 7–8, 55, 57, 62, 73, 75, 76
biography of a family, 114–32 *passim*,
124n10
diaspora, 106, 114, 128–9, 129n15
dress, 130
identity, 101–7, 110–11, 193–5, 193n1
in Iran, 166

Index

Index

muhtar (local state official), 17, 17n1,
    19n4, 22, 23n9, 113
multicultural(ism), 2, 87, 165
music, 39–40, 42–3, 50, 66, 70, 72, 72n7,
    131n17
Mustafa Kemal, *see* Kemal

namaz (ritual prayer), 2, 65, 73, 76, 139,
    164
Nasır, N., 160, 196
nationalism, 7–8, 62, 62n13
    alliance with right-wing Muslims, 144
    ambivalence of Islamists towards, 91,
        143
    Arab nationalism, 32
    'history thesis', 33–33n16, 89
    importation of alien forms of, 91
    'new nationalism', 78
    of Kurds, 98, 102, 129–31, 181–2
    of state, 32–4, 86, 99, 106, 122, 130–1,
        131n16, 159
    pan-Turkism (*Turanism*), 150–4
        passim, 175n2
    Turkish as world language, 152
    Western *v* Eastern, 86–7, 168–9
    and Kurdish Muslims, 199
    and language policy, 99–100, 99n3,
        110, 122–3, 179–81
    and racism, 144
National Action Party (MÇP), 148
National Movement Party (MHP), 74n8,
    101, 105, 175
Nü Bihar, 157, 180, 182
Nurcu (Light) movement, 149, 187
Nursi, Bediuzzaman Said, 149, 150n3

Ocalan, Abdullah, 125
Önçü A., 21, 127, 128
orientalism, 86, 137, 137n2, 165
Ottoman(s), 11, 31, 90, 143–4, 150–1,
    161, 172, 179
    Caliphate, abolition of, 13, 143
    cuisine and style, 50
    Empire, 32–3, 69, 143–4
    modernization (*Tanzimat*), 50n2,
        68n2
    neo-Ottomanism, 13, 14, 33, 50–1,
        183, 192
    Pax Ottomana, 57

treatment of ethnic minorities, 91, 172,
    183, 192
Öztürk K., 140, 142

PKK (Kurdish Workers Party), 117, 119,
    182
    alleged as Armenian front, 149n1
    Kurdish Islamic critique of, 188
    Kurdish support for, 125, 186–7
    Marxist credentials of, 108–9
    motivation for joining, 186
    program of, 185–6
    television channel (Med TV), 127–9,
        127n13
    and feudal society, 117, 186–7
    and Islam, 57, 185–6
    and Islamism, 182
    and terrorism, 148, 154, 161
    and war with state, 71, 87, 96, 105,
        106, 114, 114n2, 115n2, 116
Pamak, M., 102–3, 104, 142, 180
political parties,
    see Kurdish Workers Party (PKK),
        Motherland Party (*Anavatan*),
        National Action Party (MÇP),
        National Movement Party (MHP),
        Republican People's Party (CHP),
        Social People's Party (SHP), Welfare
        Party (Refah), Workers Party (*Işçi
        Partésé*)
populism, 49–53 *passim*, 55
Prophet, the, 28, 32, 33, 77, 93n6, 179,
    184
    following example of (*sünnet*), 54–5,
        54n5
Prost, H., 12, 137n1
race/racism, 153, 158–158n1, 159, 164,
    193
    condemnation by Islam, 144–5, 150–1
    see also ırk

Ramazan (Ramadan), 46, 65, 66, 77, 117
Refah (Welfare) Party, 1, 2, 31, 32, 79–81
    passim,
    ambivalence towards nationalism, 78,
        143–4, 148
    closure by state, 147
    electoral success, 1, 34n17, 178
    flirtation with neo-Ottomanism, 33

Index

Index

sünnet (following personal example of the Prophet), 54–5, 54n5

Tan, A., 178, 182–5 *passim*
Tanzimat (Ottoman modernization), 42m 50n2, 137n1
Tapper R. and Tapper, N., 75, 77n10, 93n6
tarikat (Sufi order), 44n7, 53–4, 147
Taylor, C., 142n5, 195n2
Tekellioğlu, O. 39, 131n17
television, 42, 43, 46, 71, 183, 195
  Med TV, 127–9, 127n13
  women as presenters, 66n1
TOBB Report on Kurdish Question, 86, 95, 141, 141n4, 193
tolerance, 81, 184
  claim of Islamists, 14, 33
  in Kuzguncuk, 24, 25, 25n11, 26, 28
  in Turkish Islam, 154
  under Ottomans, 91
touristifying/touristification
  of Islam, 11, 13
  of Istanbul, 11, 20
  of Kuzguncuk, 24
Tunç, O., 172–4
Türkdoğan, O., 99, 100, 101, 110

Ummah/ümmet (community of all believers),
Ummah (Arabic term), 30, 45, 58, 60, 91, 176
Ümmet (Turkish term), 22, 53, 55, 140n3, 144, 159, 161, 165–76 *passim*
ümmetcilik (unity of the Islamic polity), 174–9 *passim,* 181, 188, 191, 193,
Üsküdar, 1, 17, 25, 54n5, 65, 66, 67

Varli, A., 172, 195

Westernization,
  Atatürk on, 54n6, 159
  as civilizing project, 20, 52, 74, 192
  as imperialism, 161, 167, 182
  under Ottomans, 50
women,
  case-study of young Islamist woman, 59–60, 61
  dress, 16, 41, 43–6 *passim*, 56, 78
  enfranchised by Republic, 89
  Islamist role of, 22, 43n6, 44–5, 44n7, 46, 56, 56n8, 66, 140n3, 144n6
  Koran courses for girls, 54, 54n5, 57
  Kurdish practices, 119, 119n7
  public reading out of Koran, 169n3
  religiosity of, 54, 78
  republican role of, 22, 44–5, 46
  as TV presenters, 66n1
Workers Party (*İşçi Partısı*), 55, 108

Yalçin-Heckmann, L., 77n10, 78n11, 108n7, 193
Yeni Şafak, 44, 44n7, 68, 87, 90, 90n4, 115n3, 131n16, 141, 148, 152, 154, 159, 160, 196
Yeni Yüzyil, *78, 81n12, 95, 121, 127n14*
youth,
  Refah 'youth wing', 72, 148
  State Youth Day, 69–71, 73
  and Republicanism, 69–71, 73
Yüksel, M., 105, 116, 117, 143, 154, 179–80

Zaman, 20n5, 149, 151, 154
Zaman (Australia), 150, 152, 158n1
Zazaki (Kurdish dialect), 129–30

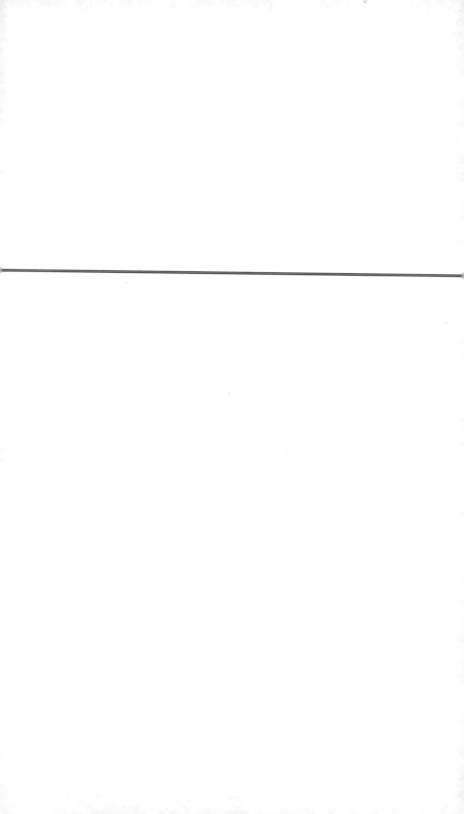